AQA History

AS
Unit 1

Russia and Germany, 1871–1914

Exclusively endorsed by AQA

Sally Waller
Steve Waugh
Simon Peaple

 Nelson Thornes

Published in 2009 by:
Nelson Thornes Ltd
Delta Place
27 Bath Road
CHELTENHAM
GL53 7TH
United Kingdom

09 10 11 12 13 / 10 9 8 7 6 5 4 3 2 1

A catalogue record for this book is available from the British Library

978-0-7487-8263-5

Illustrations by: Angela Knowles, David Russell Illustration

Page make-up by Thomson Digital

Printed in Croatia by Zrinski

Contents

AQA introduction

Nelson Thornes and AQA

Nelson Thornes has worked in collaboration with AQA to ensure that this book offers you the best support for your AS or A level course and helps you to prepare for your exams. The partnership means that you can be confident that the range of learning, teaching and assessment practice materials has been checked by the senior examining team at AQA before formal approval, and is closely matched to the requirements of your specification.

How to use this book

This book covers the specification for your course and is arranged in a sequence approved by AQA.

The features in this book include:

Timeline

Key events are outlined at the beginning of the book. The events are colour-coded so you can clearly see the categories of change.

Learning objectives

At the beginning of each section you will find a list of learning objectives that contain targets linked to the requirements of the specification.

Key chronology

A short list of dates usually with a focus on a specific event or legislation.

Key profile

The profile of a key person you should be aware of to fully understand the period in question.

Key term

A term that you will need to be able to define and understand.

Did you know?

Interesting information to bring the subject under discussion to life.

Exploring the detail

Information to put further context around the subject under discussion.

A closer look

An in-depth look at a theme, person or event to deepen your understanding. Activities around the extra information may be included.

Sources

Sources to reinforce topics or themes and may provide fact or opinion. They may be quotations from historical works, contemporaries of the period or photographs.

Cross-reference

Links to related content within the book which may offer more detail on the subject in question.

Activity

Various activity types to provide you with different challenges and opportunities to demonstrate both the content and skills you are learning. Some can be worked on individually, some as part of group work and some are designed to specifically 'stretch and challenge'.

Question

Questions to prompt further discussion on the topic under consideration and are an aid to revision.

Summary questions

Summary questions at the end of each chapter to test your knowledge and allow you to demonstrate your understanding.

AQA Examiner's tip

Hints from AQA examiners to help you with your study and to prepare for your exam.

AQA Examination-style questions

Questions at the end of each section in the style that you can expect in your exam.

Learning outcomes

Learning outcomes at the end of each section remind you what you should know having completed the chapters in that section.

■ Web links in the book

Because Nelson Thornes is not responsible for third party content online, there may be some changes to this material that are beyond our control. In order for us to ensure that the links referred to in the book are as up-to-date and stable as possible, the web sites provided are usually homepages with supporting instructions on how to reach the relevant pages if necessary.

Please let us know at **kerboodle@nelsonthornes.com** if you find a link that doesn't work and we will do our best to correct this at reprint, or to list an alternative site.

Introduction to the History series

When Bruce Bogtrotter in Roald Dahl's *Matilda* was challenged to eat a huge chocolate cake, he just opened his mouth and ploughed in, taking bite after bite and lump after lump until the cake was gone and he was feeling decidedly sick. The picture is not dissimilar to that of some A level history students. They are attracted to history because of its inherent appeal but, when faced with a bulging file and a forthcoming examination, their enjoyment evaporates. They try desperately to cram their brains with an assortment of random facts and subsequently prove unable to control the outpouring of their ill-digested material in the examination.

The books in this series are designed to help students and teachers avoid this feeling of overload and examination panic by breaking down the AQA history specification in such a way that it is easily absorbed. Above all, they are designed to retain and promote students' enthusiasm for history by avoiding a dreary rehash of dates and events. Each book is divided into sections, closely matched to those given in the specification, and the content is further broken down into chapters that present the historical material in a lively and attractive form, offering guidance on the key terms, events and issues, and blending thought-provoking activities and questions in a way designed to advance students' understanding. By encouraging students to think for themselves and to share their ideas with others, as well as helping them to develop the knowledge and skills they will need to pass their examination, this book should ensure that students' learning remains a pleasure rather than an endurance test.

To make the most of what this book provides, students will need to develop efficient study skills from the start and it is worth spending some time considering what these involve:

▪ Good organisation of material in a subject-specific file. Organised notes help develop an organised brain and sensible filing ensures time is not wasted hunting for misplaced material. This book uses cross-references to indicate where material in one chapter has relevance to material in another. Students are advised to adopt the same technique.

▪ A sensible approach to note-making. Students are often too ready to copy large chunks of material from printed books or to download sheaves of printouts from the internet. This series is designed to encourage students to think about the notes they collect and to undertake research with a particular purpose in mind. The activities encourage students to pick out information that is relevant to the issue being addressed and to avoid making notes on material that is not properly understood.

▪ Taking time to think, which is by far the most important component of study. By encouraging students to think before they write or speak, be it for a written answer, presentation or class debate, students should learn to form opinions and make judgements based on the accumulation of evidence. These are the skills that the examiner will be looking for in the final examination. The beauty of history is that there is rarely a right or wrong answer so, with sufficient evidence, one student's view will count for as much as the next.

Unit 1

The topics offered for study in Unit 1 are all based on 'change and consolidation'. They invite consideration of what changed and why, as well as posing the question of what remained the same. Through a study of a period of about 50 to 60 years, students are encouraged to analyse the interplay of long-term and short-term reasons for change and to consider not only how governments have responded to the need for change but also to evaluate the ensuing consequences. Such historical analyses are, of course, relevant to an understanding of the present and, through such historical study, students will be guided towards a greater appreciation of the world around them today, as well as developing their understanding of the past.

Unit 1 is tested by a 1 hour 15 minute paper containing three questions, from which students need to select two. Details relating to the style of questions, with additional hints, are given in Table 1 and links to the examination requirements are provided throughout this book. Students should familiarise themselves with these and the marking criteria given below before attempting any of the practice examination questions at the end of each section.

Answers will be marked according to a scheme based on 'levels of response'. This means that the answer will be assessed according to which level best matches the historical skills displayed, taking both knowledge and understanding into account. All students should have a copy of these criteria and need to use them wisely.

Marking criteria

Question 1(a), 2(a) and 3(a)

Level 1 Answers will contain either some descriptive material that is only loosely linked to the focus of

Table 1 *Unit 1: style of questions and marks available*

Unit 1	Question	Marks	Question type	Question stem	Hints for students
Question 1, 2 and 3	(a)	12	This question is focused on a narrow issue within the period studied and requires an explanation	Why did… Explain why…	Make sure you explain 'why', not 'how', and try to order your answer in a way that shows you understand the inter-linkage of factors and which were the more important. You should try to reach an overall judgement/conclusion
Question 1, 2 and 3	(b)	24	This question links the narrow issue to a wider context and requires an awareness that issues and events can have different interpretations	How far… How important was… How successful…	This answer needs to be planned as you will need to develop an argument in your answer and show balanced judgement. Try to set out your argument in the introduction and, as you develop your ideas through your paragraphs, support your opinions with detailed evidence. Your conclusion should flow naturally and provide supported judgement

the question or some explicit comment with little, if any, appropriate support. Answers are likely to be generalised and assertive. The response will be limited in development and skills of written communication will be weak. *(0–2 marks)*

Level 2 Answers will demonstrate some knowledge and understanding of the demands of the question. They will **either** be almost entirely descriptive with few explicit links to the question **or** they will provide some explanations backed by evidence that is limited in range and/or depth. Answers will be coherent but weakly expressed and/or poorly structured. *(3–6 marks)*

Level 3 Answers will demonstrate good understanding of the demands of the question providing relevant explanations backed by appropriately selected information, although this may not be full or comprehensive. Answers will, for the most part, be clearly expressed and show some organisation in the presentation of material. *(7–9 marks)*

Level 4 Answers will be well focused, identifying a range of specific explanations backed by precise evidence and demonstrating good understanding of the connections and links between events/issues. Answers will, for the most part, be well written and organised. *(10–12 marks)*

Question 1(b), 2(b) and 3(b)

Level 1 Answers may **either** contain some descriptive material which is only loosely linked to the focus of the question **or** they may address only a part of the question. Alternatively, there may be some explicit comment with little, if any, appropriate support. Answers are likely to be generalised and assertive. There will be little, if any, awareness of differing

historical interpretations. The response will be limited in development and skills of written communication will be weak. *(0–6 marks)*

Level 2 Answers will show some understanding of the focus of the question. They will **either** be almost entirely descriptive with few explicit links to the question **or** they may contain some explicit comment with relevant but limited support. They will display limited understanding of differing historical interpretations. Answers will be coherent but weakly expressed and/or poorly structured. *(7–11 marks)*

Level 3 Answers will show a developed understanding of the demands of the question. They will provide some assessment, backed by relevant and appropriately selected evidence, but they will lack depth and/or balance. There will be some understanding of varying historical interpretations. Answers will, for the most part, be clearly expressed and show some organisation in the presentation of material. *(12–16 marks)*

Level 4 Answers will show explicit understanding of the demands of the question. They will develop a balanced argument backed by a good range of appropriately selected evidence and a good understanding of historical interpretations. Answers will, for the most part, show organisation and good skills of written communication. *(17–21 marks)*

Level 5 Answers will be well focused and closely argued. The arguments will be supported by precisely selected evidence leading to a relevant conclusion/judgement, incorporating well-developed understanding of historical interpretations and debate. Answers will, for the most part, be carefully organised and fluently written, using appropriate vocabulary. *(22–24 marks)*

Introduction to this book

At first glance, Russia and Germany would seem to be two very different countries in the last quarter of the 19th century: the former an ancient state which could trace its heritage back to 882 when Kiev became the capital of a recognisable Russia; the latter a new creation which did not exist as a single country until 1871. While Russia was ruled by a Tsar who claimed to represent God on Earth and could do as he pleased, Germany had a Kaiser and a constitution, with an elected parliament. While Russia was economically backward, with an 85 per cent peasant population, many of whom were still cutting the corn with medieval sickles and sharing their huts with their animals, Germany was already steadily advancing towards its 'second industrial revolution', with many developing towns and cities, a prosperous middle class and a modernising agriculture. While Russia looked eastwards, in its commitment to preserving Slav culture and the teachings of the **Orthodox Church**, Germany shared a western culture and saw the value of industrialisation and urbanisation.

Although they set out from very different starting points, these two countries would come to have much in common as they moved from the 19th to the 20th century. Both faced the impact of rapid industrialisation, albeit at different levels, and both had to come to terms with its social and political consequences. Both found themselves trying to cling to the past as these forces of change swept them into uncharted territories and both faced political storms as a result. Above all, both were led by rulers who had little real understanding of the changes that were going on around them. While their economies and social structures changed, they remained 'political dwarves'.

Externally, the Germany of 1871 was concerned only to maintain peace with its neighbours, whereas Russia still had an eye towards expansion to the south and east – for reasons of trade, greed, security and to restore its shattered prestige after defeat in the Crimea in 1855–6. However, in the early 20th century all this began to change. Thwarted in their ambitions to expand eastwards after defeat in the Russo-Japanese war of 1904–5, the Russians looked increasingly towards an expansion of influence in the Balkans, among their fellow Slavs. The Germans too started to look outwards from the 1890s, when it was decided that the country should belatedly join the colonial race and pursue 'Weltpolitik' – world policy – and claim 'a place in the sun'. Both countries sought alliances and by 1907, Britain, France and Russia were linked in a Triple Entente ranged against the Triple Alliance of Germany, Austria-Hungary and Italy. Thus it came about that these two nations, despite their internal difficulties, both turned to war as a means of escape and to prove themselves 'Great Powers'. What both were to prove, of course, was that the regimes which their respective rulers, Tsar Nicholas II and Kaiser Wilhelm II, had been running, were insufficiently robust to withstand the demands which wartime conditions brought. Neither survived the conflict. Tsardom collapsed in 1917, the Kaiserreich in 1918.

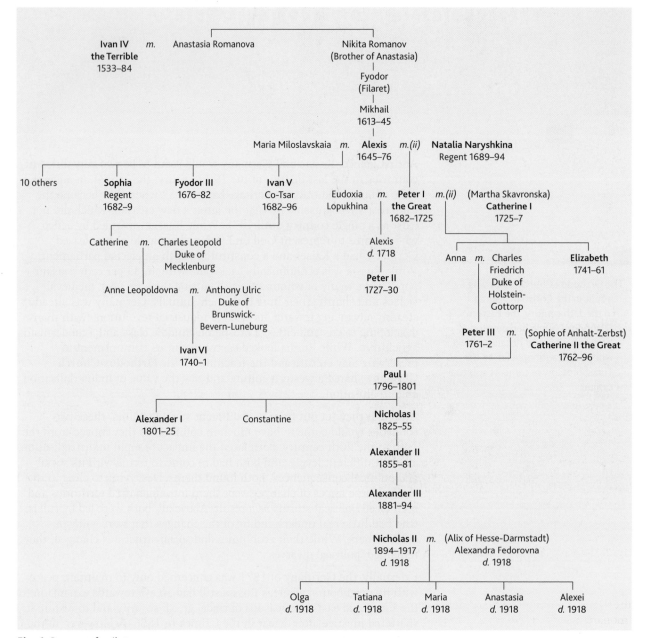

Fig. 1 *Romanov family tree*

In 1881, Alexander III came to power in Russia. He was a Romanov and the penultimate member of a dynasty established by Mikhail Romanov in 1613. It was Mikhail's grandson, Peter the Great (1682–1725) who had, according to a contemporary, transformed Russia, 'from nothingness into being'. Borrowing ideas from the west, he had given the country a glittering new capital at St Petersburg, built up a powerful army and navy and, as a result of a great victory against Sweden, at Poltava in 1709, had adopted the title of Emperor in 1721. This inheritance was added to by Catherine the Great (1762–96), whose reign saw Russia acquire the Crimea and a Black Sea coastline as well as Lithuania and parts of Poland. The multinational Empire was not always easy to control. In 1773–4, Catherine faced the Pugachev revolt, for example, and, following the French Revolution in the west, from 1789, new liberal ideas about freedom and equality began to circulate among members of

Fig. 2 *Tsar Alexander II emancipating the serfs in 1861*

the upper class 'intelligentsia'. However, Catherine claimed to offer 'monarchy without despotism' and although the foundations of autocracy (where a ruler's power had no limits) and serfdom (where individuals were owned by their master) remained unchanged, her reign was 'enlightened' by the standards of the time.

After the undistinguished reign of Catherine's son Paul, who was strangled in his bedchamber by noble assassins, Alexander I (1801–25) led the Russians in a heroic defence of their country against the Napoleonic invasion of 1812 and he took his place with the victors at the subsequent Congress of Vienna in 1815. Out of that Congress came a Russia strengthened by the acquisition of Poland and reassured by the 'Holy Alliance' in which Austria and Prussia also pledged themselves to rule according to *'the sublime truths taught by divine law'*.

In the ensuing years, Russia turned more in on itself as it became disillusioned by the spread of liberalism in the west and relied on the Holy Alliance to crush outbreaks of rebellion. Nicholas I (1825–55) maintained a reactionary regime with the slogan 'Orthodoxy, Autocracy and Nationalism'. He set up the notorious 'Third Section' (secret police)

Cross-reference

Autocracy is further discussed in Section 2, on Russia.

■ Cross-reference

More information on **'The Pale'** is provided on page 71.

to spy on his subjects and root out opposition and maintained a strict censorship over education and all publishing. Severe restrictions were imposed on Russia's other nationalities and Jews were required to reside in 'The Pale'. Abroad, he acted as the 'gendarme of Europe', supporting legitimate rulers and helping defeat revolts in Poland in 1830 and Hungary and Romania in 1848–9. His reign culminated in military defeat in the Crimea, which acted as a wake-up call to a country which had long ignored demands for change.

Nicholas's son, Alexander II (1855–81), was the first Tsar to make any serious attempt to reform Russia's archaic political and social structure. He did so less out of a sense of belief in liberal ideas than out of a fear for his nation's survival. Until 1861, approximately 85 per cent of the Russian population had remained peasants, with two thirds tied to their lands, either as serfs – the personal property of their landowning masters – or as state peasants, working lands owned by the Crown. By the mid-19th century, serfdom had not only become morally unacceptable, it was preventing economic progress, as seen, for example, in Germany, where farm workers were increasingly turning themselves into wage-earners and contributing to industrial development.

The emancipation edict of 1861 was not as far reaching as some supporters had hoped for. The newly emancipated serfs were required to pay for their freedom in the form of 'redemption dues', over a 49-year period. Until then, they were tied to the village commune (mir). However, the edict was backed up by other reforms which, together, earned Alexander II the nickname, the 'Tsar liberator'. *Zemstva* – local government assemblies, elected by an indirect voting system which favoured the landowners without excluding the peasants – were instituted in 1864, and similar assemblies in towns in 1870, in an attempt to provide for some local democratic initiative, although the franchise was sufficiently restricted to ensure the dominance of the nobility. Legal reforms brought a jury system, equality before the law and a greater openness and independence of proceedings. Military conscription was reduced from 25 to 6 years and the conditions in which conscripts served improved, while the universities were given greater autonomy and the number of students allowed to increase.

Even this degree of limited reform had its consequences. Opposition groups emerged – some suggesting Russia should follow a more western route, others determined to preserve Russia's 'Slavophile' inheritance. The peasants grew restless, the non-Russian peoples sought greater independence, liberals demanded a constitution and the universities became centres of radical thinking. It was in this atmosphere that in March 1881, Alexander II was blown up by a terrorist organisation known as the 'People's Will' and Alexander III succeeded to the throne.

There was no such 'Great Power' heritage to the country of Germany which emerged in 1871. Most of the states which filled the area between the Baltic, the Rhine, the Alps and the Danube had been small players on the European scene until swept into the new German state by the most dominant of their number, Prussia. The 1815 Congress of Vienna had created a **confederation** ('Bund') of 39 German states, each with its own ruler, but with a permanent central '**Diet**', the *Bundesrat*, established at Frankfurt under an Austrian presidency.

Prussia had played a significant part in Napoleon's defeat and had consequently made some important gains at Vienna. Although it lost some eastern territories, it acquired the Rhineland and Westphalia, half of Saxony and Pomerania. Such acquisitions were to have far-reaching

■ Key terms

Confederation: a group of states which had separate internal governments with control over domestic policies but which worked together in matters of common interest.

Diet: a ruling body.

consequences. Prussia had gained control of areas of huge economic and industrial potential, its population had been doubled and it had been transformed from an eastern European power into a central one. Although, at the time, Austria saw no rival in Prussia, with its split possessions, the next 50 years were to see a struggle between these two powers to dominate the area of 'Germany'.

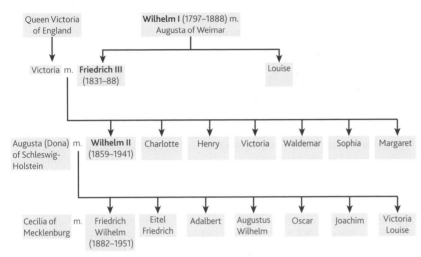

Fig. 3 *Hohenzollern family tree*

Although the 1815 settlement had stipulated that individual states should establish constitutions with parliaments, not all did. In Prussia, Friedrich Wilhelm III remained staunchly conservative. He relied heavily on the Prussian '**Junker**' class of landowning aristocrats who provided his civil servants and army officers and who remained hostile to the forces of liberalism.

However, in the years up to 1848, economic development began to change the German Bund. The Prussian Rhineland led the way in a frenzy of industrial expansion. The coal, iron and textile industries boomed and turned villages into cities. Steam engines transformed production and by 1838 Prussia had built its first railway line from Berlin to Potsdam (a full 13 years before Russia had a line between St Petersburg and Moscow). Furthermore, by 1834, Prussia had developed an internal customs union, or *Zollverein*, whereby 18 of the German states agreed to abandon customs barriers and create a free trade zone, with tariffs, or duties, on goods entering the zone from elsewhere. To its economic and political loss, Austria remained outside this union, while within it, greater economic integration bred not only prosperity and social change, but a stronger sense of unity.

During the '**Vormärz**' years between 1815 and 1848, liberal and nationalist ideas grew in Germany. Liberalism became entwined with nationalism so that a sense of a common heritage and a pride in contemporary Germanic achievement, particularly among the middle classes and in the universities, created a commitment to the unity of German-speaking peoples. Since Prussia led the Zollverein, it was to Prussia that these nationalists looked, as the potential leader of a united Germany.

However, an outbreak of revolutions in many German states in 1848–9 did not bring unity any nearer. Despite some initial success, and the setting up of a '**Vorparlament**' to create a unified Germany, debates about whether to include or exclude Austria protracted its discussions. By March 1849, when Friedrich Wilhelm of Prussia was eventually offered the throne of a united Germany, he refused to '*pick up a crown from the gutter*'.

Key terms

Junker: a term used to describe Prussian aristocrats. The Junker class was specifically the class of large Prussian landowners who lived east of the River Elbe and dominated the institutions of Prussia. They were conservative in outlook.

'Vormärz': literally means 'before March' and refers to the years before the outbreak of revolution in Germany in March 1848.

Vorparlament: a German parliament to draw up a constitution.

Fig. 4 *Otto von Bismarck*

■ Key terms

Landtag: under the Prussian constitution granted in 1850, there were 2 parliamentary houses. The Landtag was the lower chamber and its members were elected by a suffrage system based on tax-paying ability.

The events of 1848–9 taught German liberals a lesson. They could not impose a new future on Germany, without an army or support from the princes. Both were to be found by Otto von Bismarck, who was appointed Minister-President of Prussia in 1862. He served Wilhelm I, who had come to power in January 1861 and had endorsed some major army reforms proposed by his war minister, von Roon. Bismarck was summoned to deal with the new Prussian '**Landtag**', which was refusing taxation to support these. Bismarck's solution was to ignore the opposition. He simply took the taxes illegally, and arrogantly told that body:

> The great questions of the day will not be decided by speeches and the resolutions of majorities – that was the great mistake of 1848 and 1849 – but by iron and blood.

Bismarck was no liberal but he wanted to strengthen Prussia and in so doing, unified Germany. He used a dispute over the administration of the Danish provinces of Schleswig and Holstein to engineer a war with Austria in June 1866 and defeated them at Sadowa in just 6 weeks. The old 'Bund' was abolished and the North German states annexed to Prussia to form the 1867 'North German Confederation'. Forgiven for his illegal handling of the budget, Bismarck found himself the unexpected hero of the 'National Liberals' and in return allowed the North German Confederation to be ruled through a parliament with universal manhood suffrage, a secret ballot and parliamentary control of the budget.

Another quarrel over the candidature for the vacant Spanish throne was used to provoke war with France, when Bismarck published an edited version of the Ems telegram sent him by the Kaiser, recording an apparent exchange of insults with the French ambassador.

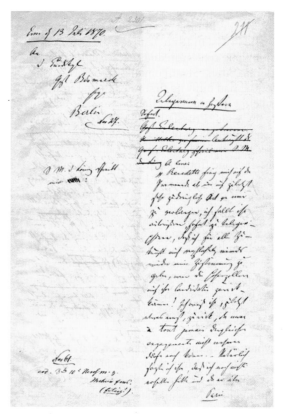

Fig. 5 *The Ems Telegram, which led to war between Germany and France*

The French were resoundingly beaten at Sedan and at the resultant Treaty of Frankfurt in May 1871, were forced to cede Alsace and Lorraine to Germany as well as paying a high level of reparations. Not only had Prussia proved its strength, but, thanks to this victory, the southern German states (which were more Catholic and pro-Austrian than the north) were persuaded to throw in their lot with the Prussians and Wilhelm found himself being offered the crown of a united Germany. By 1871, the unification of Germany (excluding Austria) was complete and, what is more, it had been accomplished by Prussian power and supported by the conservative elite.

While their backgrounds were different, the future paths of both Russia and Germany from the 1870s were to have a number of similarities. Two inherently conservative countries were to face industrial upheaval, political unrest and the consequences of Great Power ambition. Both were to miss vital opportunities and both were to slide to war against each other in 1914. As you read this book, you should reflect how, in each state, traditional authoritarian rule was challenged by modern democratic trends and how foreign policy increasingly became an outlet for internal frustration and stagnation. As well as examining the key political developments of these countries, think about the broader economic, social and international trends that were influencing them. By examining the interplay of forces which affected both states, you should acquire a full and rich understanding of both Germany and Russia as each found itself moving towards the First World War.

■ Timeline

The colours represent the geographical locations of the events in the timeline as follows:
Green: German; Red: Russian; Blue: International

1871	1871	1872	1872	1873	1875	1878	1878
German Empire is proclaimed at Versailles. Wilhelm I becomes Kaiser	Treaty of Frankfurt: Germany annexes Alsace and half of Lorraine	The *Dreikaiserbund* (League of Germany, Russia and Austria-Hungary) is created	Jesuit activity is forbidden in Germany	May Laws directed against the influence of the Catholic Church in Prussia	Founding of the SAPD (Socialist Workers' Party) at Gotha	Assassination attempt on Kaiser Wilhelm I	Anti-Socialist Law passed; Conservative gains in Reichstag elections

1884	1884	1887	1888	1889	1889	1890
Dreikaiserbund is again renewed (until 1887)	University statute removes all autonomy granted by Alexander II and student clubs banned	Bismarck negotiates a secret Reinsurance Treaty with Russia	March–June: Reign of Kaiser Friedrich III; Kaiser Wilhelm II succeeds	Old Age and Invalidity Insurance Law is passed	Land Captains are established	Bismarck is dismissed and Caprivi becomes Reich Chancellor

1900	1901	1903	1904	1904	1905
Von Bülow becomes chancellor	The Social Revolutionary Party is founded	The Social Democratic Party splits into Bolsheviks and Mensheviks	Von Plehve, Minister of Internal Affairs is assassinated; Russo-Japanese war breaks out	Britain and France sign *Entente Cordiale*	Russians defeated by Japan in the Far East. Father Gapon leads a march on 'Bloody Sunday' and protestors are killed. Series of strikes and unrest follows. The St. Petersburg Soviet is set up; the Tsar issues the October Manifesto promising an elected parliament

1909	1911	1911	1912	1912-13	1913	1913	1914
Bethmann-Hollweg becomes chancellor	Stolypin is assassinated	The second Moroccan Crisis breaks out when the Kaiser sends 'Panther' to Agadir	The SPD become the largest party in the Reichstag	The Balkan Wars intensify the conflicts between Austria-Hungary and Serbia	The fourth *Duma* is elected	The Zabern Affair rouses protests against military dominance	Archduke Franz Ferdinand is assassinated in Sarajevo. Germany offers Austria-Hungary a 'Blank Cheque'. Germany declares war on Russia and France

1878	1879	1879	1881	1882	1883	1884
The Congress of Berlin; Austrians gain protectorate over Bosnia and Herzegovina	Passing of Protectionist legislation by the Reichstag	The Dual Alliance is formed between Germany and Austria-Hungary	Alexander II is assassinated; Alexander III is crowned Emperor; the *Dreikaiserbund* is renewed	The Triple Alliance links Germany, Austria-Hungary and Italy	Sickness Insurance law is passed	Accident Insurance law is passed

1891	1892	1893	1894	1894	1898	1898
Construction of Trans-Siberian Railway begins; Jews evicted from Moscow and anti-Semitic campaign begins	Sergei Witte is appointed Minister of Finance	Franco-Russian military agreement	Pan-German League is established; Hohenlohe-Schillingsfürst becomes Reich Chancellor	Alexander III dies and is succeeded by Nicholas II	Founding of the Navy League and first Naval Law	The Social Democratic Labour Party (forerunner of the Communist Party) is founded by Plekhanov and includes Lenin

1905	1906	1906	1907	1907	1908	1908
The first Moroccan Crisis breaks out	The first *Duma* assembles; Stolypin becomes Prime Minister and begins land reform	At the Conference of Algeçiras Germany is isolated	The second *Duma* meets but is dissolved after three months. New electoral law is introduced and the third *Duma* is elected	Russia and Britain settle their differences; the Triple Entente is formed	The *Daily Telegraph* interview causes an outcry in Germany	Rising of the 'Young Turks'; Austria-Hungary incorporates Bosnia and Herzegovina

1 Germany

1 Bismarck and the New German Empire, 1871–90

Fig. 1 *The proclamation of the German Empire at Versailles, 18 January 1871. Can you identify Wilhelm I and Bismarck?*

In this chapter you will learn about:

- the main features of the new German Constitution, set up in 1871

- Bismarck's policies against the Catholic Church, known as the '*Kulturkampf*'

- the significance of the political changes of 1878–9

- Bismarck's attempts to suppress socialism

- Bismarck's relationship with the Reichstag during his chancellorship.

On 18 January 1871, in the Hall of Mirrors, in the great palace of Versailles outside Paris, King Wilhelm I of Prussia was proclaimed Emperor of a united Germany, known as the **Second Reich**. The Franco-Prussian War was in its final stages. Indeed, within ten days France had surrendered.

Activities

Group activities

1 In groups, examine the painting at the beginning of this chapter. What message does it give about the new empire?

2 Why do you think the Kaiser was concerned about the difference in the royal titles – as given in the 'Did you know?' on page 11 box?

Key profiles

Kaiser Wilhelm I

Wilhelm I (1797–1888) became King of Prussia in 1861. As the second son of Friedrich Wilhelm III, he had not been expected to ascend the throne. He developed a reputation as a very brave soldier, fighting in the Napoleonic wars. During the Revolutions of 1848 he crushed a revolt using cannons which earned him the nickname of the Prince of Grapeshot. In 1857, his elder brother, Friedrich Wilhelm IV suffered a stroke and Wilhelm took over as Regent, becoming king on his brother's death three years later. In his memoirs, Bismarck described Wilhelm as an old-fashioned, courteous, infallibly polite gentleman and a genuine Prussian officer, whose good common sense was occasionally undermined by 'female influences'.

Otto von Bismarck

Otto von Bismarck (1815–98) came from a Junker family living in the district of Brandenburg in Prussia. At the age of seven he was sent to a boarding school where he suffered from homesickness. He enjoyed sport and became a deadly shot with both rifle and pistols, able to blow the head off a duck at 100 metres. At university in Göttingen he even joined an illegal duelling club, fighting many duels and becoming a top swordsman with the nickname 'Achilles the Unwoundable'. Initially he worked as a civil servant and then as a squire on the family estates before becoming a Prussian deputy to the Federal *Diet* (parliament) followed by Prussian Ambassador to Vienna, St Petersburg and finally Paris. In 1861 he nearly died from an injury to his leg and inflammation of the lungs. In 1862 Wilhelm I of Prussia, in dispute with the Prussian National Assembly, appointed Bismarck as Minister-President in the hope that he would resolve the conflict.

Key term

The Second Reich: Reich means German state (or Empire) and that founded in 1871 was known as the Second Reich to distinguish it from the First Reich of the Holy Roman Empire (that covered the lands originally ruled by Charlemagne from the 9th to the 19th century). The Third Reich (1933–1945) was the period of Nazi rule in Germany.

Did you know?

Wilhelm, the King of Prussia, had set his heart on the title of 'Kaiser (Emperor) of Germany'. However, Bismarck, in order to gain the support of the King of Bavaria, had agreed that the title would be 'German Kaiser'. At the official ceremony on 18 January 1871, Wilhelm showed his disappointment by ignoring Bismarck.

The German political structure in 1871

The new German Reich was a confederation comprising 25 separate states which retained their own sovereignty – or right of self-government. Twenty-two of these states even retained their own monarchies. Prussia was by far the largest single state with over 60 per cent of the area of the Reich and a similar proportion of its population, followed by Bavaria. The latter had joined the Reich reluctantly and managed to preserve a considerable degree of state autonomy, including the right to maintain its own army in peacetime. The Reich also included the mainly French speaking provinces of Alsace-Lorraine in the West, and mainly Polish speaking areas in East Prussia.

Bismarck had several key aims when drawing up the new German constitution which was to lay down the manner in which the Reich would be ruled:

- To retain as much power as possible for the Kaiser and chancellor
- To limit the influence of the German Parliament
- To ensure a pre-eminent position for Prussia.

Did you know?

The new German Constitution was virtually the same as the system which Bismarck had devised for the North German Confederation of 1867 – when only the northern states of Germany had been unified. Some alterations were made in November 1870 when Prussia made treaties with the south German states and the new constitution was finally made law on 20 April 1871.

The new constitution

Kaiser	Government (chancellor and ministers)
■ Was the hereditary monarch (and always the King of Prussia too). ■ Appointed/dismissed chancellor and other ministers (Secretaries of State). ■ Could call/dissolve the Reichstag. ■ Commanded the army directly. ■ Controlled foreign policy, including the right to make treaties and alliances and declare war if attacked. ■ Gave assent to all laws (with the chancellor). ■ Devised policies and laws in consultation with his chosen chancellor, ministers and the Bundesrat. ■ Had the final say in any dispute over the constitution. 	■ Was appointed and dismissed by the Kaiser (and responsible only to him, not to the Reichstag). ■ Decided outlines of policy with the Kaiser/ Bundesrat. (Were not required to take account of the Reichstag's views/resolutions.) ■ Chancellor (and Kaiser) gave assent to all laws. 
Reichstag (parliament, also known as the Lower House)	**Bundesrat (also known as the Upper House)**
■ Members (deputies) elected by males over 25 years. ■ Deputies had the right of free speech. ■ Elections held every three years by an indirect voting system which varied in different regions. ■ Gave consent to all laws (including the annual budget which assessed the raising and spending of taxes). ■ Could question, debate, agree to or reject a law proposed by the chancellor. ■ Could not amend a law. ■ Could not demand the dismissal of the chancellor or any other ministers. 	■ 58 representatives from the 25 state governments in proportion to size of state (Prussia, as the largest state, had 17 members). ■ Presided over by the chancellor. ■ Could initiate legislation. ■ Decisions decided by majority vote except for any proposal to alter the constitution, which needed a majority of 14. ■ Had to approve new laws (along with the Reichstag, Kaiser and chancellor). ■ Could veto all legislation except a budget approved by the Reichstag. ■ Had to give approval to the Kaiser for a declaration of war (in cases where Germany was not under attack). 

Fig. 2 *Bismarck's constitution*

Political features

Through Activity 2, you will have seen how, in many respects, the German constitution was undemocratic, authoritarian and Prussian-dominated. However, some aspects of it were quite liberal. You may, for example, have been surprised to discover that Bismarck gave the vote to all men over the age of 25 years. One explanation is that Bismarck was simply trying to win support by appearing to be forward looking. He seems to have believed that the ordinary German peasants and workers had traditional views similar to his own and that their support could help him keep the demands of the more radical, middle class liberals at bay.

Nevertheless, this opportunity for the broad mass of the people to express their views was a modern concept.

There were certainly signs of emergent democracy in Germany and the political framework laid down by Bismarck produced some flourishing political parties and lively debates. The constitution guaranteed freedom of speech and the law was held in high regard. So, despite its limitations, it would be wrong to describe the 1871 constitution as wholly illiberal. If political groups were anxious to fight for a place in the Reichstag, they must have felt the prize worth having!

However, in 1871 the German political 'parties', as outlined below, were not quite like British political parties. They were not competing for the right to rule the country and preparing manifestos which offered broad policy proposals. They were actually more like pressure groups representing the interests of different sections of the community and wanting to be in a position to be able to advance the concerns of their followers.

The table below indicates the main political groupings of the Bismarckian era.

Activities

Thinking and analysis

1. Look at Bismarck's aims, given on page 11. How far do you think the new constitution fulfilled his objectives?

2. How far is it correct to describe the constitution as 'liberal and democratic'?

Cross-reference

For details of the **socialist grouping** in 1871, read pages 22–3.

Table 1 *The main political groupings from 1871*

Party	Key features
National Liberals (NL)	Formed in 1867 by those who favoured Bismarck's policy of German unification. This was the party of the Protestant middle classes. It was supported by wealthy, well-educated men such as bankers, merchants and civil servants. It stood for free trade, a strong Germany and a constitutional liberal state. After 1875 it grew more conservative as its members felt threatened by the growing strength of the Social Democratic Party.
Centre Party (*Zentrum*)	Founded in 1870, this party represented the German Catholics and the minorities opposed to Bismarck. The party was strong in the southern German states, particularly Bavaria and also in the Rhineland. It was determined to preserve the position of the Catholic Church, especially in education. It was conservative regarding the constitution and favoured greater decentralisation, but it was quite liberal in its attitude to social reform.
Social Democratic Party (SPD)	There was already a socialist grouping in 1871 but the SPD itself was not founded until 1875. This party represented the working classes and worked with the trade unions. It supported a reduction in the power of the elite and the extension of welfare reforms. Its most extreme members wanted a total overthrow of the constitution, but the majority were prepared to work within it in order to bring about better conditions for the masses.
German Conservative Party (DKP)	Conservative elements adopted the DKP name in 1876. This group mainly represented the Protestant and aristocratic Prussian Junker landowners. It was the most right wing of the political groups and detested the Reichstag because it was elected by universal suffrage. It was dominant in the Prussian Landtag (state government).
Free Conservatives or *Reichspartei* (FKP)	Formed in 1871, the FKP represented landowners, industrialists and businessmen. Its members were strong supporters of Bismarck and its geographic base was wider than the DKP.
The Progressives or *Fortschrittpartei* (DFP)	A party which believed in a liberal, constitutional state but disliked centralism and militarism so were not very supportive of Bismarck. They wanted to extend the powers of the Reichstag.

Fig. 3 *Bismarck sweeps Germany clean. Why do you think Bismarck is portrayed in this way?*

Bismarck's new constitution ensured that he held a pivotal position at the centre of government. He controlled the governments of Prussia and the German Empire and he was at the centre of policy making. He harangued the Reichstag to get them to accept his proposals and if they failed to comply, he sought the Kaiser's permission to dissolve the lower house and hold new elections – with the intention of getting more supporters there. Although Bismarck was supposed, by law, to discuss proposed legislation with the Kaiser, Wilhelm I came to be totally dependent on his chancellor so that he more or less allowed him to go his own way. Since the Kaiser was so desperate to keep his services, whenever there were differences of opinion (as did happen on a number of occasions), Bismarck could usually get what he wanted by threatening to resign! Indeed Lady Emily Russell, wife of the British ambassador, was to write in 1880:

> The initiated know that the emperor has allowed Prince Bismarck to have his own way in everything; and the great chancellor revels in the absolute power he has acquired and does as he pleases. He lives in the country and governs the German Empire without ever taking the trouble to consult the Emperor about his plans, who only learns what is being done from the documents to which his signature is necessary, and which his Majesty signs without questions or hesitation. Never has a subject been granted so much irresponsible power from his sovereign, and never has a minister inspired a nation with more abject individual, as well as general, terror. No wonder, then, that the Crown Prince should be so worried at the state of things which he has not more personal power or influence to remedy than anyone else in Prussia, while Prince Bismarck terrorises Germany with the Emperor's tacit and cheerful consent.

1

A closer look

Bismarck's power

There is much debate over the extent of power influenced by Bismarck. On the one hand, he seemed to have had almost dictatorial powers. As a result of the Constitution, he was Prussian Prime Minister, Foreign Minister, Reich Chancellor and he also presided over the Bundesrat. He manipulated Wilhelm I and interfered in the appointment of Ministers (giving them little power beyond the carrying out of his instructions). He did not consult with others and he did not use a cabinet system (whereby Ministers jointly decide policy). Indeed, it would seem that the government was more Bismarck's than the Kaiser's.

However, there were limitations to his power. He was ultimately answerable to the Kaiser. If he lost the support of the Kaiser, as did, in fact, happen after 1888, when Wilhelm I died, he had no power in his own right. In addition, the new Germany was a federal state and the individual states which made up the Confederation retained a great deal of independence. Bismarck could not ignore the Reichstag either, since he needed to ensure that he had majority support there, especially when the army budget was up for renewal. He found it increasingly difficult to keep the Reichstag 'on side' as his rule progressed and there were sometimes some quite ugly scenes. Bismarck's control of day-to-day decision making was finally limited by his frequent absences from Berlin because of his ill health, which caused him to retreat to his country estates.

A closer look

Prussia

Prussia controlled two thirds of the territory of the new German Empire, commanded three fifths of its population and possessed many of its industrial and mineral resources. The King of Prussia was the Emperor, and the Minister-President of Prussia, the chancellor. Prussia also dominated the Bundesrat, with 17 of the 58 votes there (Bavaria was next highest with 6) and the civil service and bureaucracy of the Empire followed the pattern already established in Prussia. The Imperial army was modelled on the Prussian army and law codes were based on the Prussian ones. Yet Prussia was a strongly authoritarian state. It had its own 'three class' franchise system which led to a Prussian parliament dominated by aristocratic Junkers. Consequently Prussian influence acted as a brake on democratic change, while at the same time providing a source of strength, since Prussia's traditions of military prowess and administrative efficiency gave the German people something to be proud of and served as a patriotic focus. It is perhaps no coincidence that Bismarck chose to wear a Prussian military uniform, whenever possible, throughout his time as chancellor.

Domestic politics of the Bismarckian era, 1871–90

Bismarck and the 'Kulturkampf'

In his first seven years as chancellor, Bismarck pursued a **Kulturkampf** in Germany, directed against the Catholics. Since he believed that Germans should put their loyalty to the state above all else, this is, perhaps, unsurprising. Thirty-nine per cent of Germans were Catholics, as against 61 per cent Protestants. Prussia, the Junker class and Bismarck himself had this Protestant background. Catholicism, on the other hand, was strong in the southern German states. These southern states were inclined to look for guidance from Austria (whom they had supported in 1866) and had been the last, and most reluctant, of the states to join the German Empire.

Bismarck's anti-Catholicism was also a reaction to the development of the Catholic Centre (*Zentrum*) Party, which had been set up to protect Catholic interests in 1870 and which gained 58 Reichstag deputies in 1871. The Centre was supported not only by the southern Catholics, but by the Poles in the east and the French of Alsace-Lorraine.

In the 1864 'Syllabus of Errors', the Pope had declared the Catholic Church to be opposed to liberalism, nationalism and 'recent' civilisation. In 1870 he went on to proclaim the 'Doctrine of Papal Infallibility' which stated that on matters of morality and faith, the Pope could not be wrong. This placed Catholics in a difficult position and meant that they could face difficult choices between the demands of their church and their country.

Bismarck feared that the Centre Party would encourage civil disobedience among Catholics whenever the policies of the state conflicted with those of the Pope. These fears grew even more acute when, in 1874, the Centre Party won 91 Reichstag seats under a new leader – the able politician Ludwig Windhorst. It became the second largest party in the Reichstag, threatening Bismarck's ability to control the majority. Such a development confirmed Bismarck's determination to crush Catholic influence in Germany.

Summary question

Why did many liberal German politicians criticise the German Constitution of 1871?

Cross-reference

For the events of 1866, re-read the Introduction.

Key term

Kulturkampf: literally this means 'struggle for culture' or 'struggle of civilisation'. This was the name given to Bismarck's attack on the Catholic Church and its political influence in Germany, particularly through the Centre Party.

THE BERLIN BULLFIGHTER.

Fig. 4 *Bismarck as a bullfighter subduing the Catholic Church. Notice that the bull is wearing a papal crown*

Cross-reference

The **Centre Party** is outlined on page 13.

Exploring the detail

The Pope and the Catholic Church

The Pope is the head of the Catholic Church and resides in the Vatican in Rome. All Catholics looked to the Pope as their spiritual leader. The Catholic Church was traditionally conservative and the momentous changes that were affecting Europe in the 19th century caused it considerable alarm. Industrialisation was producing a more vociferous 'working class' and new theories were challenging the Church's teaching. In 1859, Charles Darwin had published 'The Origin of Species' suggesting a non-Biblical explanation of the creation of species, while between 1867 and 1894 Karl Marx was to publish *Das Kapital*, encouraging workers to rise against their masters and create a classless society. The Pope's own temporal (earthly) power had been challenged by the unification of Italy. The new doctrinal statements were, in part, an attempt to reinforce control.

Key profile

Ludwig Windhorst

Ludwig Windhorst (1812–91) was born into a Catholic family in Hanover. He became a deputy and Minister of the Interior there and opposed Bismarck's annexation of his state. In 1874 he became leader of the Centre Party. It was chiefly owing to his skill and courage as a parliamentary debater that the party increased in numbers. He was attacked by Bismarck who attempted, unsuccessfully, to discredit him. After 1879, however, he became reconciled and even friendly to Bismarck.

Kulturkampf campaign

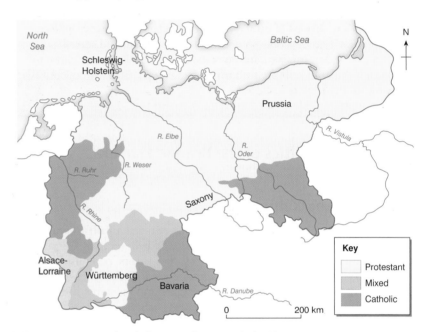

Fig. 5 *Protestant and Catholic areas of Germany in the 1870s*

Some German Catholics had refused to accept the new doctrine of Papal Infallibility. There were only about 50,000 of these so-called 'Old Catholics', but Bismarck saw them as a useful ally against the rest of the Catholic Church in general, and the Centre Party in particular, especially when 'Old Catholic' teachers and professors were dismissed from schools and universities by Catholic bishops. The National Liberals, who wanted to replace religious with state control of education, also offered support and the campaign cemented the 'alliance' of 1871–8.

Claiming to be acting in the interests of the 'Old Catholics', in 1873, Bismarck launched the Kulturkampf, declaring to the Reichstag:

> The question before us is, in my opinion, not a religious, ecclesiastical question. It is a political question. It is not, as our Catholic citizens are being persuaded, a matter of a struggle between a Protestant dynasty and a Catholic Church. It is not a matter of a struggle between belief and unbelief. It is a matter of conflict, which is as old as the human race, between monarchy and priesthood. What is at stake is the defence of the state.

Activity

Making a timeline

As you read through this section, make a timeline of the key events of the Kulturkampf.

Activity

Source analysis

Study Source 2. What arguments does Bismarck use to try to justify his Kulturkampf and to dispel criticism?

2

Since 1871, a climate hostile to the Catholics and Centre Party had already started to develop in government. For example, there had been a series of newspaper articles against the Centre Party and the Catholic section of the Prussian Ministry of Religion and Education had been abolished. Clergy had also been ordered to avoid any mention of politics while preaching. In May 1872, diplomatic relations with the Vatican had been broken off and the Jesuits, a religious order which pledged to spread Catholicism and who were strong supporters of Papal authority, were forbidden from preaching or entering schools. This had led to the expulsion of almost all Jesuits from Prussia and an anti-Jesuit campaign had gradually begun to spread through the rest of Germany.

It was in a series of laws passed in Prussia between 1873 and 1875 that Bismarck intensified this Kulturkampf. In May 1873, the 'May' or 'Falk' Laws were introduced by the Prussian Minister of Religion and Education, Adalbert Falk. These laws brought the Catholic Church more closely under government control. Catholic education came under state supervision, including the education of priests themselves. Only those who had studied in Germany and passed a state exam could become priests and existing priests were required to retrain and prove their loyalty to the state. The appointment of clergy was to be made by the state (rather than the Pope), and a civil marriage ceremony was made compulsory in Prussia and subsequently, the rest of the Empire. All other religious orders were dissolved, state financial aid to the Catholic Church was ended, and Prussian Catholics were deprived of legal and civil rights.

In 1874, the registration of births, marriages and deaths in Prussia was removed from the Church and taken over by the state. All states were given the right to restrict the freedom of movement of the clergy and any banned priest caught preaching could be placed under house arrest or even expelled from Germany. Finally, in 1875, the Prussian government was given the power to suspend state subsidies to **dioceses** where the clergy were resisting the new laws and every religious order, except for nursing orders, was abolished.

At first, Wilhelm I was lukewarm in his support for the Kulturkampf. However, when Pius IX wrote to him in 1873, complaining about the Kulturkampf and adding that anyone who had been baptised belonged to the Pope, Wilhelm was much offended and showed some support. Nevertheless, many members of the royal family, including the Crown Prince Friedrich and his English wife, Victoria, regarded the campaign with disfavour.

> ■ Key term
>
> **Diocese:** a unit of Church administration which was part of an ecclesiastical area headed by a bishop or archbishop.

Fig. 6 *Bismarck and Kaiser Wilhelm I*

Die Nacht am Rhein.

Wahl-Lokal

Fig. 7 *The Catholic Church stood up to Bismarck's persecution, forcing him to abandon his Kulturkampf*

Results and end of the Kulturkampf

The Pope sent a letter to all German bishops instructing them to disobey the anti-Catholic laws. Although Bismarck forbade the bishops to print the letter, by 1876, all the Catholic bishops of Prussia and all Polish bishops had either been imprisoned or exiled and 1,400 out of 4,600 Catholic parishes were without priests.

However, despite this repression, the Catholic Church continued to thrive. Bismarck had underestimated the strength of Catholicism and the extent of popular support which it enjoyed. Persecution created martyrs and encouraged even greater resistance. Many ordinary Catholics rallied to the cause of their Church and became more convinced than ever that they should support the Centre Party in order to defend their interests. The Centre Party's leader, Windhorst, rose to the challenge, organising meetings and 'national resistance tours' to attack the Kulturkampf and unite the Catholic voters. The party was extremely successful in whipping up support which cut across both class and regional divisions and by 1874, it had increased its number of Reichstag seats to 91– fewer than the Liberals who held 155 – but nearly twice as many as the next largest party, the Progressives.

Far from unifying the newly created empire, Bismarck had intensified its divisions. In 1874, a Catholic barrel maker tried to assassinate Bismarck. Furthermore, there were growing problems in the minority areas, among the Poles and peoples of Alsace-Lorraine. German protestants were even expressing unease with Bismarck's attack on religious freedoms, while within the dominant National Liberal Party, there were those of Jewish blood, who disliked the way the campaign was also provoking more anti-Semitism in Germany.

By the late 1870s, Bismarck must have realised that the campaign had been a mistake. His frequent absences from Berlin, occasioned by his own poor health, made it difficult for him to keep control of the situation, and he seemed keen to find an excuse to bring this destructive campaign to an end.

Other factors also favoured the ending of the Kulturkampf:

■ Bismarck wanted a closer alliance with Catholic Austria and he feared that his anti-Catholic policies would stand in the way.

■ Bismarck suspected that the Centre Party was giving support to those in France seeking revenge for Germany's seizure of Alsace-Lorraine in 1871.

■ **Cross-reference**

Anti-Semitism in Russia in the same period is discussed on pages 70–2.

- Bismarck wanted to change his economic policy and abandon free trade, after the agricultural and industrial depressions of the 1870s. Since this would lose him the support of the National Liberals, he could not afford to have the Centre Party (which favoured protection) as an 'enemy'.

- Bismarck wanted to build up the support of the Protestant Conservatives, who had grown increasingly hostile to the Kulturkampf because it was promoting anti-clericalism in Germany.

- Bismarck felt that increasing working class support for socialism posed an even greater threat to German unity and his own position than the Catholic Church. He could not hope to wage a war successfully against both Catholicism and socialism and since the Catholic Church had declared against socialism, Bismarck felt that he might be able to utilise the Centre Party and Catholicism against this new 'enemy'.

Cross-reference

Bismarck's economic policy, including the issues of free trade and protection, and the political changes of 1878–9, are discussed on pages 20–1. His policies against socialism can be found on pages 22–4.

The death of Pius IX in 1878 and the election of a new and more liberal Pope, Leo XIII, provided Bismarck with the excuse he needed to change to a policy of conciliation. One of Leo XIII's first acts was to write to Bismarck, expressing his wish for a reconciliation and an end to the struggle. Bismarck began long and difficult negotiations with the Pope's envoy. He put all the blame for the May Laws on Dr Falk, who was forced to resign. In 1880, the repeal of the May Laws began, together with the removal of the ban on foreign-trained priests within Germany. Catholic clergy gradually returned to their parishes. However, not all the laws were repealed. Civil marriages continued and the Jesuits were not allowed in Germany.

The struggle had several consequences:

- Bismarck's subsequent relations with the Papacy were good and in 1885 he even proposed the Pope as a mediator in Germany's colonial dispute with Spain.

- The Centre Party, which gained 93 seats in 1877, 94 in 1878 and 100 in 1881, transformed itself into a purely religious party and was no longer seen as the refuge of Bismarck's 'enemies' (*Reichsfeinde*). Leo XIII encouraged the Centre Party to support the existence of the German Empire and thus, in the long term, unity was strengthened.

- Closer relations with the Papacy and the support of the Centre Party facilitated an alliance with Austria, signed in 1879.

- The change of policy in 1878–9 enabled Bismarck to make himself independent from the National Liberals (whose prestige fell).

- The Kulturkampf highlighted Bismarck's qualities as a politician. His actions showed him to be a supreme opportunist who was able to move from persecution to conciliation to strengthen his position in the Reichstag and facilitate the policy changes he desired.

Activity

Critical analysis

The points given above provide some positive outcomes of the Kulturkampf. In pairs, prepare a balance sheet which evaluates both the positive and negative aspects of the Kulturkampf.

Summary question

How successful was Bismarck in dealing with the threat from the Catholic Church in Germany in the years 1871 to 1878?

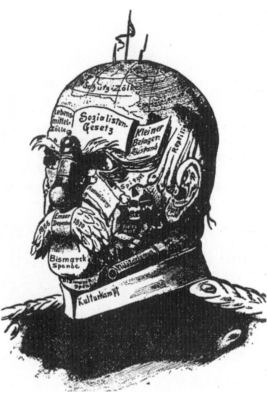

Fig. 8 *Having abandoned the Kulturkampf, which can be seen on his collar, Bismarck turned his attention to protectionism and anti-socialism, as seen on his head and brow*

Political changes 1878–9

Bismarck's political realignment in 1878–9 has been described as a turning point in his domestic policy. It included:

■ the abandonment of the Kulturkampf
■ the reintroduction of tariffs on the imports of foreign goods
■ the ending of the political alliance with the National Liberals
■ the creation of a Conservative/Centre support base in the Reichstag
■ the beginning of a new political struggle against socialism.

Reintroduction of tariffs on the imports of foreign goods

In the 1870s Bismarck, in order to keep the support of the National Liberals, had followed a policy of **free trade**. The German economy had experienced a rapid boom in the early 1870s and had appeared strong enough to withstand foreign competition. However, in 1873, it suffered a serious financial crisis, when prices started falling throughout the world and this was followed by several years of much slower growth. German manufacturers were alarmed and blamed the strong opposition which they faced from foreign competitors. Consequently, they started to demand **protection**.

Most European countries, with the exception of Britain, had moved towards protection by the late 1870s and in 1878, some of the leading German manufacturers formed the 'Central Association of German Manufacturers' to campaign for the introduction of tariffs on imports in Germany. Agriculture was also suffering from a depression due to a series of bad harvests at the end of the 1870s and increased foreign competition from cheap American and Russian wheat. Peasant farmers and landowners alike feared for their incomes and survival. Like the manufacturers and industrialists, they began to campaign for protective tariffs against cheap foreign grain.

By 1878, Bismarck had decided to reintroduce protective tariffs. There were a number of reasons for this:

■ As a Junker landowner himself, Bismarck was sympathetic to the demands of the agriculturalists. A threat to agricultural incomes would undermine the economic position of the Junker aristocracy (who supplied the officers for the army and on whom the imperial state rested).

■ Bismarck favoured German self-sufficiency, especially in wheat. He did not want Germany to become dependent on foreign imports and felt it essential that the country could feed itself, in case of war.

■ Tariffs could provide the government with much needed revenue. The Reich government could not tax its citizens directly but was dependent on contributions from individual states. Since all other taxes had to have Reichstag approval, Bismarck favoured any means of gaining income which did not require dependency on an annual Reichstag vote.

■ Bismarck was keen to work more closely with the German Conservative Party and the Centre Party (which included Junkers and factory-owners). He needed their support against the growing threat of socialism.

■ Russia, which supplied Germany with wheat, had adopted a policy of protection. However, relations with Russia had become strained over issues in the Balkans in the years 1877–8 and protection could act as a form of retaliation.

■ Key terms

Free trade: having few or no duties or tariffs on imports or exports. Those who supported this, such as the National Liberals, believed it encouraged economic growth because it kept the price of imported raw materials low which, in turn, reduced the cost of manufactured goods. Consequently, these could be sold abroad at a more competitive price. It was also hoped that free trade would encourage other countries to reduce or remove duties.

Protection: the introduction of duties (tariffs) especially on imports. This would increase the price of imported goods, especially manufactured goods, and encourage consumers to buy home-produced goods. However, it could lead to retaliation, with other countries introducing similar tariffs and so have an adverse effect on exports.

In February 1878, Bismarck announced to the Reichstag the first stage of a comprehensive financial reform that would involve the introduction of tariffs. In May 1879, Bismarck declared to the Reichstag:

> The only country which persists in a policy of free trade is England and that will not last long. France and America have departed completely from this line; Austria instead of lowering her tariffs has made them higher; Russia has done the same. By opening the doors of our state to the imports of foreign countries, we have become the dumping ground for the production of those countries. Since we have become swamped by the surplus production of foreign nations, our prices have been depressed. The development of our industries and our entire economic position has suffered as a consequence.
>
> Let us finally close our doors and erect barriers, as we have proposed to you, in order to reserve for German industries at least the home market, which because of German good nature, has been exploited by foreigners. I see that those countries that have adopted protection are prospering and those countries which have free trade are deteriorating.

3

Questions

1 Summarise Bismarck's arguments as given in Source 3.

2 What arguments might the National Liberals and other supporters of free trade have used against those of Bismarck?

Ending of the National Liberal Alliance and creation of a Conservative/Centre support base

By the later 1870s, Bismarck had grown increasingly irritated by the National Liberals. They had forced him to agree to give the Reichstag the power to vote for the army budget every seven years and constantly demanded greater parliamentary powers. Their support for free trade, when others were clamouring for change, proved the final straw.

In the elections of 1877, the National Liberals had lost seats while the pro-protection Conservative parties did rather better. Consequently, when the National Liberals led a campaign against Bismarck's reintroduction of tariffs, Bismarck called another election in June 1878, aiming to deprive them of still more seats. His gamble paid off as their support fell further and the Conservatives and Centre Party emerged with the overall majority.

Cross-reference

For further details of the powers of the **Reichstag**, refer to page 12.

Table 2 *German election results, 1877–8*

Party	1877	1878
National Liberals	128	99
Centre Party	93	94
German Conservative Party	40	59
Free Conservatives	38	57
The Progressives	52	39
SPD	12	9

In 1879, Bismarck was able to pass his legislation for levying tariffs on iron, iron goods and grain and for increasing indirect taxation on selected luxury goods with the support of the Conservatives, Free Conservatives, Centre and 15 so-called 'tariff rebels' from the National Liberal Party. The unity of the National Liberal Party was destroyed. The results of these changes can be seen in the table on the following page.

Table 3 *Results of the economic changes of 1878–9*

Political	Economic
The National Liberal Party was seriously weakened by the crisis of 1878–9. There were already divisions before 1878 but these became permanent in 1879.	Although agricultural prices continued to fall, the tariff on grain protected farmers and landowners from the worst effects of the agricultural depression. Landowners became strong supporters of Bismarck.
In the 1880s Bismarck relied for his majorities in the Reichstag on an alliance between the Conservative parties and the Centre, together with the right wing of the National Liberal Party. The forces of conservatism were therefore dominant in the 1880s and there was less pressure on Bismarck to move towards a more representative system of government.	Industrialists and businessmen abandoned their support for free trade and the National Liberal Party. In the 1880s they increasingly supported the Conservative Party. This became known as the 'alliance of steel and rye'.
Bismarck had demonstrated his supreme political skill and opportunism, his control over the Reichstag and his ability to make and break alliances.	Consumers suffered from artificially high prices on basic food products such as bread. High tariffs had adverse effects on living standards, especially for the very poor. This, in turn, provided greater support for socialism and the SPD.
The Reich became more united in its support of protection since Bismarck presented tariffs as a patriotic necessity, essential for the defence of the fatherland.	

■ Summary question

Why did Bismarck change to a policy of protection at the end of the 1870s?

Did you know?

SPD or SAPD?

The Social Democratic Party was only known as the SPD after 1891. Until then it was called the SAPD, or Socialist Workers' Party of Germany. However, few books make this distinction, and to avoid confusion this book refers to the party as the SPD throughout.

The new political struggle against socialism

Bismarck perceived the emergence of the Social Democratic Party and the growing popularity of socialism as yet another threat to the unity of the Reich, as well as to his own position as chancellor.

Socialism already had a long history in Germany. There had been workers' parties in the more industrially advanced states of Germany in the 1840s and 1850s, but not until 1863 had various groups combined to form the German Workers' Association (ADAV). This group was led by Ferdinand Lasalle, and was committed to a socialist programme which included the redistribution of wealth and the abolition of private property. It had 15,000 members by the middle of the 1870s.

■ Key profile

Ferdinand Lasalle

Ferdinand Lasalle (1825–64) was a Jewish lawyer. He had begun as a liberal nationalist and had been imprisoned for his part in the 1848 revolution in Germany. However, he had become convinced that the working class needed their own political party and in 1863 founded the General German Workers' Association, Germany's first Labour Party. Although left wing, Lasalle did not believe in Marxist revolution and was prepared to work with the state for the benefit of working people. He led a flamboyant lifestyle and was killed in a duel.

Fig. 9 *Ferdinand Lasalle*

The ADAV was followed, in 1869, by a more Marxist organisation, the Social Democratic Workers' Party (SDAP), set up by Karl Liebknecht. This group had a more overtly revolutionary programme, including the abolition of class rule. By 1875 it had 9,000 members.

In 1875, these two groups met at Gotha and united to form the Social Democratic Party (SPD). A programme was drawn up stating aims such as:

There should be:

1 universal, equal and direct suffrage, with secret, obligatory voting by all citizens at all elections

2 legislation by the people

3 universal, equal and compulsory state education

4 a progressive income tax to replace indirect taxation

5 the right to form trade unions

6 a reduction in the working day

7 the abolition of child labour

8 protective laws for the life and health of the workers.

4

Underlying the SPD's short-term aims was the desire to create a workers' republic with nationalised industries and workers enjoying a share of the profits. These were Marxist ideas but the party's leaders appreciated that they were unlikely to be able to lead Germany in revolution in the immediate future. Consequently, they were content to campaign to win seats in the Reichstag and in 1877 the party won half a million votes and 12 seats. This was a negligible amount, but five times that which the separate workers' parties had polled in 1871. Bismarck was understandably concerned by the threat the new party posed to the position of Germany's Junkers and factory owners – and indeed to himself!

The Anti-Socialist Law

Bismarck believed that socialism, which was an international movement like Catholicism, was a social and political threat to the unity of the German Empire and a threat to traditional German society in which the majority of peasants showed respect and deference to the monarchy, army and Junker aristocracy. Bismarck also knew that an attack on socialism would strengthen Germany's ties with Russia and Austria (his conservative allies overseas) who were intent on suppressing international revolutionary movements.

Two assassination attempts on the Emperor in 1878 provided the opportunity he needed and Bismarck took advantage of the public alarm they caused to whip up anti-socialist feeling. He persuaded the Reichstag that the SPD should be suppressed in order to remove a major source of disloyalty.

The Anti-Socialist Law, which was passed in October 1878, declared that:

- Organisations which through Social Democratic activities aim to overthrow the established state or social order are hereby forbidden.

- All meetings in which Social Democratic activities appear to be dedicated to the overthrow of the existing state or social order shall be dissolved.

- All publications in which Social Democratic influence appears to be aimed at overthrowing the established state or social order by breaching the public peace are forbidden.

- Anyone who takes part as a member of a forbidden organisation shall be punished with a fine of up to 500 marks or with imprisonment of three months.

5

Questions for discussion

1 How revolutionary do you feel the Gotha programme was?

2 Which of these points do you think would most alarm Bismarck? Why?

Exploring the detail

Socialism

Both Karl Marx and Friedrich Engels were German. In 1848 they co-authored the 'Communist Manifesto' which put forward the idea that all history was the history of class struggles. They suggested that workers in industrialising countries would need to use force to destroy a social system based upon exploitation. In its most extreme form socialism is generally referred to as Marxism or communism. However, more moderate forms of socialism are less violent and seek to achieve greater equality by reducing private profit, extending opportunities and spreading welfare reforms.

Cross-reference

Although **Marx** and **Engels** were German, Marxist ideas took a firmer hold in Russia than in Germany. More on Marxism, including a profile of Karl Marx, can be found on pages 77–9.

Fig. 10 *The breaking up of a meeting of the Social Democrats in 1881. Among the participants were Wilhelm Liebknecht and August Bebel*

As can be seen, the law banned meetings and publications as well as laying down penalties for those considered a threat to the state. These penalties included fines, imprisonment and, at the worst, exile from Germany. Police powers were also increased with powers to search houses; arrest on suspicion; break up meetings, processions and festive gatherings; suppress books, pamphlets, newspapers and periodicals; and seize the property of organisations perceived as a danger to the state. Trade unions and cultural associations with socialist connections were also banned. However, because of the fierce Reichstag opposition, led by the National Liberals and supported by the Centre and Progressive Parties, the Law did not actually ban the SPD as a political party. Members could still take part in elections and sit in the Reichstag and federal governments.

Consequences of the Anti-Socialist Law

As with the Kulturkampf, repression had the opposite effect from that which Bismarck had intended. The law deprived many people of their livelihoods and around 15,000 were sentenced to imprisonment or hard labour and many others forced to leave the country.

Since industrial workers were made to feel the state was unsympathetic and unlikely to right their grievances, after an initial decline in support for the SPD following the Act, members and supporters returned in increasing numbers. The number of people voting for the SPD rose from 437,158 in 1878 to 1,427,928 in 1890 and the number of seats held by the SPD rose from 9 to 35 in the same period. The Act also helped divorce the Socialist deputies – who had to appeal to the broader electoral constituency – from the more militant and persecuted activists and this had the effect of broadening the SPD's appeal.

Table 4 *The effects of repression 1878–90*

Negative	Positive
■ Membership of the SPD initially declined in the immediate aftermath of the legislation.	■ Within a few years, trade unionism revived. There was a series of strikes in the industrial and mining areas and by 1890 membership had reached 278,000.
■ Trade unions were crushed.	■ The socialist vote nearly doubled between 1878 and 1887.
■ The cabinet, civil service and Prussian Diet were purged in 1880 to remove liberal sympathisers.	■ Strong leadership rallied the party and organised resistance. In 1880, the SPD rejected anarchism and terrorism.
■ 1,350 publications and 45 out of 47 socialist newspapers were suppressed.	■ A new party newspaper, *The Social Democrat*, was published in Zurich and smuggled into Germany by the 'Red postmaster' – Julius Motteller.
■ Many were exiled or imprisoned with hard labour.	■ Groups met in secret to discuss policy developments and collect financial contributions.
■ The Prussian police expelled 67 leading socialists from Berlin (1879) and prominent socialists were driven from Breslau (1879), Hamburg (1880), and Leipzig in (1881).	■ Secret conferences were organised on foreign soil including Switzerland in 1880 and Denmark in 1883.
■ Many socialists chose to emigrate, especially to the USA.	■ The SPD encouraged great loyalty from its members by organising educational courses, libraries, sports clubs and choral societies.
■ Before the election of 1881, 600 socialists were arrested. The SPD had such difficulty in finding sufficient candidates to contest the elections that one, Bebel, stood in 35 constituencies.	

State socialism

Bismarck was aware that repression alone would not reduce support for the SPD as many of the workers' grievances were legitimate. He appreciated the need to show the workers that the state was not unconcerned for their welfare and had more to offer the working class than the socialists. This is often referred to as the 'carrot and stick' approach. Can you explain why?

As he said to the Reichstag, in 1881:

> A beginning must be made in reconciling the labouring classes to the state. A remedy cannot be sought only through the repression of socialist excesses. It is necessary to have a definite advancement in the welfare of the working classes. The matter of first importance is the care of those workers who are incapable of earning a living. Previous provision for guarding workers against the risk of falling into helplessness through incapacity caused by accident or age have not proved adequate, and the inadequacy of such provisions has been a main contributing cause driving the working classes to seek help by joining the Social Democratic movement.

6

Question

What were Bismarck's motives for the introduction of state socialism?

The main measures providing for state social security are described in Table 5.

Table 5 *State social security measures, 1883–9*

May 1883	Medical insurance. This scheme was paid for jointly by employers and employees. It allowed for the payment of medical bills for workers and their families and covered 3 million workers.
June 1884	Accident insurance. This was paid for entirely by employers. It provided benefits and funeral grants to people who had been injured at work. In 1886 this was extended to cover 7 million agricultural workers.
May 1889	Old Age Pensions. These were introduced for people over the age of 70.

Bismarck's scheme was the first of its kind in the world and much more extensive than might have been expected at the time. Some workers were enthusiastic about it while others believed it was a 'sham' since the government had consistently opposed trade unions and socialism. The Marxist, Friedrich Engels, then in retirement, urged opposition to the scheme, insisting that the workers did not want concessions from an autocratic government but the removal of that government. However, his voice represented only an extreme minority. Some Liberals were also against the scheme for rather different reasons. They believed it extended the role of the state and threatened individual freedom and a 'laissez-faire' attitude.

Although Bismarck had hoped the scheme would attract workers away from the SPD, support for the socialists continued to grow and reached nearly 1.5 million by 1890. The SPD's seats in the Reichstag had fallen to 11 in 1887 but three years later, they reached 35. At the same time employers grumbled at the trouble and expense of 'sticking on eleven million stamps every Saturday morning', referring to the insurance stamps which had to be placed in an insurance book, for each worker covered by the scheme.

While there was no violent revolution in Germany before 1918, state socialism certainly failed in winning the workers' full allegiance. The Anti-Socialist Law was renewed four times, effectively making the activities of the socialist labour movement illegal until 30 September 1890. In 1889, Bismarck was so concerned that he proposed that the Anti-Socialist Law be made permanent. However, the Reichstag refused to pass this amendment, and the arrival of a new Kaiser, Wilhelm II, who believed that the workers could be won over by more social insurance schemes, led to the lapsing of the Act.

Relations with the Reichstag

The Constitution of 1871 had created a Reichstag with limited powers. Bismarck hated having to pander to the Reichstag and if he disliked sharing power with other Ministers, he resented even more having to take

Did you know?

Britain did not adopt similar state insurance schemes until 1908 (Old Age Pensions) and 1911 (Health and Unemployment Insurance). Lloyd George, the Chancellor of the Exchequer in the Liberal government of this period sent civil servants to Germany to study the German scheme. It thus became a model for that later adopted by Britain.

Question

How successful were Bismarck's attempts to curb the growth of socialism between 1878 and 1890?

Cross-reference

For further details of the **Constitution** and the powers of the Reichstag refer to page 12.

account of the views of the political parties in the Reichstag. According to the memoirs of Prince von Bülow:

> In my presence, Bismarck expressed some extreme opinions about his domestic enemies. He did not want, in the least, to govern autocratically, he said, although there are those who daily accuse him of this. He was perfectly well aware that, in Germany, in the second half of the 19th century, absolutism and autocracy would be impossible. But a parliamentary regime seemed to him just impossible. Our parties possessed neither the patriotism of the French nor the sound common sense of the English. Considering the political hopelessness of the average German, a full parliamentary system would lead to weakness and incompetence at the top and to over-confidence and ever new demands from below.

7

However, for all his misgivings, Bismarck appreciated that without Reichstag support he could not carry out his policies. It was in his interests to ensure he could command a majority there so that he could make new laws and obtain the taxes he needed for the government and the army.

The relationship was never easy, even though Bismarck tried to ensure he had groups in the Reichstag 'on his side'. Bismarck's first major struggle over the issue of military spending, took place despite his 'alliance' with the majority National Liberals; the resulting **Septennial Law** of 1874 was essentially a defeat for the chancellor. After the political changes of 1878–9, Bismarck turned to his more natural supporters – the Conservatives and, less obviously, the Centre Party – and he tried to use their fears of socialist revolution to get their support for his measures.

In 1880, when the Reichstag was proving awkward, Bismarck considered setting up an alternative Reich Council which would 'bypass' the Reichstag. As an experiment, he tried this out in Prussia, where he launched a Prussian Council with representatives from commerce, industry and agriculture. Unsurprisingly, the scheme was rejected by the Reichstag and after the 1881 Reichstag election, three quarters of the Reichstag were left hostile to the government.

In 1886–7, when the army budget was again due for renewal and Bismarck wanted a 10 per cent increase to finance army growth, he exploited the *Boulanger Crisis* of 1886 in France to create a war scare and in January 1887 he dissolved the Reichstag. The subsequent election was fought in an atmosphere of artificially contrived crisis and brought gains for those parties who supported Bismarck. Through his exploitation of the Boulanger Crisis, he skilfully engineered a majority in the Reichstag which passed the Army Bill. This marked the high watermark of Bismarck's control of the Reichstag and illustrated his skill as an opportunist.

Three years later, however, Bismarck's position was less secure. In October 1890, Bismarck proposed a new Anti-Socialist Bill which was not only intended to operate permanently but contained an extreme clause for the expulsion of socialist agitators. The National Liberals refused to support it, since it allowed the police powers to drive socialists from their homes. However, the conservatives said they would no longer support it if this clause was abandoned! Bismarck did not

■ **Key term**

The Septennial Law of 1874: an agreement whereby the Reichstag could discuss and agree (or refuse) military spending (the army budget) every seven years.

■ **Cross-reference**

The political changes of 1878–9 were discussed earlier in this chapter, on pages 20–2.

■ **Exploring the detail**

The Boulanger Crisis

The Boulanger Crisis began with the appointment in France in 1886 of a little known general, Georges Boulanger, as Minister of War. In the succeeding months he was transformed into a national cult figure as the long-awaited military saviour of France. Boulanger was one of those who wanted revenge for the French defeat of 1871 and the return of the lost provinces of Alsace-Lorraine. The arrest of a French official on the border of Alsace in April 1887 brought threats of war from the Minister. Bismarck used this as evidence of the possibility of war with France.

know what to do and rashly suggested that perhaps it was best to allow the socialists to rise in rebellion so that the army could be called upon to crush them once and for all. The Reichstag rejected the bill and another general election was held. It was to be Bismarck's last as chancellor.

Activities

Group activities

1 Make a copy of the grid below. Give a rating and brief explanation for each of Bismarck's policies.
1 = Very successful to 5 = Total failure

	Rating 1–5	Explanation
German Constitution		
Kulturkampf		
Socialism		
Relations with the Kaiser and Reichstag		

2 Hold a forum to discuss Bismarck's policies. Each member of the group could prepare a talk outlining the arguments and evidence for the success or failure of one of the policies shown in the grid.

Bismarck's resignation

Bismarck's resignation in 1890 came about following a change of Kaiser. Kaiser Wilhelm I had died in 1888 and was succeeded by his son, Friedrich. The latter, however, died in the same year from cancer of the throat.

Friedrich's son, Wilhelm, became Kaiser in 1888 and had no intention of taking a back seat role in policy making. A few weeks after becoming Emperor he said:

> I shall let the old man snuffle on for six months, then I shall rule myself.

Bismarck, who had experienced little or no interference from Wilhelm II's predecessors, made no attempt to gain the friendship of the young Kaiser and either ignored him or poured scorn on his policy suggestions.

The two differed over several key issues:

- Bismarck wanted to control policy making and maintain his position as Minister-President of Prussia. The Kaiser believed in personal rule and wanted to reduce the powers of the Minister-President.
- Bismarck wanted to repress socialism and workers' agitation. Wilhelm II was more sympathetic and believed he could win over the industrial workers where Bismarck had failed.
- Bismarck wanted to maintain close relations with Russia. The Kaiser favoured Austria.
- The chancellor cared nothing for popularity and was happy to fight the 'Reichsfeinde' and remain aloof in politics. Wilhelm wanted to be loved and honoured by all classes in society and perceived himself as the 'People's Emperor'.

In the 1890 elections, the SPD and Progressives increased their seats, while the conservatives (who were favourable to Bismarck) lost seats.

Exploring the detail

In January 1887, Friedrich developed an inflammation of the throat and a persistent cough. He could only talk in a hoarse whisper. His doctors were convinced that he was suffering from cancer of the throat. A leading consultant examined him and said that there was no evidence of cancer but this was almost certainly a lie, to save Friedrich from an operation that would have almost certainly killed him. By February 1888, Friedrich had lost the power of speech and he died on 13 June 1888, having ruled for only 99 days.

Fig. 11 *The young Kaiser Wilhelm II*

Fig. 12 *'Dropping the pilot', Punch 1890*

Table 6 *Comparison of election results, 1887 and 1890*

Party	1887	1890
National Liberals	99	42
Centre Party	98	106
SPD	11	35
German Conservatives	80	73
Free Conservatives	41	20
Progressives	32	76
Others	33	38

Bismarck was desperate and tried to introduce two bills, one increasing the army and the other banning the socialists, which he knew the Reichstag would reject, so as to be able to find an excuse to change the constitution. The chancellor seemed to have lost touch with reality. The measures he had proposed would have wrecked the Empire that he had devoted his life to creating and Wilhelm II rejected this scheme out of hand.

Two further incidents finally ended Bismarck's career. Firstly, he argued with the Kaiser about whom Ministers should approach first – Kaiser or chancellor. Secondly, Bismarck tried to prevent a visit by the Kaiser to Russia and accused Wilhelm II of 'meddling in foreign affairs'. Angrily, Bismarck submitted his resignation, but he was surprised when Wilhelm II accepted it. Thus, in March 1890, the 'grand old man' departed from the German Chancellory.

Bismarck's letter of resignation said:

> I would have asked to be relieved of my offices to Your Majesty long ago if I had not had the impression that Your Majesty wished to make use of the experiences and abilities of a faithful servant of your ancestors. Since I am now certain that Your Majesty does not require them I may retire from political life without having to fear that my decision may be condemned as untimely by public opinion.

 8

■ Did you know?

Bismarck celebrated his 75th birthday two days after his resignation. Wilhelm II even sent him a present; an enormous portrait of himself! Bismarck found retirement dull and boring. He did try to return to politics by being elected to the Reichstag, but he never took his seat. He wrote his memoirs and, briefly, wrote articles for a Hamburg newspaper which criticised Caprivi, the next German chancellor. His main hobby was the migration of birds, which he observed on his vast estates. His health began to deteriorate, especially after the death of his wife in 1894. He suffered from severe pains in the toes and, by 1897, could only walk a few paces. In July 1898 he died from inflammation of the lungs.

■ Activity

Talking points

In groups, examine the cartoon.

1. What message is the cartoonist trying to get across?
2. How does the cartoonist put across this message?
3. Can you explain the caption?
4. On a separate sheet of paper, suggest some suitable 'speech' bubbles for both the Kaiser and departing chancellor.

■ Summary question

How successful was Bismarck as chancellor of Germany between 1871 and 1890?

Germany under Kaiser Wilhelm II, 1890–1914

In this chapter you will learn about:

- the personality and political power of Kaiser Wilhelm II
- the Reich chancellors and their policies
- the growing militarism of the Kaiserreich
- the reasons for Germany's industrial growth
- the impact of economic change on society.

Fig. 1 *Kaiser Wilhelm II, on the right in this photograph. This picture unusually shows the Kaiser's withered left arm*

Cross-reference

Kaiser Wilhelm II's family tree is shown on page 5.

Kaiser Wilhelm II (1859–1941) was the grandson of Wilhelm I. His parents were Friedrich of Prussia, who had become Kaiser for 99 days before his premature death, and Victoria, the eldest daughter of Queen Victoria of Great Britain. This posed a contradiction. While his Father inculcated in him a love of the Prussian military tradition, his mother encouraged a 'liberal' outlook on life. However, Wilhelm never liked his mother and her preference for all things English antagonised him.

A difficult breach birth left him with a withered arm, defective hearing and paralysis on the left side of his body. Subconsciously or not, he blamed his mother – and England!

Wilhelm was subsequently subjected to a strict and painful upbringing in an attempt to force him to overcome these disabilities. Painful medical treatments, unapproachable parents and the demands of a surly personal tutor, Hinzpeter, combined to create a child that was both introverted and emotionally ill at ease. Wilhelm was given no peace in the attempt to force him to master the military skills expected of a Prince and he painfully learnt the art of horse-riding and, to his credit, became an able horseman and competent sailor. He was sent to Bonn University, but was much more influenced by his experience of military life, first with the Prussian Foot Guards and then as Colonel of the Guard Hussars where he developed his enthusiasm for uniforms. Throughout his life Wilhelm II was always happiest in the company of soldiers, while despising civilians, politicians and socialists.

Wilhelm suffered from deep personal insecurity and suffered frequent fits of rage. It has been suggested that this was caused by a condition which is now recognised as 'Attention Deficit Disorder', or that he was a repressed homosexual. Nevertheless, he married Princess Augusta Viktoria of Schleswig-Holstein-Sonderburg-Augustenburg in 1881 and fathered six sons and a daughter.

■ Activity

Research exercise

Undertake some further research into Wilhelm II's character and upbringing and make a poster presentation to share with your class. You should then write a short answer to the following question:

How far did Wilhelm II's upbringing and personality prepare him for the role of Kaiser?

■ Domestic politics under Kaiser Wilhelm II, 1890–1914

Kaiser Wilhelm II's personal power

Wilhelm II was determined to play an active role in politics and 'rule' rather than just 'reign'. He did not want to be lectured to by a chancellor and had even less intention of bowing to public opinion or the Reichstag, which he regarded with contempt. Consequently, he chose men whom he believed he could control as chancellors, and sought advice only from those whom he personally favoured, such as Philipp Fürst zu Eulenburg and his circle. However, Wilhelm II had neither the concentration nor judgement to run the government effectively. While his courtiers had to cover up criticism of Wilhelm's actions, Wilhelm ensured that he wielded ultimate power. This became even more marked after he dismissed his first choice of chancellor, General Leo Caprivi.

Key profile

Philipp Fürst zu Eulenburg und Hertefeld

Philipp zu Eulenburg (1847–1921) had wanted to become a poet or painter, but was forced by his Prussian father into a military career. He trained as an officer, but joined the foreign office in 1877 and subsequently worked as a diplomat. He got to know the future Kaiser Wilhelm II in 1886, and became one of Wilhelm's favourites. The Eulenburgs' landed estate in Liebenberg became a centre of power where a circle of friends, including Count von Moltke, met. The circle was referred to by jealous enemies as the 'camarillo' and its members possessed considerable influence. In the 1880s, Philipp was a government minister and became German ambassador in Vienna from 1894 to 1902. In 1892 Philipp's cousin, Count Botho zu Eulenburg, became Minister-President of Prussia, breaking Bismarck's tradition of the Imperial Chancellor also holding this office and extending the influence of the Eulenburg family further.

Fig. 2 *Philipp Fürst zu Eulenburg, one of the Kaiser's favourites*

It was the camarillo's suggestion that led to Caprivi's removal as chancellor and his replacement with von Bülow. In 1908 Philipp zu Eulenburg, by then a happily married man and father of eight children, was accused by a German journalist of being homosexual, and charged with perjury during a libel case. Homosexual activity was illegal at that time in Germany and the accusations and trial which followed destroyed his public image and his health. In the end, the trial was indefinitely adjourned, but it was noted that Wilhelm made no attempt to defend his friend and after this, his influence over Wilhelm ceased.

■ Key chronology

German chancellors, 1890–1914

1890–1894 General Leo von Caprivi

1894–1900 Prince Chlodwig zu Hohenlohe-Schillingsfürst

1900–1909 Count Bernhard von Bülow

1909–1917 Theobald Bethmann Hollweg

The Reich Chancellors and their policies

Table 1 *Election Results, 1887–1912*

Party	1887	1890	1893	1898	1903	1907	1912
Conservatives	121	93	100	79	75	84	57
Other right wing parties	3	7	21	31	22	33	19
National Liberals	99	42	53	46	51	54	45
Centre	98	106	96	102	100	95	91
Progressives (left wing liberals)	32	76	48	49	36	49	42
Social Democrats	11	35	44	56	81	43	110
Minorities, (e.g. Poles, Danes, Alsatians)	33	38	35	34	32	29	33

General Georg Leo von Caprivi, 1890–94

■ Key profile

General Leo von Caprivi

Caprivi (1831–99) was of Italian and Slovenian origin. He had entered the Prussian army in 1849 and served in the Austro-Prussian and the Franco-Prussian Wars. From 1883 to 1888 he was the Chief of the Imperial Admiralty. He was an intelligent man and soon demonstrated his abilities as an administrator of mildly progressive views. He was briefly appointed commander of the Tenth Army Corps in Hanover 1888–90 before he was summoned by Wilhem II to succeed Bismarck as chancellor.

Having quarrelled with Bismarck over the continuation of the Anti-Socialist Bill, Wilhelm was looking for a chancellor who would adopt a more moderate, conciliatory approach to the problems raised by socialism. Wilhelm favoured a military figure and personally selected Caprivi from a list of generals. He had administrative experience and was regarded as a moderniser, but, more importantly, Wilhelm believed that he would be controllable and amenable to Wilhelm's own direction.

Caprivi set out a 'new course' for German politics which he intended to follow. It included:

■ giving ministers more influence over policy making and developing greater cooperation with the Reichstag

■ bringing about social reform to reconcile the working classes with the established order

■ lowering tariffs to improve Germany's export trade and enable industry to expand.

■ Questions

1 Why do you think Caprivi's proposals were described as a 'new course'?

2 Do they justify this description?

As part of this new programme, Caprivi allowed the Anti-Socialist Bill to lapse in 1890 and he introduced a series of reforms in an attempt to take support away from socialism and reduce social tension:

■ Industrial Tribunals (courts) were set up to arbitrate in wage disputes in July 1890. Caprivi invited trade union representatives to sit on these tribunals.

■ Hours of work for women were reduced to a maximum of 11.

■ In 1891, Sunday working was forbidden and a guaranteed minimum wage established.

■ The employment of children under 13 years of age was forbidden and 13–18-year-olds were restricted to a maximum day of 10 hours.

■ A finance bill introduced progressive income tax whereby the more a person earned, the more he paid.

■ Duties on imported wheat, rye, cattle and timber were reduced under two trade treaties of 1891 and 1894. (Duties on industrial imports remained.)

These measures were generally welcomed by the working classes, the socialists, industrialists, Centre Party supporters and Liberals. However, the conservative Junkers disapproved and, led by the Eulenburgs, Holstein, the Agrarian League and the camarillo, they did all they could to bring Caprivi down.

■ Cross-reference

The **Agrarian League** is explained on pages 53–5.

The **camarillo** was outlined earlier in this chapter in the key profile on page 31.

Key profile

Baron Friedrich von Holstein

Friedrich von Holstein (1837–1909) was a strong right wing nationalist who took control of foreign affairs from 1890, when Bismarck resigned. Since Caprivi had little interest in this area, Holstein easily found a place for himself and although he was officially only a political counsellor in the foreign office, he wielded a great deal of influence and advised the Kaiser directly. Although Wilhelm II relied heavily on him, he remained almost totally unknown outside government circles.

The hostility of the Conservatives towards Caprivi was increased by the chancellor's compromise agreement with the Reichstag in 1893. This was made in order to get support for the Army Bill of 1892, drawn up at the Kaiser's demand, in order to increase the size of the army by 84,000. To gain the Reichstag's approval, Caprivi agreed to reduce military service from three to two years and to allow the Reichstag to discuss the military budget every five instead of every seven years. To the Conservatives this was a humiliating surrender.

Caprivi found it difficult to work with the Kaiser. When the chancellor tried to take the initiative and to follow his own policies, the Kaiser would often interfere. So, for example, Caprivi tried to reverse an aspect of the Kulturkampf and allow both Protestant and Catholic Church authorities more control over education. However, Wilhelm, who did not want to have to rely on the Centre Party to pass the bill, forced him to withdraw the proposed legislation. The modern historian Layton says that he was '*more astute and independent-minded than the Kaiser had bargained for*' while his rivals Porter and Armour have referred to him as '*an intelligent man with a mind of his own*'. This is not what the Kaiser had been wanting.

■ Exploring the detail

Military spending

The Kaiser was determined to increase military spending because he feared that one day Germany might have to face a war against France, which remained bitter about the loss of Alsace-Lorraine, and Russia, which had been allied to Germany in the time of Bismarck but which had developed closer relations with France since 1890. Von Schlieffen, the German Chief of Staff had drawn up the 'Schlieffen Plan' in 1892, on the assumption that if a war broke out, Germany would need to defeat France before Russia could mobilise in order to win. If this plan was to be effective, it was necessary to expand the army reserve and, although its details were not disclosed to the Reichstag, Wilhelm demanded Caprivi win approval for higher taxes to support increased military expenditure.

Socialism was also an issue on which the chancellor and Kaiser came to disagree, despite their initial consensus that socialism could be killed by reforms and that repression was counter-productive. The SPD continued to grow. They made considerable gains in the 1893 election and this, in addition to a wave of attacks by anarchists throughout Europe, convinced Wilhelm that an Anti-Socialist Subversion Bill was needed once again. When Caprivi refused to introduce this legislation, Philipp zu Eulenburg encouraged Wilhelm to present the bill to the Reichstag anyway. He suggested that if the Reichstag refused it, Wilhelm should rule without a parliament. This was the end for Caprivi. He managed to talk the Kaiser out of taking such a course of action, but then resigned. He complained:

> My relations with the All Highest have become intolerable. You cannot imagine how relieved I will feel to get out of here.

Fig. 3 *Caprivi introduced social reforms to try to improve the position of the growing population in Germany*

Caprivi's departure was Germany's loss. Caprivi had genuinely tried to plot a new course and to change the confrontational political atmosphere left by Bismarck to one of compromise and advance. Had he succeeded in his aim of winning over the industrialists and integrating the working classes and their organisations into German political life, the future of that country might well have been different. Indeed, the historian Stürmer has suggested that: *'Industrial Germany might have become, instead of an uncertain giant, the centrepiece of European stability'*. Caprivi's sincere attempts at reform, however, had alienated the traditional forces of power and influence and it was clear that, without the support of the court favourites and the Kaiser, his position was impossible.

Caprivi's dismissal demonstrated the decline that had taken place in the role of chancellor since the days of Bismarck. Thereafter Wilhelm avoided independent-minded chancellors and, instead, his own personal influence became even more marked.

Prince Chlodwig zu Hohenlohe-Schillingsfürst, 1894–1900

Wilhelm chose as his new chancellor Prince Chlodwig zu Hohenlohe-Schillingsfürst. He was 75 years of age and was selected, not for his

■ **Summary question**

Explain why Caprivi resigned in 1894 as chancellor of Germany.

personal abilities, but because he posed no political threat to those who surrounded the Kaiser.

Key profile

Prince Chlodwig zu Hohenlohe-Schillingsfürst

Prince Chlodwig zu Hohenlohe-Schillingsfürst (1819–1901) was a Bavarian aristocrat. He was a Catholic, but disliked the Centre Party and he had refused to oppose the Kulturkampf. Although he had limited political experience and no obvious policies of his own, he was regarded as mildly liberal although happy to take up the conservative demand for action against the 'socialist threat'.

Hohenlohe-Schillingsfürst was seen as little more than a figurehead chancellor and the Kaiser described him as his 'straw doll'. Accordingly, Hohenlohe tried to do as the Kaiser asked and introduced bills to curb socialist 'subversion'. Two bills were attempted, in 1894 (Subversion Bill) and 1899 (Anti-Union Bill). These proposed stiffer penalties for subversion and trade union activity but both were thrown out by the Reichstag. The Conservatives, who, in earlier years might have been relied upon to carry such measures, no longer commanded a majority in the Reichstag. Indeed, their representation fell by 21 per cent between 1893 and 1898. It seemed as though constitutional government had reached breaking point. The Kaiser was not prepared to bow to the wishes of the Reichstag majority, while the Reichstag was not prepared to accept the Kaiser and chancellor's proposed legislation.

'Sammlungspolitik' and the policy of concentration

The Kaiser's advisers led by Philipp zu Eulenburg pressed for a change of approach from 1897. They encouraged the Kaiser to bypass the chancellor and choose his own Ministers. Hohenlohe despaired in a letter of 1897:

> Without authority, government is impossible. If I cannot get the Kaiser's consent to measures I regard as necessary, then I have no authority. I cannot stay if His Majesty removes ministers against my will. Likewise I cannot stay if the Kaiser appoints ministers without consulting me. I cannot govern against public opinion as well as against the Kaiser. To govern against the Kaiser and the public is to hang in mid-air. That is impossible.

1

Activity

Source analysis

To what extent does Source 1 justify the view that:

1 Hohenlohe was simply a figurehead chancellor?

2 1897 marks the beginning of a changed approach to government?

Cross-reference

Weltpolitik is further described on page 45 and in Section 3, page 130.

This change coincided with the Kaiser's developing interest in *Weltpolitik* – a drive to achieve world power status through the expansion of naval power and colonial annexations. Wilhelm's court circle believed that Weltpolitik had the power to unite peoples of different political and economic backgrounds and so overcome the difficulties government was facing in the Reichstag. Although Hohenlohe officially remained as chancellor, in practice, the Kaiser began to act as his own chancellor and worked with his preferred ministers to determine Imperial policy. The main personnel to influence decisions in these years were:

- Dr Joannes von Miquel, Prussian Finance Minister who was made Vice-President of the Prussian Ministry of State in 1897
- Ernst von Koller, former Prussian Minister of the Interior (who had been dismissed in 1895 by the Prussian Ministry of State, after it came to light that he was revealing cabinet discussions to the military)
- Bernhard von Bülow, Foreign Minister from 1897 (and chancellor from 1900)
- Admiral von Tirpitz, Navy Secretary from 1897
- Count Arthur von Posadowsky-Wehner, Interior Minister from 1897.

A new policy, known as *Sammlungspolitik*, or the 'policy of concentration' emerged. Sammlung literally means 'rallying together' and it was a policy intended to rouse, or concentrate, nationalist sympathies, bringing the landowners and industrialists together in the face of the perceived threat from socialism and anarchism and in support of the Empire's ambitious foreign policy.

Cross-reference

To review the alliance of landowners and industrialists, refer back to pages 20–1.

Caprivi's tariff reforms, which had hit at the farmers, had broken the alliance which Bismarck had brought about between landowners and industrialists while his social reforms had failed to win over the working class and had, instead, alienated the middle classes. The Kaiser's advisers believed that this damage could be undone by highlighting the threat from socialism. They hoped to win back the middle classes in support of the Kaiser and reunite landowners and industrialists in a new alliance of 'steel and rye'. This policy of 'concentration' deliberately polarised German society into two hostile camps – the forces of law, order and respectability on the one hand, and the forces of radicalism and socialism on the other.

Cross-reference

The establishment of the **Navy League** in March 1898 and the construction of the new German navy is covered on pages 54–6 and 144–8.

Von Bülow, at the Foreign Office, responded with enthusiasm to the Sammlungspolitik principle and declared in 1897:

> I am putting the main emphasis on foreign policy. Only a successful foreign policy can help to reconcile, pacify, rally, unite.

Part of this drive, involved the construction of a new naval fleet. Admiral von Tirpitz took a personal interest in this and two naval bills were introduced in 1898 and 1900 which committed Germany to the construction of 38 battleships, 8 battle cruisers and 24 cruisers. Tirpitz, supported from March 1898 by the 'Navy League', successfully launched a huge press campaign to win popular support for the programme.

It was over an issue concerning Germany's colonial policy towards China that a disagreement between the Kaiser and his chancellor gave Hohenlohe the excuse to resign. He was probably glad of the opportunity to escape his unpredictable master and he left just as a new quarrel was breaking in the Reichstag over tariffs.

Count Bernhard von Bülow, 1900–9

Key profile

Count Bernhard von Bülow

Count Bernhard von Bülow (1849–1929) was an aristocratic Junker who had served as a member of the Prussian civil service and had experience as a diplomat and at the foreign office. In 1887, he had advocated the ethnic cleansing of all Poles in the German Empire. He served as foreign secretary from 1897 to 1900 where he favoured an adventurous foreign policy and was responsible for the policy of colonial expansion.

Count Bernhard von Bülow had been groomed as Hohenlohe's replacement by Wilhelm's inner circle of courtiers, particularly Philipp von Eulenburg. As early as 1895, Wilhelm had written:

> Von Bülow shall become my Bismarck and as he and my grandfather pounded Germany together externally, so we two will clean up the filth of parliamentary and party machinery internally.

2

Fig. 4 *Count Bernhard von Bülow, Chancellor of Germany 1900–9*

Von Bülow had gone out of his way to flatter the Emperor and win his backing, as seen in this letter, from von Bülow to Eulenburg in 1897:

> I am completely open, sincere and honest with our dear master. But I don't mean to play schoolmaster towards him. First because it hurts me to see His beautiful sad eyes, but then also because for Him everything depends on His retaining trust and friendship for me. I am entering more and more into His ideas, am trying to turn everything round for the best.

3

Von Bülow was the first chancellor whom the Kaiser trusted absolutely. He visited Wilhelm every morning and used his skills of flattery to remain in the Kaiser's favour. This earned him the nickname of 'the eel'. Von Bülow abandoned the anti-Socialist aspect of Sammlungspolitik, and instead worked to generate broader political support by focusing on the foreign policy, appealing to the people's patriotism, through Weltpolitik, the development of the fleet and the promotion of Wilhelm II himself as the great Emperor. No wonder that in July 1901, Wilhelm told Eulenburg:

> Since I have him (Bülow), I can sleep peacefully. I leave things to him and know that everything will be alright.

4

Activity

Using Sources 2, 3 and 4, summarise the relationship between von Bülow and Kaiser Wilhelm II. In what respects was this relationship different from the Kaiser's relationship with Caprivi?

However, von Bülow could not escape the controversy that was raging over tariffs when he took control. In 1902, he chose to reverse the tariff reductions arranged by Caprivi, partly to help provide sufficient revenue for the developing navy. A new tariff law restored the 1892 duties on agricultural products and a few key manufactures. This pleased the conservative Junkers, although it fell short of what they had demanded. Since industrialists were set to benefit from the huge naval expansion programme that was just developing, this change in economic policy was important in helping to create the alliance of 'steel and rye' that Germany's leaders had been seeking.

Despite this, it was not popular with the socialists, or the electorate, who believed that, by keeping out cheap Russian grain, it would increase the price of foodstuffs. Perhaps not surprisingly, in the 1903 elections, the SPD's vote jumped from two to three million, and the party gained an impressive 81 seats.

Nevertheless, the government did not resort to repression. Instead, rather as in Bismarck's time, a series of social reforms was introduced.

■ In 1900 the period for which workers could claim accident insurance was lengthened.

■ In 1901 industrial arbitration courts were made compulsory for towns with a population of more than 20,000.

■ In 1903 health insurance was extended and further controls imposed on child labour.

Other reforms included the introduction of a polling booth law, which improved the secret ballot in 1904 and the establishment of payment for Reichstag deputies in 1906.

However, despite such changes, von Bülow was fundamentally a Conservative and a nationalist, who was intolerant of the national minorities and enthusiastically reversed Caprivi's policies. He made German the only teaching language in Prussian schools and in 1908 an expropriation law was passed in Prussia which made possible the confiscation of Polish property, which was then given to German farmers. It was during these years also that an increasing interest was shown in quasi-scientific studies, which purported to demonstrate the superiority of the German race. Houston Stewart Chamberlain's *Foundations of the 19th Century* was published in 1899, and its anti-Semitic message certainly found favour with some Conservatives, although its overall influence should not be exaggerated.

Von Bülow's difficulties

By 1905–6, relations between von Bülow and the Kaiser were no longer as harmonious as they had been at the outset of the chancellorship. Von Bülow had been held responsible for foreign policy failures and he was unable to fulfil the Kaiser's demand for more money for military spending, since it had become clear that he was no better than his predecessor in controlling the Reichstag. The income raised by the new tariff laws proved insufficient, yet when he tried to force increased taxes, von Bülow found the Centre Party, on whom he had previously been able to rely, as well as the SPD, voting against him. He resorted to a small tax on legacies in 1906, which both the SPD and Centre Party voted through, although they complained that it did not go far enough, but the Conservatives and Bundesrat were horrified by such action.

In 1907, von Bülow negotiated a new coalition, known as the 'Bülow Bloc' of Conservatives, members of the Agrarian League and Liberals. His aim was to be able to get legislation passed without relying on the Centre Party. Following the 'Hottentot election' of 1907, this Bülow Bloc won an overwhelming victory, leaving the Centre Party with 95 rather than 100 seats and reducing the number of SPD seats from 81 to 43.

Cross-reference

The **Agrarian League** is explained on pages 53–5.

Exploring the detail

The Hottentot election

The election was fought on the issue of support for von Bülow's policies in South-West Africa. The Centre Party and SPD had been critical of the government's imperial policies and it was they who forced this election. However, a huge campaign was mounted against these two parties, branding them as 'unpatriotic' and this swung the vote.

Not surprisingly, the Centre Party was deeply resentful of its treatment and became even more determined to oppose von Bülow at every stage. Von Bülow had placed himself in a very difficult position. Having brought the Liberals (which included the Progressive, left wing Liberals) into the ruling coalition, he faced pressure from them for electoral reform and this was in addition to the continuing financial problems. By 1908, the **National Debt** was twice that of 1900 and while the Conservatives and Agrarian League favoured increased taxation on consumer goods, the Socialists and Progressive Liberals supported an increase in property and **inheritance taxes**. When von Bülow introduced a bill trying to combine elements of both in June 1909, it was defeated by a combination of the Conservatives, the Centre Party, Progressive Liberals and Socialists. He seemed to have succeeded in uniting both the right and left against himself and, as a result, when von Bülow was dismissed a month later, the budget remained in deficit.

Von Bülow's fall from power

Von Bülow's reputation had suffered a blow in 1907, when details of a homosexual scandal had been released, but the specific reason for von Bülow's fall was linked to an interview given by the Kaiser to the British newspaper, the *Daily Telegraph*, in October 1908. In this, Wilhelm II suggested that the Germans were anti-British and that he was personally restraining this sentiment. The report of this piece of personal 'meddling' by the Kaiser, which von Bülow had failed to suppress despite being given the opportunity to do so, worsened relations with Britain and led to another outcry in the German press. The Reichstag demanded curbs on Wilhelm's activities, forcing him to give an undertaking to moderate his conduct in future. Although he would not admit it publicly, the whole affair damaged the Kaiser's confidence in von Bülow so when the latter submitted his resignation after his finance bill had been rejected, Wilhelm readily accepted it.

A closer look

The Kaiser and the *Daily Telegraph* Affair

During a visit to Britain in 1907, Wilhelm II stayed with the pro-German Colonel Stuart-Wortley. The latter subsequently produced an article for the *Daily Telegraph* based on his conversations with the Kaiser. He hoped it would improve relations between the two countries. The Kaiser was quoted as saying that during the Boer War, he had remained neutral despite strong anti-British sentiment in Germany and that he had personally prevented the fomation of an anti-British coalition. He claimed that he had also contacted Queen Victoria with advice on how to win the war. The Kaiser suggested that, while he himself was pro-British, German public opinion was not.

Stuart-Wortley had sent the article to the Kaiser to have it checked before publication, but the Kaiser had passed it to von Bülow and the latter had returned it, largely unread. Its publication, on 28 October 1908, brought severe criticism, both in Britain, due to Wilhelm's perceived arrogance, and in Germany, where there were demands for constitutional reform to curb the Kaiser's interference. Even though the affair was primarily due to von Bülow's negligence, once the storm broke, von Bülow joined in the attacks on the Kaiser's 'personal government'. Wilhelm was forced to issue a statement saying that he promised to respect the constitution and had complete confidence in his chancellor. However, the damage had been done.

Key terms

National Debt: money which has been borrowed by a government and will therefore need to be paid back, with interest.

Inheritance tax: a tax on the value of land and possessions paid after a person's death.

Exploring the detail

The Eulenburg affair and von Bülow scandal

In 1907–9, the problems of the Empire were added to by a series of courts-martial and five trials in which prominent members of Kaiser Wilhelm II's circle were accused of homosexuality. The journalist Maximilian Harden claimed to have discovered evidence of homosexual conduct between Philipp zu Eulenburg and General von Moltke, while another journalist, Brand, claimed that von Bülow had been observed kissing and embracing at male gatherings hosted by Eulenburg. However, despite rulings which cleared these men, the media interest caused much public speculation. It is possible that the accusations were the product of those jealous of the Kaiser's circle or of von Bülow's foreign policy, but whatever their origins and truth, the reputations of those implicated were severely damaged.

Summary question

How successful was von Bülow in achieving political stability in Germany in the years 1900–9?

Fig. 5 *Theobald von Bethmann Hollweg, Chancellor of Germany, 1909–17*

Theobald von Bethmann Hollweg, 1909–17

Theobald von Bethmann Hollweg

Bethmann Hollweg (1856–1921) was an aristocrat, educated at the universities of Strasburg and Leipzig. He entered the Prussian administrative service in 1882 and rose to the position of the President of the Province of Brandenburg in 1899. He served as Prussian Minister of Interior from 1905 to 1907, and as Imperial State Secretary for the Interior from 1907 to 1909. In 1909, von Bülow recommended Bethmann Hollweg to succeed him. Bethmann Hollweg was intelligent, a careful administrator and a man of honour, but he admitted that he possessed little knowledge of foreign and military affairs and he was far too entrenched in conservatism to see the need for (still less carry through) fundamental political reforms. He presided over the disastrous July crisis which led Germany into war in 1914 and eventually resigned in 1917 under pressure from the supreme command led by Hindenburg and Ludendorff. Wilhelm accepted his resignation with reluctance.

■ Activity

Thinking point

As you read this section, try to decide whether Bethmann Hollweg's problems were more:

1 the result of von Bülow's legacy as chancellor

2 the result of Bethmann Hollweg's own failings as chancellor.

Von Bülow's fall marked the end of the Kaiser's attempts to conduct a 'personal rule' at least as far as domestic affairs were concerned. He had chosen Bethmann Hollweg because he was known to be a good administrator and Wilhelm did not mind his lack of experience in military and foreign affiars because this gave the Kaiser a free rein to take contol of such areas himself! Although Wilhelm never had quite the same relationship with Bethmann Hollweg that he had enjoyed with von Bülow, he was still quite enthusiastic about his new appointment, saying:

> He is as true as gold. A man of integrity, also very energetic. He will straighten out the Reichstag for me. Besides, it was with him in Hohenfinow that I shot my first roebuck.

However, despite his personal qualities, Bethmann Hollweg soon found himself faced not only with a difficult Reichstag, but also with an increasingly uncontrollable and demanding military.

Reform of the Prussian Parliament

Although the Imperial Reichstag was elected on a one-man-one-vote system, within the individual states that made up the Empire, voting systems varied and often favoured the wealthy. In Prussia, for example, the lower house of Parliament was elected on a three class system by means of an open ballot. This meant that the votes of the lower and middle classes were worth less than those of the Junkers. This ensured that the Junkers were always able to control the Prussian Parliament. For example, in the election of 1908, Socialist candidates won 23 per cent of the votes, but gained only 7 seats. The Conservatives, on the other hand, who won 16 per cent, gained 212 seats.

Von Bülow had unsuccessfully suggested reforms in 1908, but Bethmann Hollweg devised a deliberately more moderate bill in 1910, aiming to strengthen the position of the growing middle class in the electorate. It was a very carefully thought through measure which would have ended indirect elections and increased votes to those with educational and other qualifications (although it still retained open voting and three classes). However, his plans met with such hostility that they had to be dropped. They were too radical for the Conservatives and the Centre Party, while not far-reaching enough for the more forward-thinking parties.

The 1912 elections

The elections of 1912 were a blow to Bethmann Hollweg's hopes of forging a working majority in the Reichstag. The Socialists won 34.8 per cent of the total vote, giving them 110 deputies and making them the largest party in the lower house. One in three Germans had voted Social Democrat and together with the Progressive Liberals (who received 12.3 per cent of the vote) the left wing formed a majority in the Reichstag. The Conservatives and others supporting Bethmann polled only just over 12 per cent, the Centre Party 16.4 per cent and National Liberals 13.6 per cent.

Increasing indirect taxes, higher tariffs and a rise in the cost of living had all played their part in swinging the vote towards the left, but the result must also have been partly caused by Bethmann Hollweg's refusal to play on people's patriotism in the way von Bülow had done.

After 1912, the chancellor could no longer guarantee majorities for his policies and he was forced to lobby for support on measures as they arose rather than relying on any fixed groupings of parties.

Military spending

Bethmann Hollweg faced the impossible task of balancing a budget deficit with demands for increased military expenditure. Between 1909 and 1912 government spending was just about manageable, but with the growth in international tension after 1912, matters grew more acute.

In July 1913, despite fierce opposition from the SPD, the Reichstag was persuaded to agree to a large increase in the size of the army, but there was much argument over the raising of an additional 435 million Reichsmarks to finance the measure. Bethmann Hollweg's solution was a special 'defence tax' on the value of property. This was carried by the votes of the left wing Liberals and socialists even though the conservative parties strongly opposed it. Their opposition was such that additional proposals to increase inheritance tax, had to be abandoned, as under von Bülow.

The Army Bill created even more problems for the government:

- The national debt reached 490 billion marks and the deficit for 1913 alone was over 400 million marks.
- Bethmann Hollweg had angered the left, through his support for army reform, and the right through his support for inheritance tax.

To compound these problems, in December 1917, Bethmann Hollweg found himself having to defend Wilhelm's behaviour over the Zabern Affair, in which it seemed as though Wilhelm was prepared to allow the military to do as they pleased with no respect for the rule of law. However, although the Reichstag passed a vote of no-confidence against the chancellor by 293 votes to 54, he survived because he still had the Kaiser's support. Nevertheless, the affair demonstrated the position which the army had by then acquired and further highlighted the weakness of the Reichstag.

■ A closer look

The Zabern Affair

Zabern, a town in Alsace province, was garrisoned by German soldiers with the help of local recruits. It became known that a German officer, 20-year-old Lieutenant von Forstner, who had been teased for his boyish appearance, had, while instructing his men, insulted the French flag and called the Alsatian recruits 'Wackes', a hated nickname meaning 'square-heads'. He had admitted this and had been punished with several days' confinement in a military prison.

A report of the incident appeared in Zabern's two newspapers and there were demonstrations in the town. On 29 November 1913, a crowd assembled in front of the barracks. The soldiers were ordered to disperse the crowd and charged wildly across the square. Fifteen people were arrested, including the President, two judges and the State Attorney of the Zabern Supreme Court, who had just come out from the court building and were caught up in the crowd.

There was outrage in Germany and an outcry against militarism. The army officers were accused of placing the army outside the law. The army claimed that it was answerable to the Kaiser alone – and Wilhelm II condoned the action. The Reichstag was furious but Bethmann Hollweg refused to side with them and supported the Kaiser and the military. He defended the military authorities saying:

Fig. 6 *The actions of the German soldiers in Alsace during the Zabern Affair, 1913. What type of magazine do you think produced this cartoon?*

The military authorities have always and justly believed that they cannot allow such insults as were directed against them, especially in this affair in which there was not a single incident but a whole chain of similar occurences. I beg you gentlemen not to forget, in this serious and in many respects sad incident, that the Army has the right to protect itself against direct attack. It not only has the right, it has the duty. Otherwise, no army in the world could continue to exist.

6

■ Activity

Pairs task

Put together a reply from the members of the Reichstag who opposed Hollweg's comments on the Zabern Affair.

■ Summary question

How important was the Zabern Affair in the breakdown of constitutional government in Germany before 1914?

The massive anti-government feeling in the Reichstag boded ill for the future of Imperial government. Within the Social Democratic Party, an active left wing had emerged, that was calling for Marxist revolution and although the majority socialists remained committed to less radical change, the situation was so tense that it might have led to some sort of revolution, but for the outbreak of war in 1914. The Kaiser's prestige was evaporating, the SPD was growing in support and after the tax compromises of 1913, Bethmann Hollweg had given up trying to carry the Reichstag with him and was relying on decrees rather than legislation. The debt crisis was mounting. There were massive strike movements not only for better wages and conditions, but also for the reform of the Prussian voting system. There were problems from minority groups, particularly the Poles who were up in arms against the blatant discrimination they faced, while the working class was critical of the lack of reform and the police were having to resort to repression and censorship to maintain control. In such circumstances, it is easy to see why it might be suggested that the Kaiser was keen to go to war as a way of diverting attention from the growing crisis at home and uniting the nation in a common cause.

Power in Germany, 1890–1914

The issue of where power resided in Wilhelmine Germany was at the heart of the many disputes of the period. The Bismarckian constitution had placed ultimate authority with the Kaiser, and Wilhelm II had maintained a very personal involvement in government, almost to the extent of over-stepping his constitutional position.

His decisions regarding the appointment and dismissal of chancellors, while breaking from the tradition established by Wilhelm I, were essentially constitutional. However, there is controversy over whether Wilhelm's actions between 1897 and 1908, during von Bülow's time as chancellor, when the Kaiser reached the high point of 'personal rule', were truly 'constitutional'. During these years he dictated policy, controlled all appointments, all legislation and all diplomatic moves and while it could be argued that he was doing nothing more than the constitution allowed, his behaviour provoked considerable difficulties with another essential part of the constitution – the Reichstag.

Although the Reichstag could not itself introduce, or even amend legislation, it nevertheless held a very important power within the constitution – the Kaiser and his ministers had to have its approval for legislation. Consequently, government could only work through a system of agreement – or at least compromise – between the Reichstag majority and the Kaiser's ministers. Unless a minister could be sure of a majority in the Reichstag for legislation, he could not get laws agreed. The deputies in the Reichstag also saw this logic in reverse. If a majority in the Reichstag wanted a particular policy or law, they felt that ministers should be prepared to respond to their views.

Hence, the period of the Kaiser's personal rule provoked endless discussion about power and rights, as outlined in these comments by Friedrich Naumann, a Lutheran pastor and liberal politician, in 1900.

> In present-day Germany there is no stronger force than the Kaiser. The very complaints of the anti-Kaiser democrats about the growth of personal absolutism are the best proof of this fact, for these complaints are based on the repeated observation that all policy, foreign and internal, stems from the will and word of the Kaiser. No monarch of absolutist times ever had so much real power as the Kaiser has today. He does not achieve everything he wants, but it is still more than anybody would have believed possible in the middle of the last century.

7

The obstruction of the Reichstag and the increasing separation between the 'Kaiser's government' and the demands of the masses – as reflected in the growing socialist vote – made the Bismarckian

Activities

Challenging your thinking

1 Construct a timeline for the period 1890–1914. Plot the key domestic policies, highlighting those that you believe were successful in one colour and those that you believe were unsuccessful in another.

2 In pairs; decide which chancellor was the most successful in the years 1890–1914 and prepare a speech to justify your choice.

Fig. 7 *Kaiser Wilhelm addressing the Reichstag in 1890*

constitution increasingly difficult to operate. The Reichstag might have been able to exert still more power, had the political parties been able to cooperate more effectively, but while they remained divided, there was always the chance that a chancellor would be able to retain the upper hand.

By 1908, the Kaiser seemed to have given up on trying to make his personal rule work and he subsequently grew less interested in domestic government. He seemed to abdicate responsibility as the political situation grew more difficult, leaving a 'political vacuum' at the head of government, which only made the situation even more chaotic. This left the Kaiser's ministers, the Junkers, the industrialists, the civil service, the military, the politicians and people of all classes trying, in different ways, to influence the future direction of Germany. They did so, not only through the obvious constitutional channels, but also through pressure groups, unions, demonstrations and displays of lawless behaviour which made government increasingly difficult.

Ministers dared not demand too much of a Reichstag that they could not control, while within the Reichstag, the political parties became sharply divided (or polarised) between left and right. By 1914, Germany had the largest Socialist party in Europe, and also the largest army. The support for the SPD was counter-balanced by support for extreme national and anti-Semitic groups. The Kaiser's association with military figures increased the feeling that the government did not represent the wishes of the people and the struggles of the different interest groups made agreement almost impossible.

■ Summary question

Explain why the German government became polarised between left and right by 1914.

■ A closer look

Wilhelm II – Historiography

In the 1960s, John Röhl put forward the view that Wilhelm II deliberately set out to create a personal rule and that his personal interests had a profound impact on the direction of German policy. However, in 1973, Hans-Ulrich Wehler produced a 'structuralist' view of the Kaiserreich, in which he suggested that developments stemmed from Germany's rapid economic development. He believed policies were shaped by elite groups defending their particular interests and trying to cling to power. According to Wehler, Wilhelm was just a 'shadow Emperor' (*Schattenkaiser*) who reigned but did not rule. Although he acknowledged that the Kaiser tried to establish a personal rule, he suggested that Germany was, in practice, a 'leaderless **polycracy**' as the Kaiser was ineffectual.

■ Key term

Polycracy: a system of government in which there are many competing power-bases.

■ Summary question

How far was Wilhelm II merely a 'shadow Emperor'?

While Fritz Fischer and V. R Berghahn have supported Wehler's view, Richard Evans, David Blackbourn and Geoff Eley have suggested that the real pressure in society came from the growing power of the working and lower middle classes.

Growing militarism and political problems

The German army played an increasingly central role in the Second Reich. There was an army of half a million men in 1890 and it enjoyed a high prestige. This was partly because of the Prussian military tradition and the role that the army had played in the unification of Germany, during which time it had enjoyed glorious victories against the Austrians at Sadowa and the French at Sedan. On 'Sedan Day', the anniversary of the 1870 victory, captured French guns were paraded through the streets of Berlin to cheering crowds. The glorification of war and conquest was a current theme in German writing and culture. The Socialist leader August Bebel claimed:

> The whole nation is still drunk with military glory and there is nothing to be done until some great disaster has sobered us.

The domination of the army was, of course, linked to that of the aristocracy. Many nobles served in the army and between 1898 and 1918, 56 per cent of all army officers were titled. Since money for the army was voted on only every seven years until 1892 and every five years thereafter, the officer corps avoided civilian control.

The Kaiser, with his love of the Prussian tradition, had always favoured the army. The troops took a personal oath of loyalty to the Kaiser, rather than the state, and in his first public speech as Kaiser, Wilhelm II addressed himself to the German army, rather than the German people, with the words:

> We belong to each other – I and the army – we were born for each other and will always remain loyal to each other, whether it be the will of God to send us calm or storm.

Wilhelm chose military personnel as his companions and he allowed them to become increasingly dominant in policy making particularly from the later 1890s. Count Philip zu Eulenburg wrote of Wilhelm II:

> He sucked in like an infant at the breast the tradition that every Prussian officer is not only the height of honour, but of all good breeding, all culture and all intellectual endowment. How a man so clear-sighted as Wilhelm II could have attributed the last two qualities to everyone in guard's uniform has always been a puzzle to me. We will call it a combination of military Hohenzollernism and self-hypnotism.

Weltpolitik

The Kaiser's ambition for Germany – to win colonies and have German power respected abroad – required military might, and the expansion of military influence in this period was both the cause and product of Germany's search for world power, or 'Weltpolitik'.

Weltpolitik was encouraged by the Pan-German League, the Colonial League and the Navy League, all of which favoured German expansionism and militarism. It was also supported by German industry, which sought raw materials and export markets and, from 1897, von Bülow, von Tirpitz and Holstein became the protagonists of this policy with the backing of the military.

Activity

Research task

Try to get hold of some of books about Wilhelm II and read for yourself what historians have had to say about his reign. You will then be able to make up your own mind which you feel is the most convincing interpretation.

Cross-reference

For the victory at **Sedan** in 1870, see the Introduction, page 7.

August Bebel is profiled on page 52.

To recap on the **military budget**, re-read page 33.

Cross-reference

For more detail on these **right wing pressure groups**, see pages 53–5.

For the **Navy League**, see page 146.

Military influence expanded with the passing of the Navy Laws of 1897, 1900 and 1906. In 1897, Wilhelm had threatened to march the army into the Reichstag and disband it when it had proved reluctant to meet his estimates, but Admiral von Tirpitz managed to force a change of heart and a year later the Navy League was founded to helped win over the public.

The formal adoption of the 1892 Schlieffen Plan in 1904 was an example of the supremacy of the military in decision making. The plan, which involved marching through Belgium (in order to defeat France quickly), a country whose neutrality had been guaranteed by Germany, among others, was politically unacceptable. It meant that Germany would have to break an international agreement. Nevertheless, von Bülow raised no objections and it became the basis for all German military planning. It led to Army Bills being forced through the Reichstag and by 1914 the army had grown to more than 4 million soldiers and expenditure on the army in 1913–14 had reached £60 m.

Allowing the military to have such dominance that it overrode civilian authority was a very dangerous step. It undermined the democratic institutions which the 1871 constitution had introduced, and placed decision making in the hands of men whose outlook was increasingly at variance from that of the general public. According to the historian Perry:

> Germany became a state of soldiers and war rather than one of citizens and law. The army not only remained independent of any control other than that of the monarch himself but also through prolonged and universal military service it was able to influence the thinking of the greater part of the German nation. German society was one in which the upper classes were soaked in the ethos of the barrack square, in which social distinction was measured almost entirely by military rank.

9   *Quoted in R. Wolfson, **Years of Change: European History 1890–1945**, 1978*

On 8 December 1912, Wilhelm II convened a war council meeting at his castle in Berlin, during the diplomatic crisis produced by the Balkan Wars. He invited his chief military and naval advisers but excluded civilian decision makers. According to the report of one who was present:

> General von Moltke (Chief of the Army General Staff) said, 'I believe a war is unavoidable. But we ought to do more through the press to encourage the popularity of a war against Russia. The Emperor supported this and told the State Secretary Tirpitz to use his press contacts too to work in this direction. In the afternoon I wrote to the Reich Chancellor about the influencing of the press.'

10   *Quoted in F. McKichan, **Germany 1815–1939: The Rise of Nationalism**, 1992*

That the civilian leaders were not present at such a crucial meeting and that the chancellor Bethmann Hollweg was merely 'informed' says much about the power of the military at this time.

■ Cross-reference

The **Schlieffen Plan** is described on pages 143–4.

The **Army Bills** are outlined on page 41.

■ Cross-reference

The **Balkan Wars** are covered on pages 154–7.

Economic and social change and its political impact

Economic development, 1871–1914

Industrial growth

Consider the following statistics:

Table 2 *Output of coal and steel*

Year	Coal (millions of tons)	Steel (millions of tons)
1871	29.4	0.2
1890	109.3	2.2
1913	191.5	17.9

Table 3 *Length of railway line*

Year	German railway line in kilometres
1871	21,471
1880	33,838
1890	42,869
1913	63,000

Table 4 *Population growth in Germany in thousands*

Year	Population	% Rural	% Urban
1871	41,059	63.9	36.1
1880	45,234	58.6	41.4
1890	49,428	57.5	42.5
1900	56,367	45.6	54.4
1910	64,926	40.0	60.0

Fig. 8 *The production of cannon in Germany around 1900*

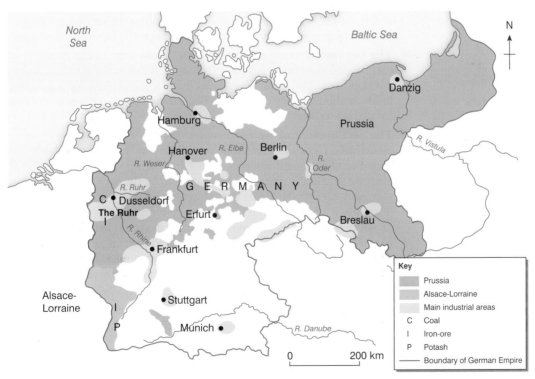

Fig. 9 *German economic development, 1879–90*

Clearly, the German economy was growing – and growing fast! This growth was the product of a number of interrelated factors.

■ **A huge growth in the German population.** This provided both the market and the labour force for the expanding economy. Furthermore the balance of the population was towards younger generations who were more mobile and willing to adapt to new skills. Germany had a population of 67 million by 1914 – a figure surpassed in Europe only by Russia.

■ **The availability of raw materials within the newly united state.** There was coal from the Ruhr, Saar and Silesia, iron ore from Alsace-Lorraine and the Ruhr and potash from Alsace-Lorraine.

■ **Germany's geographical advantages.** These included navigable rivers like the Rhine and Elbe, and the broad flat northern plain which was well-suited to the construction of railways. The railway system, essentially complete by 1880, proved invaluable for the transport of raw materials and manufactured goods. The canal and river system stimulated the shipbuilding industry which, in turn, facilitated the growth of overseas trade. By 1908 the total tonnage of the German merchant navy was to be second only to Britain.

■ **A highly developed education system.** German elementary education was deemed the best in the world, while higher education made increasing provision for the development of the technical skills necessary in industrial development. In 1870, for example, there were more science graduates at just one German university – Munich – than the total number of science graduates at all English universities.

■ **Unification and state involvement.** This in itself had given a boost to economic growth, while the tariffs on imports introduced by Bismarck in 1878 helped protect German industry from foreign competition and stimulated further development. Caprivi negotiated trade treaties and the influence of the industrial and agricultural elite ensured that matters of economic development were kept at the forefront of politics.

■ **The German banking system.** German banks were free from state control and they became heavily involved in industrial research and development. The number of banks increased and close links between banks and businesses developed. Their own representatives were often invited on to boards of directors of firms.

■ **The development of 'new industries' such as chemicals and electricals.** Germany became a world leader in the newer industries. There were abundant reserves of coal and potash which became the basis for numerous chemical products and by the early 20th century Germany had established a virtual world monopoly in the production of synthetic dyes, artificial fibres, some photographic materials, some drugs, plastics and new explosives. In the electrical field, German firms such as Siemens led the way in the production of such things as dynamos. The production of electrical energy increased by 150 per cent between 1901 and 1915 and, by 1913, Germany controlled half the world's trade in electricals. Machinery and the motor car industry boomed. Advances were made by Daimler, Diesel, Benz and Mercedes and in the aviation industry by Zeppelin. Germany's industrial production tripled and, by 1914, Germany was alongside Britain and the USA as one of the world's leading industrial nations.

■ **The expansion of overseas trade.** This provided markets for expanding German industry and German merchants penetrated the markets of North and South America, Africa and Asia. Food, raw materials and particular types of manufactured goods had to be imported. To pay for these Germany sold chemicals, metal goods and machinery, textiles

Cross-reference

Bismarck's introduction of tariffs in 1878 is covered on page 20.

Exploring the detail

The development of cartels

Although Germany suffered from the world-wide depression between 1873 and 1894, this helped German industry in some ways as it encouraged greater cooperation rather than rivalry between businesses. Some associations were established to encourage lobbying and to put pressure on the government to introduce protection. Some firms went even further in order to reduce internal competition – they formed cartels or associations of producers in similar trades or processes. These increased from eight in 1875 to seventy by 1887. By 1905, 366 cartels existed and whole areas of Germany had been 'cartelised'. In the Ruhr coalfield, ten giant collieries produced some 60 per cent of output by 1910. In iron and steel, huge firms like Krupp and Thyssen dominated entire cities such as Essen.

and coal abroad. In 1890, Germany was buying nearly £200 m worth of foreign goods and selling £153 m. By 1913, imports had risen to £526 m and exports to £495 m. Although there was a 'trade gap' between imports and exports, the difference was easily made up by the 'invisibles'. These comprised the money earned through foreign investments which were worth over £1,000 m and the considerable revenues brought in by shipping and banking.

Agricultural change

As German industry grew, agriculture declined in comparison. However, the extent of this decline should not be exaggerated:

Table 5 *Assessing the extent of agricultural decline*

Evidence for decline	Evidence against decline
▪ Decline in agricultural prices and, consequently, in the incomes of farmers and landowners.	▪ The growth of towns and the protection given to German grain growers after 1879 created opportunities for the more enterprising farmers to supply food to a growing domestic market.
▪ A series of bad harvests in the late 1870s which led to an increase in the import of grain from the USA.	
▪ The building of new railways and roads which broke down the isolation of rural communities and exposed farmers to competition from outside.	▪ Farm machinery and fertilisers were beginning to become available and those farmers who had the money to invest in such innovations could and did greatly raise their yield.
▪ The growing number of peasants who abandoned agriculture and moved to the industrial towns. (The percentage of the population employed in agriculture fell from 50% in 1871 to 35% in 1907.)	▪ More than 4 million acres of land were brought under cultivation between 1880 and 1900. By 1914 German agriculture, in terms of yield per hectacre, was the most productive in the world.
▪ Landowners who failed to modernise production methods or did not adapt to changing market conditions were forced to sell up or mortgage farms.	▪ Root crops like potatoes and sugar beet, which accounted for almost 20 per cent of arable land by 1913, encouraged a revolution in German agriculture. They facilitated more rapid crop rotation, encouraged greater use of fertilisers and machinery and provided additional fodder for livestock.
▪ In the 1880s the share of agriculture in the GNP (Gross National Product) was 35–40 per cent while industry's share was 30–35 per cent. By 1914, agriculture had fallen back to 25 per cent with industry at 45 per cent.	▪ There was a more business-like cultivation of the land, with heavy reliance on large numbers of cheap seasonal workers.

Social change

In simple terms rapid industrial change meant that millions of ordinary people had to come to terms with fundamental changes in their way of life. Yet, surprisingly, German society seems to have remained divided along traditional class lines and what mobility there was tended to be within a class rather than movement between classes.

Part of the reason for this was that the very speed of Germany's industrialisation meant that society was less able to adjust to it than in Britain and Belgium, where the process had taken place over a much longer period of time. In Germany, industrialisation reinforced the existing divisions. The working class, for example, strengthened its identity and expanded in size, which served to intensify the suspicions of the social elite.

Industrialisation encouraged urbanisation as many peasants left their farms for the towns even though they often only travelled a few miles. Some made longer journeys, travelling, for example, from the eastern provinces of Prussia to Berlin or even further to the industrial towns of the Ruhr valley. Large factories, like those in Essen, attracted thousands of peasants' sons, forced to leave their family farms by the decline of peasant agriculture. By 1910, 60 per cent were city dwellers compared with 47 per cent in 1890 and 36 per cent in 1871. In 1871, only eight German towns had more than 100,000 inhabitants. In 1910 there were 48, accounting for 21.3 per cent of the population.

Activity

Pairs activity

Working in pairs draw a spider diagram of the main reasons for industrial development. Using different colour lines show links between some of these reasons, explaining briefly, on the line, how one factor encouraged the other.

Activity

Challenging your thinking

What links might be expected between industrial and social change?

Table 6 *Growth of major cities, 1875–1910, in thousands*

City	1875	1890	1910
Berlin	967	1,588	2,071
Cologne	135	282	516
Dresden	197	276	548
Dusseldorf	81	145	359
Essen	55	79	295
Hamburg	265	324	931
Kiel	37	69	212
Leipzig	127	295	590
Munich	193	349	596

*Quoted in Simpson, W., **The Second Reich – Germany 1871–1918**, 1995*

There was a vast regional transfer of population, not only from country to town, but from east to west, as Germans left the land in their millions to seek work in industrial areas. By 1907, the population of the industrial Rhineland and Westphalia had increased by one million.

Middle classes

The main beneficiaries of industrialisation were the middle class, especially the great industrialists such as the Krupps, Thyssens and Hugenbergs who became the elite or upper middle class. The middle ranks of the middle classes were also expanding. White collar workers in industry, education and the bureaucracy were in great demand for their scientific, technical or administrative skills. The numbers of lawyers, teachers and civil servants, for example, grew as business and its demands became more complex.

The lower middle class or 'Mittelstand' embraced a wide variety of occupations and standards of living. This included small businessmen, shopkeepers, artisans (skilled workers or craftsmen) and minor officials. Their position was less secure than those above them. They could, for example, be squeezed by a downturn in the economy, or challenged from below by the unionised working class and from above, by the larger, more productive enterprises of big business.

Working classes

Industrialisation brought both benefits and losses to the working classes which, as a group, expanded vastly in this period. Although many workers were forced to live in cramped inner city streets, statistics suggest that, after the initial industrial 'take off' of the Bismarckian era, standards of living improved substantially. There were new job opportunities, particularly with the spread of white collar positions, and state welfare schemes grew, providing support in times of sickness, accident and old age.

Employment rates in the cities were high and average real wages (what could be bought by money wages, taking the cost of living into account) increased by 25 per cent between 1895 and 1913. There were also medical improvements, innoculations and developments in hygiene which enabled people to live healthier and longer lives. Leisure opportunities improved with the spread of transport and the advent of the cinema and new devices like the telephone, the typewriter and the electric tram network helped speed communications. However, it was the more skilled workers who reaped the greatest benefits and it was probably also the case that the prospect of higher living standards tempted workers to want to improve their lot by joining trade unions and the socialist movement. If the country was flourishing economically, they wanted a greater share of the wealth that they had helped to create.

Nevertheless, despite the improvements, life could be hard and conditions of both living and working compared unfavourably with those in industrialised Britain and the USA. The average German worked nearly 2 hours a day longer than the average British worker in the 1890s and even by 1912, the average working day was longer than the British one of 1877. Despite the wage increases, German workers earned nearly a third less than their British counterparts and there were pockets of acute poverty where families had to share rooms and live with the threat of unemployment just around the corner.

Landowners

Although the pace of change was much slower in the countryside than the cities, even the villages and small towns of rural Germany were undergoing change. The position of the Junker landowners was threatened by falling incomes from agriculture. The smaller the estate and the further east it was situated, the greater the levels of debt it was likely to experience. Some landowners were forced to sell their estates to the newly rich upper middle class families from the cities. Nevertheless, the political and social dominance of the Junker class in Prussia remained as strong as ever and local government remained in the hands of this landowning Junker class.

Peasants

It is difficult to generalise about the impact of economic growth in the countryside, since conditions varied enormously between one area and another. In some regions over-population encouraged large numbers to leave the rural community to move to the big cities. Elsewhere (for example dairy and vegetable areas near the towns) the rural economy flourished, although changed by the greater dependence on a money-based economy, the spread of communication and education (which brought near-universal literacy) and the influence of central and local state government policies. Overall, the constraints which had made rural life harsh and isolated disappeared and there was greater interaction between town and countryside.

Activity

Class activity

Each member of the class should choose one of the following people and undertake some additional research in order to prepare a short presentation for the rest of the group, giving that person's view of life in Germany 1890–1914. The group should pose questions to each speaker and, at the end, discuss which person seemed to be in the best and which in the worst position. Choose from:

- a Junker
- a factory owner
- a factory worker
- a farm labourer
- an unemployed city dweller
- a middle class woman.

Political impact of economic and social change

One significant consequence of economic change was increasing support for socialism and the Social Democratic Party. Neither Bismarck's persecution nor the development of 'state socialism' had prevented the

■ Cross-reference

The **emergence of socialism** and Bismarck's attempts to repress it are detailed in Chapter 1.

■ Cross-reference

Caprivi's change of direction in this area is covered in Chapter 3.

■ Questions

1 Which of the demands in the Erfurt Programme might appear 'revolutionary' and why?

2 Who might be alarmed by this programme?

party's growth. Caprivi's 'new course' (1890–4), during which the Anti-Socialist Laws had lapsed had encouraged a growth in membership and in the 1890s, the Party organised a series of well-attended conferences, including one in Halle, 1890 and one in Erfurt, 1891.

At the 1891 Erfurt Congress, the party produced a statement of party principles known as the Erfurt programme:

Extracts from 'The Erfurt Programme'

■ The Social Democratic Party of Germany fights for the abolition of class rule and of classes themselves and for equal rights and duties for all.

■ The Party demands the vote for all men and women over 21.

■ The making of new laws and the appointment of high officials to be controlled by the people.

■ Decisions for war and peace to be made by the representatives of the people.

■ All taxes on goods to be abolished as they are an unfair burden on the poor.

■ The costs of government to be paid from income tax, property tax and inheritance tax, to ensure the rich pay most.

■ Eight hours to be the maximum working day.

11

Despite the apparent radicalism of the Erfurt Programme, the SPD became increasingly moderate in the Wilhelmine era, aiming to help workers with social reform, rather than contemplating the overthrow of society. August Bebel, the most prominent party leader, encouraged members to work through the Reichstag rather than against it.

■ Key profile

August Bebel

August Bebel (1840–1913) was the son of a Rhineland officer who trained as a turner. He met Karl Liebknecht in 1865 and they co-founded the Saxon People's Party – a workers' party. He was elected to the Reichstag of the North German Confederation in 1867 and was the only person to be returned at every election between then and 1912. In 1869, Bebel and Liebknecht formed the Social Democratic Workers' Party (SDAP) which merged with Lasalle's ADAV in 1875 at Gotha. In 1892, Bebel was elected one of the two Presidents of the SPD.

Fig. 10 *August Bebel, one of the founders of the SPD*

He was opposed by socialists such as Karl Liebknecht and Rosa Luxemburg who clung on to their Marxist belief in more revolutionary methods and, in 1900, they defeated a proposed amendment to the Erfurt programme, stating the socialists' desire to work through the Reichstag. While, in practice, this made little difference to the course the SPD adopted, the continuance of the party's revolutionary slogans made it harder for other parties, such as the Liberals, to support them and provided an excuse for the imperial militarist Reich elite to attack them. The government's attempt to combat the socialists' steady rise by portraying them as enemies of the state in 'Sammlungspolitik', however, simply prevented compromise and helped split German society into two opposing extremes.

The SPD was popular, not only because it promised to advance the working man's cause in the Reichstag, but also because it helped provide the German working class with a new sense of identity. There were local socialist societies for sport, music and educational purposes. The SPD organised festivals, rallies and holidays, produced newspapers, founded libraries and ran welfare clinics. Their May Day parades were the largest in Europe and a blatant display of working class solidarity and confidence.

The SPD also helped promote Germany's extensive system of welfare support, giving Germany the most comprehensive system of social insurance in Europe by 1913. They pressed successfully for some constitutional changes like the secret ballot (1904) and payment of MPs (1906), which permitted lower middle and working class men, with no other income, to put themselves forward as deputies for the Reichstag. In 1911, they supported measures whereby Alsace-Lorraine was given Reichstag representation and universal male suffrage at 21 years was introduced. They also successfully resisted the taxation proposals that would hit harder at the working man and promoted progressive taxes, whereby those with the most would be forced to pay more.

From 1912, the SPD was the largest party in the Reichstag, with 110 out of 397 seats. However, they still failed to press for fundamental constitutional change and in 1914, they accepted a political truce between the parties, known as the *Burgefrieden*, and voted for the funds needed to wage war.

Trade Unions also grew rapidly in this period and supported the reformist policies of the SPD. In 1890, the General Federation of Trade Unions was founded by Karl Legien and it became Europe's largest labour organisation. Trade Unions campaigned for better working conditions, shorter hours and more pay and encouraged workers to strike to achieve their aims. The Free Trade Unions (organised in associations for each branch of industry) had 50,000 members in 1890, 680,000 in 1900 and more than 2.5 million in 1913. However, a sizeable body of workers remained outside the Trade Union movement. They were known as the 'Lumpenproletariat', and some indulged in militant activity, conducting 'lightening' strikes and other violent activity to achieve their ends, while others were the poor and disinterested who remained firmly on the fringes of politics.

 Question

How successful was the SPD between 1890 and 1914 in promoting the cause of the working class?

Growth of the right wing pressure groups

Social and economic change also produced groups on the right of politics, which detested the rise of the left and were determined to preserve the traditional social hierarchy and the power of the Emperor. The Junkers, military officers and large factory owners shared a common interest in maintaining and extending their own wealth and power. They were fiercely nationalistic and determined to promote the expansion of German influence throughout the world as a way of controlling socialism.

Cross-reference

Sammlungspolitik is explained on page 36.

Fig. 11 *The mythical Germania supervises the rise of the German Imperial Navy between 1895 and 1905*

In the course of the 1890s, a number of these right wing elite formed themselves into pressure groups, with the aim of influencing government policy.

Table 7 *Right wing pressure groups, 1876–1912*

Date	Group	Aim
1876	Central Association of German Industrialists (CVDI)	High tariffs to protect German industry
1882	German Colonial League (DKG)	To promote the development of German colonies
1890	Pan German League (ADV)	Unification of all Germans (to include those living outside the Empire)
1893	Agrarian League (BdL)	Tariff protection for agricultural products
1894	German Eastern Marches Society (HKT)	To expand the German Empire
1895	Industrialists' League (BdI)	Tariffs reduction – to promote exports
1898	Navy League (DF)	Naval expansion and growth of colonies
1904	Imperial League against Social Democracy	To curb the growth of socialism
1912	Army League	To promote the expansion of the German army

■ Cross-reference

For more detail on the **Navy League**, see page 146.

■ Question

What common themes can you detect in the demands of these right wing pressure groups?

■ Cross-reference

For more on **Weltpolitik**, see pages 45 and 130.

These patriotic societies and right wing interest groups came to exert a direct influence on policy making. This was partly because their leadership comprised influential men with wealth and contacts and partly because their concerns were fundamentally in tune with those of the Kaiser and his ministers. Although there were social differences between the traditional Junker land-owning aristocracy and the newly wealthy industrialists, they shared a common interest in preserving and advancing their own positions and under their leadership, these pressure groups were able to attract other, conservative elements in society – middle class bureaucrats, academics, small businessmen, office employees and even members of the working class, particularly in the more rural areas where the peasantry associated their own interests with those of their landlords.

Employers' organisations as well as the Junker-led Agrarian League mounted campaigns for protective tariffs in the wake of Caprivi's relaxing of Bismarck's protectionist laws. Perhaps even more importantly, both Junkers and big business interests came together in the nationalistic and imperialist organisations which sought to expand Germany's wealth and influence overseas and to channel public energies into support for a more aggressive foreign policy. They advocated Weltpolitik and justified and publicised nationalist demands. Among the most radical was the Pan-German League that wanted to unite all ethnic Germans around the world. From around 1900, this League became increasingly confrontational and opposed any reformist policies. They called for the suppression of the SPD and stronger leadership, accusing the Kaiser's government of being too moderate.

Right wing pressure groups lobbied ministers, sought members within the Reichstag, and employed comparatively modern techniques (advertising, the press and even the cinema) to spread their message and win converts. Their campaigning branded opponents as unpatriotic and they were consequently able to attract quite large followings. The Pan-German League could claim membership from 60 right wing Reichstag members by 1914, and although it never had more than 25,000 actual members, the status of those members gave it a disproportionately strong influence. The Navy League was deliberately sponsored by the government to promote Germany's claims for a larger navy and win support for the naval laws. By 1900 it had over a million members, which was more than any of the political parties, while the Agrarian League had attracted 250,000. In both cases, they could claim extensive support from the lower classes too.

The overall extent of influence exercised by these groups is still a matter of some controversy. The historian Geoffrey Eley in *Reshaping the German Right Radical Nationalism and Political Change* (1991) suggested that their influence was not as extensive as was once believed and that they reflected rather than formulated policy decisions. Nevertheless, their very existence adds weight to the view that politics in Germany had become strongly polarised in the early years of the 20th century. Constant pressure from groups determined to promote a strong foreign policy and resist any internal change must have made some contribution to the final breakdown of the Imperial state.

Activities

Class debate

1 Individuals or pairs should choose one of the suggested right wing pressure groups and prepare a class presentation on it. Try to address:

- its origins
- leadership and membership
- methods and influence
- success.

2 After seeing the presentations, debate the view that 'Right wing pressure groups exerted limited influence on the policies of Wilhelmine Germany, 1890–1914'.

Learning outcomes

Through your study of this section you should be aware of key developments in Germany in the years after unification. You should understand the main features of the new German Constitution and Bismarck's policies towards the Catholic Church and socialism. You should also understand the clash of personality and policy between Bismarck and Wilhelm II and the main reasons for the chancellor's resignation in 1890.

You should also be aware of the debate about the role of Wilhelm II in policy making and government in the years 1890–1914, key developments such as Weltpolitik and Sammlungspolitik and the achievements and weaknesses of the four different chancellors who served under Wilhelm II during these years.

Such political developments should be appreciated against the context of the key economic developments in Germany between 1890 and 1914.

 Examination-style questions

(a)   Explain why industry grew rapidly in Germany in the years after 1890.   *(12 marks)*

 Try to think of a range of factors which help explain the growth of industry. You may want to include some general factors such as the availability of raw materials, but try to be as precise as you can and think, for example, in what areas and why there was particularly rapid growth after 1890.

(b)   How far did the economic changes of 1871–1914 transform German society?   *(24 marks)*

 This question is asking you to evaluate the impact of economic change. You will need an introduction which defines any key terms in the question (such as 'economic changes' and 'German society') and suggests the arguments you are going to use. You will need to consider the impact of both industrial and agricultural developments on urban and rural areas, on the class structure, living and working conditions and the emergence of movements such as socialism and trade unionism. You are being asked to make a judgement, 'how far', so discuss the extent of change and continuity and try to reach a supported conclusion.

3 The reign of Alexander III, 1881–94

Fig. 1 *Alexander II being blown up by a terrorist bomb, 1881*

In this chapter you will learn about:

- the meaning of autocracy in Russia in 1881

- the policies of Alexander III and the degree of repression exerted during his reign

- the problem of the Russian nationalities and the policy of Russification

- the importance of the Orthodox Church within Russia

- the extent of opposition to the autocracy by 1894.

Workers of Russia!

Today, 13 March, Alexander the tyrant has been killed by us, socialists. He was killed because he did not care for his people. He burdened them with taxes. He deprived the peasant of his land. He handed over the workers to plunderers and exploiters. He did not give the people freedom. He cared only for the rich. He lived in luxury. The police maltreated the people and he rewarded them instead of punishing them. He hanged or exiled any who stood up on behalf of the people or on behalf of justice. That is why he was killed. A Tsar should be a good shepherd, ready to devote his life to his sheep. Alexander II was a ravening wolf and a terrible death overtook him.

1   *Quoted in J. Ryan (ed.)* **The Russian Chronicles,** *1998*

This statement by the assassins of Alexander II on the day after the Tsar's assassination was followed, ten days later, by an open letter, addressed to the dead man's son, Alexander III.

Your Majesty,

While fully comprehending your deep sorrow, there is something higher than the most legitimate of personal feelings – the duty to our country, to which all individuals' sentiments must be sacrificed.

There are but two ways – either revolution or the voluntary transfer of supreme power into the hands of the people. We do not impose conditions, as these have been imposed by history; we merely state them. The conditions are:

■ a general amnesty for all political crimes, as those were not crimes, but rather the fulfilment of social duty

■ the summoning of representatives of the whole nation to consider the existing social and economic order and its modification in accordance with the nation's desire.

2

Quoted in J. Ryan (ed.) ***The Russian Chronicles,*** *1998*

The mourning Alexander III was in no mood for such requests, or for clemency. Within days, 150 members of the opposition movement responsible for the assassination had been arrested. Everywhere there was a clampdown on clandestine meetings as known centres of trouble were raided by the forces of the secret police. Censorship and security were tightened and the Tsar retired to the fortified castle of Gatchina lest some 'madmen' try to kill him too. Thus began the reign of Alexander III.

■ The Tsarist political structure in 1881

Key

Extent of the Russian Empire, c.1881

Fig. 2 *The Russian Empire in 1881*

It is hard to appreciate just how large Imperial Russia was in the late 19th century. It covered an area of approximately 8 million square miles, twice the size of Europe, and was the largest consolidated state territory in the world. It stretched 5,000 miles from Poland in the west to the Pacific Ocean in the east, and 2,000 miles from the Arctic Ocean in the north to Persia, Afghanistan and India in the south. It spanned Europe and Asia, contained the largest population in Europe – around 100 million people in 1881 – and the world's largest army of around 1.5 million. It was Europe's main exporter of agricultural produce and possessed vast mineral reserves.

The Russian Empire contained infinite variety – from the tundra, forests and barren landscapes of the north and east to the fertile 'black earth' areas of south and west. The people too comprised many different nationalities, fewer than half of them Russian. Three quarters of them lived within European Russia (to the west of the Urals) on less than a quarter of the total land mass.

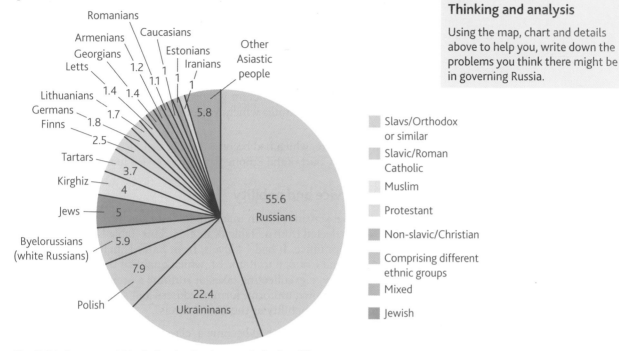

Fig. 3 *Ethnic groups within the Russian Empire, population in millions*

Activity

Thinking and analysis

Using the map, chart and details above to help you, write down the problems you think there might be in governing Russia.

The Tsar

This vast Empire was ruled by a Tsar who took the title, 'Emperor and Autocrat of all Russia'. According to the *Collected Laws of the Russian Empire* compiled by Nicholas I in 1832:

> The Emperor of all the Russias is an autocratic and unlimited monarch; God himself ordains that all must bow to his supreme power, not only out of fear but also out of conscience.

Cross-reference

To compare the position of the Tsar with that of the German Kaiser, refer back to Chapter 1.

3

All political authority was vested in the Tsar; his imperial edicts (or *ukaze*) were the law of the land. In modern constitutional terminology, he was the supreme legislative, executive and judicial power. Furthermore, he was the titular Head of the Russian Orthodox Church and he ruled the country according to his own consciousness of duty and right, guided by God. Indeed the Russian belief was that the Tsar was the embodiment of God on earth. The land of Russia was his private property and the Russian people, his children. According to tradition, there was an unbreakable bond between the Tsar and his people. They loved and obeyed him as children to their father and God.

Fig. 4 *The coronation of Alexander III*

Obviously, in practice, the Tsar was bound by precedent and relied on advisers to guide him in the task of running his vast Empire. All advisers and Ministers were chosen by the Tsar himself and none could do anything without his approval. Furthermore, they did not work collectively and there could be quite extreme differences of opinion between the members of these bodies, which consisted of:

- ■ the Imperial Council or Chancellery – a body of 35–60 nobles especially picked by the Tsar to advise him personally and provide their 'expert' opinion
- ■ the Committee of Ministers – a body which comprised between 8–14 Ministers in charge of different government departments. They could issue ministerial statutes which, with the Tsar's approval, had the force of law.

(The former Senate, which had become defunct had, in 1864, been replaced by the Supreme Court of the Empire which supervised judicial proceedings.)

The civil service and nobility

The Tsar's civil servants which made up the bureaucracy running his Empire were selected from a 'Table of Ranks'. This Table laid down the requirements for office. It had 14 levels, from Rank 1, held by members of the Ministerial Council to Rank 14, which qualified the educated for minor state office, e.g. collecting taxes or running a provincial post office. Each rank had its own uniform, form of address and status – which included hereditary nobility at the higher levels.

By 1881, this bureaucracy had become a 'class apart' and suffered from internal corruption and incompetence. Complicated procedures proved stifling and worked against individual initiative. All orders were passed downwards from the centre to the governors of the 50 provinces and in turn to the district governors and the commandants of towns. Essentially, it was a one-way operation, with no provision for suggestions to travel upwards from the lower ranks. In any case, to obtain promotion, length of service was more important than efficiency.

In addition to the paid bureaucracy, the Tsarist regime depended on the provincial nobility for support. These were the landowners who made up around 10 per cent of the population but owned 75 per cent of the land. It was more than a century (1785) since nobles had been obliged to serve the state, although many continued to do so, for example as Provincial Governors, but their sense of obligation remained strong and all landowners were relied upon to keep order on their estates. Finally, when circumstances demanded, Tsars might choose to appoint a special committees to carry out an investigation or prepare a report. Such committees were usually headed by trusted nobles but, even so, there was no need for the Tsar to take any notice of what they found!

Maintaining the autocracy

The police state

Until 1880, the state security network had been run by the 'Third Section' of the Emperor's Imperial Council but when Loris-Melikov was appointed Minister for Internal Affairs that year, its functions were given to the Department of State Police which operated within his Ministry. A special section dealt with internal security and answered directly to the Minister. This became known as the 'Okhrana' and its agents kept a strict surveillance over the population, maintaining a rigid control and ensuring that any subversive activites were exposed. Political parties were banned and political meetings and strikes forbidden but the Okhrana worked under cover to discover illegal political organisations and to root out political crimes before they were committed. They had unlimited powers to carry out raids, and arrest, imprison or exile people, often on the word of an informer.

The police state prevented freedom of speech, freedom in the press and freedom to travel abroad. Censorship existed at every level of government and was carried out by the state departments and the Church as well as by the police. There was even a committee which censored the censors! The censors ensured all books and newpapers were vetted so that anything prejudicial to the regime could be suppressed. Any revolutionary language was forbidden and all writers were closely watched.

The Orthodox Church

Another prop of the autocracy was the Russian Orthodox Church which taught people to display loyalty to their Tsar and accept conditions on earth as the will of God. The Patriarch of Moscow, who worked in close harmony with the Tsar provided spiritual guidance, while the Over-Procurator of the Holy Synod, a post created in 1721, was a government minister, appointed by the Tsar to run church affairs. The archbishops and bishops at the head of the church hierarchy were subject to his control over appointments, religious education, most of the church's finances and issues of administration.

The army

The Tsarist regime also relied on its huge army, which absorbed around 45 per cent of the the government's annual expenditure. Since 1875, the army relied, for its rank and file, on a universal military service requirement for six years for all males over 20. Some of the worst military brutality had been outlawed that year, but the ranks of conscripted peasants were still subject to vigorous discipline. The higher ranks of the military were reserved for aristocrats who bought and sold their commissions. Under their command, the army was used to put down risings and disturbances while the elite regiments of mounted Cossacks acted both as the Tsar's personal bodyguards and as police reinforcements. They enjoyed special social privileges and served as border guards on national and internal ethnic borders.

Financing the autocracy

Government revenue came from taxes and dues, and was largely borne by the peasantry, since the nobility and clergy were exempt from the Poll tax. This was a tax on every male peasant in the Empire and had been introduced to provide money for maintaining Russia's large army in 1719. It was loathed because it was blatantly unfair. The richest peasant paid exactly the same as the poorest, but it did provide a substantial income to the state. Other indirect taxation included taxes on such 'essentials' as vodka and salt, and altogether the peasantry provided 90 per cent of the imperial revenue. Customs duties were another source of income and when these sources proved insufficient, the government would negotiate a loan.

Apart from the 45 per cent of income that went on the military, 17 per cent went on paying back such loans while 31 per cent was absorbed by the costs of running the government. The remaining 7 per cent went to finance the Tsar's household expenses – maintaining his palaces, court and entertainments.

Reform

The autocratic system of government was not without critics. As early as the reign of Alexander I (1801–25), a representative assembly to advise the Tsar (possibly one with law making powers) had been considered. However, while Alexander had pondered the idea without putting it into practice, his brother Nicholas I (1825–55) had totally rejected such a thought. Alexander II (1855–81) had undertaken some reforms including, in 1864, the setting up of the *Zemstva* (singular: *Zemstvo*), which were local district and provincial councils (elected by an indirect system) which favoured the landowners but did not exclude the peasants. The Zemstva had assumed responsibility for transport and a variety of social services including health, education and the poor. They were granted some funding out of local rates and although they had no official executive power, they were a focus for liberal reform, when not obstructed in their work by the Ministry of Internal Affairs.

The establishment of the 'mir' as the agency responsible for the collection of peasant taxes and redemption dues was a further change instituted by Alexander II which helped the autocracy in the smooth-running of the Empire. The mir was also responsible for court cases involving peasants and issued passports, without which a peasant was unable to move away from the commune. It was a cheap and efficient means of control.

Towards the end of his life in 1880, Alexander II had contemplated proposals for further governmental reform. Loris-Melikov, the Minister for Internal Affairs, produced a report which considered the inclusion of elected representatives of the nobility, of the Zemstva and of the town governments in the discussions of the drafts of some State decrees. The project became known as the 'Loris-Melikov's Constitution', although it was not really a constitution for the running of the state at all. Alexander II signed the report on the morning of 13 March 1881 and called for a meeting of the Council of Ministers to discuss the document. The same day the Emperor was killed by a bomb.

Key term

Mir: the village commune in which the peasants worked and which they were not allowed to leave until their redemption dues were paid.

Summary question

How important was the part played by the okhrana in maintaining the autocratic government in Russia around 1881?

Activity

Thinking and analysis

Make a diagram to illustrate where power and authority resided within the Russian state in 1881, by copying and completing the following outline chart.

The position and power of:

The Tsar	The Central Institutions of Government
The Civil Service	Local Government
The Secret Police (okhrana)	The Orthodox Church
The Army	

Domestic politics under Alexander III, 1881–94

Key profile

Alexander III

Alexander III (1845–94) was the second son of Alexander II. He pursued an army career until he became heir to the throne after the death of his elder brother, Nicholas, in 1865. After the assassination of his father, he became 'Emperor of All Russia' on 1 March 1881. He had watched his father die and was consequently so fearful of revolutionary activity that he refused to live in the Winter Palace in St Petersburg and instead spent most of his time at a palace designed like a fortress in Gatchina, which had belonged to his great-grandfather. He was a large, but ungainly, man, 6 feet 4 inches tall and immensely strong. He could tear a pack of cards in half, bend an iron pole over his knees and crush a silver rouble with his bare hands. He married a Danish Princess, Dagmar (Maria Feodorovna), and had six children. He died of a kidney ailment, possibly brought on by heavy drinking, in Livadia in the Crimea, and was buried in the Cathedral of St Peter and St Paul Fortress in St Petersburg.

Fig. 5 *Alexander III*

A change of direction

Since two decades of cautious reform had ended with his father's assassination, Alexander III felt that it was imperative to reassert 'traditional' Tsarist authority for the good of his people. Tutored by Konstantin Pobedonostev, Alexander had been brought up with a very strong sense of commitment to his future role and he took his duties as head of the great Russian Empire very seriously. After a three day trial, the conspirators involved in his father's assassination were rounded up and five were publicly hanged.

There is little doubt that Alexander III's early decision to reject the plans for consitutional reform drawn up by his father's Interior Minister, Loris-Melikov, were taken out of a determination to reassert the principles of personal rule. Although he took some weeks to consider the way forward, rather than simply rejecting the proposals out of hand, it is well known that Alexander was keen to avoid any barrier which might get in the way of a direct relationship between himself and his people. He believed that western-style democracy was alien to the 'Russian way' and that it was not wanted by the peasants, who comprised around 85 per cent of his subjects.

In April 1881, he issued a manifesto, probably drafted by Pobedonostev:

> We call upon all Our faithful subjects to serve Us and the state in fidelity and truth for the eradication of the vile sedition disgracing the Russian land, for the strengthening of faith and morality, for the proper upbringing of children, for the extermination of falsehood and theft and for the introduction of truth and good order in the operations of the institutions given to Russia by her benefactor, Our beloved Father.

4

Key profile

Konstantin Pobedonostev

Konstantin Pobedonostev (1827–1907) was a former Professor of Law at Moscow State University who had been chosen to tutor Alexander from 1865. He became very close to Alexander and his presence behind the throne led to his nickname, 'the Black Tsar'. He probably wrote Alexander's accession manifesto which reasserted the Tsarist autocracy and, using his position as Over-Procurator of the Holy Synod (from 1880), he spoke out forcibly in favour of absolutism, nationalism and anti-Semitism, for example referring to Judaism as the 'Hebrew Leprosy'. He also tutored Nicholas II, but lost some influence after Nicholas's accession in 1894. In 1901, a socialist, Lagovsky, tried to shoot Pobedonostev through an office window, but missed. Pobedonostev retired from public affairs during the 1905 revolution and died two years later.

The Law on Exceptional Measures of 1881 confirmed Alexander's intentions by declaring that, in an 'exceptional' situation, a Commander-in-Chief could be appointed to reassume control of a locality, using military police courts and arbitrary powers of imprisonment.

Loris-Melikov and two other reforming ministers, Alexander Abaza and Dimitri Miliutin, resigned in protest against the direction the new reign

Did you know?

The Church of our Saviour on Blood

(See page 73 for photo)
As a memorial to his father, Alexander III began the construction of a new Church in St Petersburg in 1883, on the very site of the assassination. Work progressed slowly and was finally completed during the reign of Nicholas II in 1907. Funding was provided by the Royal family with the support of many private investors. It was a huge undertaking, but the Church of Our Saviour on Blood preserved the spot where Alexander II's blood was shed as a place of veneration. A deliberate parallel to the shedding of Christ's blood on the cross was suggested.

Key terms

Reactionary: 'backward-looking' and wanting to reverse modernising changes and reforms.

Pan-Slavism: the unity of all Slav peoples under Russian protection.

Cross-reference

The **Over-Procurator** of the **Holy Synod** is introduced at the beginning of this chapter, on page 61.

For the policy of **Russification**, see page 70.

Activity

Creative thinking

Write an editorial for a newspaper commenting on Alexander III's 'reshuffle'. Make it clear whether you are a Tsarist supporter or opponent through your style of writing.

was taking, but there is no doubt that Alexander was genuinely alarmed about the growth of revolutionary activity in Russia. His determination to live outside St Petersburg is indication enough that, despite his personal bulk, the new Tsar was fearful for himself and his family. Although Alexander's reign is usually labelled as '**reactionary**', his actions were not taken out of spite or lack of concern for his country. On the contrary, he sincerely believed that he embodied God on earth and and that he alone could decide what was right for his people. Orthodoxy and earthly power were combined in his being and the duty of his subjects was not to question, but to love and obey.

Alexander naturally turned for advice and support to those of like mind. He surrounded himself with men who were committed to strengthening his autocracy, persecuting non-Russians, enforcing religious orthodoxy and developing policies which would reverse, or at least slow down, the reforming practices of Alexander II. The most important were:

- Count Nikolai Ignatiev (1832–1908). Ignatiev was chosen as Minister for Internal Affairs (1881–2). He had a diplomatic background and had encouraged **Pan-Slavism** in the Balkans, thus bringing about the Russo-Turkish war of 1877–8, which encouraged Russian nationalism.
- Count Dimitri Tolstoi (1823–89). Tolstoi was Alexander's second Minister for Internal Affairs (1882–9). Formerly Minister of Education (1866–80), he was known as an uncompromising conservative who had restricted entry to universities. He had also held the post of Over-Procurator of the Holy Synod between 1865 and 1880 and was an outspoken supporter of Tsarist authority and Russification.
- Konstantin Pobedonostev (1827–1907). Pobedonostev wielded much influence as the new Over-Procurator of the Holy Synod. He was an outspoken nationalist driven by a total commitment to the restoration of the Tsar's absolutism. His influence over Alexander in the early days of the reign was particularly strong.
- Mikhail Katkov (1818–87). Katkov was not a Minister or adviser but an influential right wing journalist who edited the Moscow News from 1863 until his death in 1887. This gave him considerable power over the literate public and he was much favoured by Alexander III for his conservative political views, support of 'Russian' interests, and opposition to Polish nationalism.

Countering Alexander II's reforms

Under Alexander III's direction, the administration of the country was strengthened, with fuller powers granted to the police and greater central control. Nationalism and Orthodoxy were enforced. Local government rights were restricted and the nobles' powers reasserted. To the Tsar and his advisers, these policies were needed in order to bring about a return to the traditional Russian ways after subversives had forced through changes during his father's reign. They were the only way to halt a tide of revolution, terrorism and violence.

The re-establishment of the nobility's powers

Alexander II's reforms had brought Russia's first experiment with an elective system of local government into being which, although weighted in favour of the nobility, allowed for some local initiatives by setting up the Zemstva and providing for elected governments in towns. These reforms had opened the way for a new style of administration which was in tune with local needs. However, the tendency of the Zemstva to criticise central government and support moderately liberalising ideas won Alexander III's distrust. He had made it clear, even while his father

Fig. 6 *Disorder in the countryside led to the overturning of Alexander II's reforms*

was alive, that he was totally against 'public' participation in government and while the Zemstva did not disappear altogether, their range of competence was handicapped by new controls.

Through a law in July 1889, a new office of 'Land Captain' was created. Land Captains were to be appointed, on recommendation from the Provincial Governor, by the Minister of Internal Affairs from among eligible herditary nobles (who had sufficient land, education and length of government service to qualify) and were made responsible for law enforcement and government in the countryside. They were given wide-ranging powers. They could override elections to the Zemstva and village assemblies and disregard decisions. They could ignore the normal judicial process and overturn the judgements of local courts and impose fines.

The independence of the Zemstva was also undermined by an Act of 1890 which changed the election arrangements to reduce the peasants' vote. The Zemstva were put under the direct control of the Ministry of Internal Affairs, which had the effect of channelling their efforts away from political discussion towards the social services – education and health in particular and also local transport and engineering projects.

In June 1892, a similar arrangement was made for the cities. The electorate in the towns was reduced to the owners of property above a certain value and the mayor and members of the town councils became state employees, subject to central government direction.

While it could be argued that these changes had been introduced in an attempt to improve local government and to ensure, for example, more efficient collection of taxes, nevertheless, by asserting central government contol, restoring power to nobles and undermining the process of election, the changes instituted under Alexander III did much to undermine what little democratisation Alexander II had been able to bring about.

V. I. Gurko, an assistant Minister of Internal Affairs, was later to look back and dwell on some of the imperfections of the Land Captains:

> Not until 1904, 15 years after the institution was established, was there an inspection of the Land Captains. From the outset it was evident that there was a multitude of problems in need of immediate solution. There was virtually no supervision over the activities of the Land Captains, other than that some of their administrative decisions were revised as a result of complaints lodged against them. One reason for this lack of supervision was that the legal supervisors, the District Marshals of nobility, very seldom carried out their duties and even avoided them, lest they offend their subordinate Land Captains who played an influential part in electing the Marshals. It also became clear that the chief sin of the Land Captains was not arbitrariness but laziness and indifference.

5

Judicial changes

The judicial reforms of Alexander II which had moved towards the establishment of fairer justice and trial by jury were partially reversed. In 1885, a decree provided for the Minister of Justice to exercise greater control over the judicial system, for example in the dismissal of judges. In 1887, the Ministry was granted powers to hold **closed court sessions** to protect 'the dignity of state power' and in 1889, it became responsible for the appointment of town judges. In 1887, the property and educational qualifications needed by jurors were raised, while in 1884, a proposal to extend the 'Volost' courts (in which peasants' cases were heard by Justices of the Peace) to all classes was rejected. Instead, in 1889, the jurisdiction of the JPs was removed and their duties fulfilled by the directly appointed Land Captains in the countryside and judges in the towns.

Education policy

As in government, so in the field of education, there was a backward move towards confining certain levels of education to certain social classes. The developments were overseen by a new Minister of Education, I. D. Delyanov (1818–97), who circulated a memorandum to all secondary schools in June 1887 which read:

> All establishments of secondary education are to cease the intake of children of coachmen, domestic servants, cooks, washerwomen, small shopkeepers and other similar persons, whose children should emphatically not be taken out of the social environment to which they belong thereby leading to disrespect for their parents, dissatisfaction with their way of life and resentment against the existing and by the very nature of things, inevitable inequality in the distribution of property.

6

Under new regulations, children from the lowest classes were to be restricted to primary education, which was to be placed in the hands of the Orthodox Church. Admittance to secondary education would work on a quota system and higher education was only available to the upper classes. The effect was to reduce the numbers of children from the lower classes passing into higher education, while increasing the proportion of children of nobles and officials. Although overall the number of schools and the numbers of those receiving some education increased – with new vocational schools and secondary schools which offered a non-classical curriculum being set up from 1888– only 21 per cent of the population were literate at the time of the first census in 1897.

Since students had been identified with radical ideas, the Education Ministry also took steps to curb the independence of the universities. By the University Charter of 1884, appointments of chancellors, deans and professors were subject to the approval of the Education Ministry. Furthermore, the criteria for appointment were no longer to be based on academic achievement but on 'religious, moral and patriotic orientation'. In 1887, a further statute established full state control over the universities, reducing the rights of higher education boards and abolishing the separate university court. Higher education fees were introduced to restrict entry and students were required to pay to attend lectures, training sessions and to take examinations. Women were barred from the universities by legislation in 1882 and 1886, and all university life was closely supervised, with students forbidden from gathering in groups of more than five.

This attempt to restrict student involvement in subversive activity did not prove particularly successful. Although there was little trouble before 1887, that year saw an outburst of rioting and students were active in illegal political movements in the 1890s. There was even a central committee, the Union Council, which coordinated student societies and encouraged unrest.

Furthermore, these education policies ran counter to the government's attempts to promote economic modernisation in Russia. It was impossible to reconcile an education policy which excluded children from poorer social backgrounds with the need for an educated workforce, or to restrict university entry when economic growth demanded a trained bureaucracy.

Censorship, orthodoxy and control

This clampdown on intellectual activity was also accompanied by a toughening up of laws on censorship. On Tolstoi's initiative, as Minister for Internal Affairs, a government committee was set up in 1882, which issued the so-called 'temporary regulations'. These provided the government with powers to close papers deemed harmful and put a life ban on editors and publishers. The freedom of the press was thus curtailed and newspapers, which had already received three warnings, were required to submit their text to a board of censors on the day before publication.

As well as schools and universities, libraries and reading rooms were also restricted in the books they were allowed to stock and all literary publications had to be officially approved. Censorship also extended to theatre, art and culture, as seen, for example, in the Russification policies, and it was firmly linked to the promotion of Russian Orthodoxy.

From 1883, members of non-Orthodox Churches were not allowed to build new places of worship, wear religious dress, except within their meeting place, or spread any religious propaganda. Any attempt to convert a member of the Orthodox Church to another faith was punishable by exile to Siberia. Anti-Semitism was rife and in 1894, an evangelical Baptist movement in the Ukraine, known as *Stundism* (after the German word for an 'hour' [of worship]), was singled out as particularly dangerous and banned. Although other religions were tolerated and a law of 1883 even allowed the non-Orthodox to engage in trade and hold minor public office, nevertheless the Orthodox priests maintained a great ascendancy and from 1893 were, quite literally, state servants, with their salaries paid by the state.

Fig. 7 *It was dangerous to keep incriminating documents. If discovered it could lead to exile or even death*

Cross-reference

The policies of **Russification** under Alexander III are discussed on page 70.

For the promotion of **Russian Orthodoxy**, see page 72.

■ Cross-reference

To recap on the **Emancipation of the Serfs** in 1861, revisit the Introduction, pages 3–4.

For the **Peasants' Land Bank**, see page 108.

■ Cross-reference

To compare the position of urban workers in Germany in the same period, look back to pages 50–1.

■ Activity

Revision

Look back at the Introduction and make a list of the reforms introduced by Alexander II. Beside each, comment on its fate under Alexander III.

■ Cross-reference

To consider repression of socialist or subversive activity in Germany, look back to page 23.

■ Exploring the detail

The Russian Gendarmerie

The Russian Gendarmerie was the uniformed security police of the Russian Empire, responsible for law enforcement and state security. The Gendarmes investigated political and criminal cases, tracked down fugitives, controlled riots, and assisted local police and officials. The corps was staffed entirely from noble army officers who relied on a network of informers and agents.

■ Cross-reference

Pogrom is defined on page 71.

Extent and impact of counter-reform

While it is clear that the overall impact of Alexander III's policies was to reverse the trends which had been set in motion by his father in the 1860s and 1870s, not all of Alexander II's reforms were reversed. The greatest of these, the Emancipation of the Serfs, for example, remained and was indeed, improved upon when in May 1881, a law reduced the redemption fees payable by the peasants and cancelled arrears. The law only applied to the 37 central provinces of the Empire and affected about 15 per cent of former serfs, but it certainly showed good intent. In May 1885, the abolition of the hated poll tax, which relieved peasants (from January 1887, when it became operative) of yet another financial and psychological burden was particularly welcomed and together with the introduction of inheritance tax, helped to shift the taxation burden a little away from the lowest classes. Such measures, together with the introduction of the right of appeal to higher courts (after trial before the Land Captain) and establishment of the Peasants' Land Bank in 1883 could be said to have been genuine reforms to improve the position of the peasantry. Although it might be argued that they were introduced merely to forestall rebellion, equally, the same accusation could be levied against Alexander II's reforms.

Urban workers also had their lot improved by some reformist factory legislation between 1882 and 1890, including the regulation of child labour, a reduction in working hours (and in particular the hours worked by women at night), a reduction in excessive fines and payment in kind, and the appointment of inspectors with powers to check up on working and living conditions. Such social reforms should not be underestimated, but they actually went very little way towards ameliorating the lives of the growing working class and were again examples of paternal (fatherly) behaviour rather than measures of any political weight.

Repression and the police

Since Alexander's government was committed to eradicating revolutionary and subversive activity, new legislation was introduced to bolster and extend the powers of the police. The Department of Police, responsible to the Ministry of Internal Affairs, was ably led by V. K. Plehve between 1881 and 1884, and from 1884 by I. P. Durnovo. They supervised the Russian Gendarmerie and the Okhrana on which the autocracy relied and all imperial police forces were subject to their authority.

■ Key profile

Vyacheslav Konstantinovich Plehve

Vyacheslav Konstantinovich Plehve (1846–1904) had served as a state official when made Director of the secret police in the Ministry of Internal Affairs in 1881–4. He was Vice-Minister for Internal Affairs (1884–99), state secretary for Finland (1899–1902), and Minister for Internal Affairs (1902–4). He was committed to upholding autocratic principles and suppressed revolutionary and liberal movements, subjected minorities to forced Russification, secretly organised Jewish *pogroms* and is said to have encourged war against Japan in 1904 to forestall revolution at home. He backed police-controlled labour unions and was assassinated by a member of the Socialist Revolutionary Party in 1904.

Police powers were bolstered by the Statute on Police Surveillance, introduced originally as a temporary measure in 1882, but in practice renewed every three years until 1917. By this decree, any area of the Empire could be deemed an 'area of subversion' and police agents could search, arrest, detain, question, imprison or exile not only those who had committed a crime, but any who were thought likely to commit crimes or knew, or were related to, people who had committed crimes. This gave them tremendous power over people's lives, particularly since any such arrested person had no right to legal representation. To enforce this statute, the number of police was increased and new branches of the Criminal Investigation Department were set up. There was also a drive to recruit spies, counter-spies (to spy on the spies) and 'agents provocateurs', who would pose as revolutionaries in order to incriminate others.

Although the Gendarmerie operated as the security police in the greater part of the country, the secret police, the Okhrana, had offices in St Petersburg, Moscow and Warsaw where they took responsibility for 'security and investigation'. They intercepted and read mail and checked up on activities in the factories, universities, the army and state, detaining suspects and resorting to torture and summary executions. Communists, socialists and trade unionists were particular subjects of their investigations but they also watched members of the civil service and government.

Fig. 8 *Prisoners were subjected to cruel treatment on their way to exile in Siberia*

For those accused of crimes, the punishments were severe. Punishments often failed to match the severity of the offence and people could be exiled to Siberia for various criminal and civil offences as well as political crimes. Political exiles represented only around 1 per cent of the total 'exile population' before 1900 and they would find themselves alongside convicts who had been exiled for anything from rape and murder to the illegal felling of trees, minor robbery and drunkenness. Such prisoners were traditionally marched on foot, held together by chains referred to as 'the golden bracelets of the Tsar' with their wives and familes travelling alongside in wagons. When they reached the penal colonies, they were installed in barracks or small peasant huts and were expected to form hard labour, usually down the mines. Work was tough, rations were meagre, healthcare minimal and punishments severe. Furthermore, this all took place in the most inhospitable of conditions as described by Leon Trotsky, exiled shortly after the death of Alexander III, in Source 7:

We were going down the River Lena, a few barges of convicts with an escort of soldiers, drifting slowly along with the current. It was cold at night and the heavy coats with which we covered ourselves were thick with frost in the morning. It took about three weeks until we came to our village which had about a hundred peasant huts. At night the cockroaches filled the house with their rustlings as they crawled over table and bed, and even over our faces. From time to time we had to move out of the hut for a day or two and keep the door wide open, at a temperature of 35 degrees below zero. In the summer our lives were made wretched by midges. They even bit to death a cow that had lost its way in the woods. In the spring and autumn the village was buried in mud.

7

Activity
Thinking point

Discuss with a partner whether you think punishments such as those described in this section were likely to increase or decrease crime.

Russification

Alexander III's reign was also marked by a powerful national policy, known as Russification, which sought to merge all the citizens of the Russian Empire into a single nation. Although elements of this idea had been present under earlier Tsars, it only became official policy under Alexander III, and continued to be followed under his successor, Nicholas II. The slogan, 'Russia for the Russians' was directed against all national minorities throughout the Empire as part of the drive to uniformity and centralised control.

Fear of the spread of liberal ideas and the Polish revolt of 1863 no doubt encouraged such thinking, and the policy was popular with nobles and government officials obsessed with order and control, with the police and army, whose task it was to watch the activities of the minority groups within the Empire and maintain the security of the Empire's borders, and with the Orthodox Church. Pobedonostev in particular was an ardent supporter of policies which weakened or destroyed alternative religious groupings.

The destruction of non-Russian national cultures was particularly marked in Poland and Finland. The Finnish senate was reorganised in 1892, in order to weaken its political influence, while the independent postal service was abolished and the use of Russian coinage became compulsory. In Poland, the Polish National Bank was closed in 1885, and in schools and universities, the teaching of all subjects except the Polish language and religion had to be in Russian. Even Polish literature had to be studied in a Russian translation! The administration of Poland was also changed to curb any independence.

Russification also extended to other provinces, such as Byelorussia, Georgia and the Ukraine. In the Ukraine, the publication of all works in the Ukraininan language was forbidden in 1883 and, in 1884, all the theatres in the five Ukrainian provinces were closed. The Ukrainian and Byelorussian languages were forbidden and their churches persecuted. Even the peoples of Siberia and the Far East were subject to attempts at Russification. Uprisings of ethnic peoples were mercilessly surpressed in Guriya in Georgia in 1892, at Bashkira in 1884, in the Uzbek district of Fergana and Armenia in 1886, and at Tashkent in 1892.

Anti-Semitism

Fig. 9 *Pogroms became a feature of life in areas of Jewish settlement*

The racial group that suffered the most from this intense nationalism was the Jews. Rampant anti-Semitism was encouraged by Ministers such as Pobedonostev, with inflammatory slogans such as, 'Beat the Yids – Save Russia'. According to the historian Flannery, he believed that '*one third should emigrate, one third die, and one third disappear*' (i.e. be converted).

Alexander himself was anti-Semitic, partly on religious grounds, seen for example when he wrote in the margin

■ **Cross-reference**

A key profile of **Pobedonostev** is on page 63.

■ **Activity**

Thinking and analysis

Make a chart to balance the potential advantages to be derived from a policy of Russification against the likely disadvantages.

■ **Cross-reference**

Anti-Semitism in Germany during this period was less organised, but it was to be found in Wilhelm II's Germany – see page 38.

■ **Activity**

Thinking point

What image of Alexander III's Russia is conveyed by this picutre? When you have read the section on anti-Semitism, judge for yourself whether this image is fair or exaggerated.

of a document urging him to lessen the persecution, *'but we must never forget that the Jews have crucified our Master and have shed his precious blood'*, and partly because it was believed that Jews had been involved in his father's murder. The right wing Russian press helped encourage the view that Alexander II's assassin had been a Jewish actress, since a close associate of one of the assassins had been a Jewess – Gezya Gelfman.

Since 1736, most Jews had only been allowed to live in an area of western Russia known as, 'The Pale of Settlement'. Alexander II had allowed the wealthier Jews to settle elsewhere, until the Polish revolt frightened him into withdrawing his concessions and reducing participation of Jews in town government. This encouraged the growth of anti-Semitism, which already existed among the poorer elements in society who not only hated Jews because of the teachings of the Orthodox Church, but also resented their money lending and personal riches.

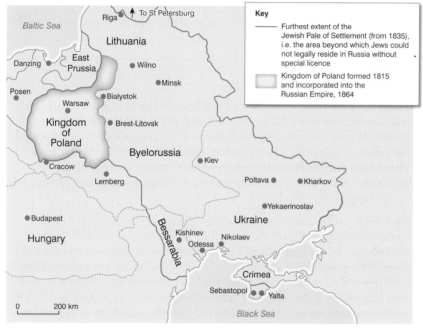

Fig. 10 *Jewish Pale of Settlement*

The Jewish concentration in the areas of the Pale made them ready targets for anti-Jewish **pogroms** which broke out in 1881. The immediate cause is unknown. They may have started because of some business competition at a time when there was jostling (in which Jews featured) for lucrative railway contracts, but it is regarded as highly probable that they were encouraged by the Okhrana using the link to Tsar Alexander II's assassination as an excuse to trigger trouble. Certainly the governing authorities did little to deter the violence and often took several days to intervene. An organisation known as the Holy League, which was supported by Pobedonostev, was certainly involved in the coordination of the early attacks, until it was banned in 1882.

The riots began in April 1881 in Yelizavetgrad in the Ukraine, where there was a large Jewish population, and soon spread to other towns, such as Kiev (where 2,000 Jews lost their homes), and Odessa. From here they spread as far afield as Warsaw and Nizhni Novgorod, causing many Jews to flee across the border into western Europe. Around

> ### Did you know?
> **Gezya Gelfman, 1852–1882**
>
> Gezya Gelfman, a Jewess, was the lover of Nikolai Sablin, one of the group of Alexander II's assassins. During the trial in 1881 she was sentenced to death by hanging, but she was reprieved as she was found to be pregnant, and under Russian law, since a foetus was considered innocent, a pregnant woman could not be hanged. She was instead sent into detention where she died in 1882.

> ### Did you know?
> **Pale of Settlement**
>
> This refers to a region in the western part of Russia, created in 1791, as an area where Jews might live. It included much of present day Lithuania, Belarus, Poland, Bessarabia, Ukraine, and parts of western Russia and comprised around 20 per cent of European Russia. A number of cities within the Pale were, however, excluded, while a limited number of categories of Jews had been allowed to live outside the Pale.

> ### Key term
>
> **Pogrom:** an old Russian word which means 'round up' or lynching. It originally denoted an assault by one ethnic group on another but after 1881 it gained the special connotation of an attack on Jews.

> ### Cross-reference
>
> For more on the **Okhrana**, see pages 60 and 68–70.

Key chronology

Anti-Semitic legislation 1882–94

1882 May Laws and Army Law. The Governor-General of St Petersburg ordered 14 Jewish apothecaries to shut down their businesses.

1886 No Jew could be elected to a vacancy on the board of an orphan asylum.

1886 Jews engaged in the sale of alcohol could only sell from their own homes or personal property.

1887 Jews who had graduated from a university outside Russia no longer possessed the right to reside outside the Pale by virtue of their qualifications.

1887 The number of Jews admitted to schools and universities was regulated by quotas – 10 per cent within the Pale, 5 per cent outside the Pale, and 3 per cent in the capitals (Moscow, St Petersburg, Kiev). Jews were prohibited from settling in Finland. Rostov-on-Don and Taganrog were removed from the Pale.

1889 Jews needed a special permit from the Minister of Justice to be elected to the Bar (the legal professional body). Any Jewish lawyer who wished to become a barrister needed the express consent of the Minister of Justice.

1891 Non-Christians were forbidden from buying property in the provinces of Akmolinski, Semirietchensk, Uralsk and Turgai.

1892 Jews were banned from participation in local elections and prohibited from the right to be elected to town 'Dumas'. The mining industry in Turkestan was closed to Jews.

1893 It became illegal for Jews to adopt a 'Christian' name.

1894 Jews who graduated from veterinary college could no longer be admitted to the service of the State. Jews were no longer eligible for any licences to sell alcohol.

16 major cities were affected where property was burnt, shops and businesses destroyed, women raped and many people put to death. Even after the main outbreaks up to 1884, there were still sporadic pogroms, as in Odessa in 1886.

The May Laws of 1882 discriminated further against the Jews, making life even harder for them, even within the Pale of Settlement.

- Article 1. Jews are forbidden to settle hereafter outside cities and towns of fewer than ten thousand people. Exception is made with regard to Jewish villages already in existence where the Jews are engaged in agriculture.

- Article 2. All contracts for the mortgaging or renting of property situated outside cities and towns to a Jew, shall be of no effect.

- Article 3. Jews are forbidden to do business on Sundays and Christian holidays; the laws compelling Christians to close their places of business on those days will be applied to Jewish places of business.

8

These laws effectively condemned the Jews to living in ghettoes in cities and towns. A separate decree of 1882 also decreased the number of Jewish doctors permitted in the Russian army because doctors possessed the rights of army officers, a privilege otherwise unattainable for Jews. These laws were supposedly temporary but, rather like the police legislation, they were constantly revised and tightened, as can be seen in the accompanying timeline.

Michael Reutern, chairman of the Committee of Ministers, set up a commission under Count Pahlen which recommended, in 1883, that Jews should be given equal rights with Russians and allowed freedom to develop their skills and contribute to society, but these recommendations were ignored. Consequently, many Jews left the country, whether of their own free will or as the result of enforced expulsions, as in Kiev in 1886. In 1890, foreign Jews began to be deported from Russia along with Russian Jews who had settled outside the Pale and in the winter of 1891–2, around 10,000 Jewish artisans were expelled from Moscow where they had legally settled during the reign of Alexander II. More expulsions followed when the Grand Duke Sergei Alexandrovich, Alexander's brother, was made Governor-General in 1892. He forced around 20,000 from the city during the Passover and closed down a newly built synagogue.

The effect of such policies among the Jews that remained in Russia was to drive a disproportionate number of them towards revolutionary groups, and in particular Marxist socialist organisations. In 1897, shortly after Alexander III's death, the General Union of Jewish Workers in Russia and Poland was set up and this was to become involved in the Marxist Social Democratic movement, playing an important part in the growth of opposition to the autocracy under Nicholas II.

Summary questions

Explain why Alexander III's government undertook a policy of Russification.

How successful were the anti-Semitic policies of the period 1882–94?

Religious policies

Alexander III's Russification policies were closely tied to his devout adherence to the principles of the Russian Orthodox Church and his belief that the Romanov dynasty had a duty to uphold and protect Orthodoxy. According to tradition, Russia was a Holy Land that had been chosen by God to save the world. The Tsar possessed not only a 'divine right' to rule, but a holiness which made him a saint on earth. However, by the late 19th century, Church administration had been moved to the **Holy Synod** and the Tsar's position had become more secular, nevertheless, Imperial Russia remained a strongly Orthodox state and the moral domination of the Orthodox Church was seen as essential to prevent revolution at a time of liberal and secular challenge. The old alliance of 'Autocracy, Orthodoxy and Nationality' was thus revived.

Priests were expected to read out Imperial manifestos and decrees, provide statistics, for example on births, marriages and deaths, root out opposition and inform the police of any suspicious activity. Even statements given in Holy Confessions, where a priest was, in Church law, bound to inviolable secrecy, were expected to be passed to the secular authorities.

The power of the Orthodox Church was not only maintained, but steadily reinforced in Alexander III's reign. Under I. D. Delyanov, the Orthodox Church was given complete control of primary schools where it could place an emphasis on religious indoctrination through the reading of Orthodox Slavonic texts and try to reinforce humility and obedience among the peasantry.

The school catechism – as written by the Holy Synod – was as follows:

> **Q. How should we show our respect for the Tsar?**
>
> ▪ We should feel complete loyalty to the Tsar and be prepared to lay down our lives for him.
>
> ▪ We should, without objection, fulfil his commands and be obedient to the authorities appointed by him.
>
> ▪ We should pray for his health and salvation and also for that of all the Ruling House.
>
> **Q. What should we think of those who violate their duty toward their Sovereign?**
>
> ▪ They are guilty, not only before the Sovereign, but also before God. The word of God says, 'Whosoever therefore resisteth the power, resisteth the ordinance of God'. (Rom: 13:2)

9

All religious books had to pass the Church's strict censorship controls and the Church Courts had complete contol over moral and social 'crimes', successfully resisting an attempt by more forward-looking bureaucrats to move cases of divorce from the Church to secular courts. Divorce could only be obtained by proving adultery in an ecclesiastical court and cases of incest, bestiality and blasphemy were also the preserve of the Church. If found guilty, the Church also had a free hand to award punishments, commonly various forms of penance or incarceration in a monastery.

Key term

The Holy Synod: a group of Bishops which forms the ruling body of the Orthodox Church. It is the highest authority on rules, regulations, faith and matters of Church organisation.

Fig. 11 *The Church of St Saviour in Blood in St Petersburg, constructed by Alexander III as a memorial to his murdered father*

Activity

Source analysis

1 From Source 9, make a list of the qualities which the Church wanted to develop in the peasant children through their education.

2 Is this catechism a form of brainwashing? Explain your answer.

Cross-reference

I. D. Delyanov is introduced on page 66.

Key terms

Old Believers: these people rejected reforms to the Orthodox liturgy in the 17th century and had fled to Siberia to escape persecution. Some remain there to this day, despite various bouts of state persecution.

Uniate Church: the Uniate Church recognises the Pope as the Head of the Church but observes the rites of the Orthodox Church.

Armenian Church: The Armenian Church has its own hierarchy and non-Orthodox practices.

Russian intelligentsia: the more educated members of Russian society who opposed the state for various cultural, moral, religious, philosophical and political reasons.

Cross-reference

For more on the attractions of socialist ideas, see pages 75–80 and 83–5.

Summary question

How important was the role played by the Orthodox Church in the maintenance of social stability in Russia in the reign of Alexander III?

Alexander's policy of Russification enabled him to promote Orthodoxy throughout the Empire. It became an offence to convert from the Orthodox to another faith, or even to publish criticisms of it. Radical sects, which had broken away from true Orthodoxy – in particular the '**Old Believers**' who had settled in remote parts of Siberia – were all persecuted by the state. The Ukrainian **Uniate Church** and the **Armenian Church** were subject to persecution and in the Volga region of Central Asia and Siberia there was enforced baptism of pagans, accompanied by scenes of ritual humiliation. More than 8,500 Muslims and 50,000 pagans were (in theory at least) converted to Orthodoxy during Alexander III's reign as well as around 40,000 Catholics and Lutherans in Poland and the Baltic provinces.

A closer look

The influence of Orthodoxy

Despite the dominance of the Orthodox Church, there is evidence to suggest that its control over the lives of the people was weakening. One 19th century priest despaired:

'Everywhere, from the most resplendent drawing rooms to smoky peasant huts, people disparage the clergy with the most vicious mockery, with words of the most profound scorn and infinite disgust.'

The provision of Churches and priests had not kept pace with the growth of urbanisation and, in any case, the Orthodox religion often seemed to have little relevance for the workers in the factories and tenement blocks, who were often more attracted by the teachings of the socialists. Even in the countryside where faith and religious practices seemed stronger, superstition frequently held a stronger sway than the Orthodox priests who were often regarded as money grasping and less than perfect role models.

Some liberal clergy expressed the wish to regenerate the Church and reform its relations with the Tsarist state but their calls were silenced by the senior conservatives and in particular by Pobedonostev, the Over-Procurator between 1880 and 1905.

Growth of opposition

Despite all the legislation and surveillance network, repression failed to prevent disturbances and the continuance of revolutionary movements, and in some respects they only served to encourage them. In June 1888, the Department of Police itself estimated 332 cases of mass disturbance in 61 of Russia's 92 provinces and districts. This included 43 disturbances in 9 out of the 12 central provinces and in 51 cases, the military had to be employed.

What is more, the intense Russification programme and in particular its anti-Semitism, drove some to emigrate and others, who might otherwise have proved loyal citizens, into the revolutionary camp. It is perhaps not surprising that the revolutionary movement in Russia in the early 20th century contained a disproportionate number of Jews, including Trotsky, Martov, Zinoviev and Litvinov.

The seeds of opposition to the autocracy had been sown long before the reign of Alexander III. The critical-thinking minority among the **Russian intelligentsia** had spent much of the century pondering the political and social direction that Russia should follow. This group divided broadly into two categories: the Slavophiles and the Westerners. The former believed that Russia had a unique culture and heritage centred on the prevailing peasant society and the tenets of the Orthodox Church, which should be preserved as the country modernised. The latter adopted the view that Russia should forget some of its traditions that were holding it back and absorb modern western values. This conflict, to some extent, resolved itself during the reign of Alexander III, as the attractions of the Slavophiles diminshed (after peaking in 1881) and the country moved forward in its march towards industrialisation, creating conditions in which western-style **socialism** began to take root.

Key term

Socialism: this implies equality and the sharing of wealth. Socialism is an element of Populist and Marxist beliefs.

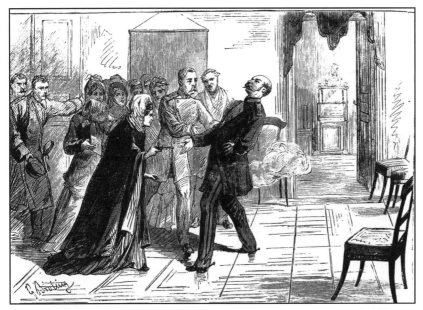

Fig. 12 *Vera Ivanovna Zasulich, a leading terrorist, shoots and wounds police chief Trepov in retaliation for his brutality. She was later tried but acquitted by a sympathetic court*

Opposition to 1881

Inspired by the works of Slavophile writers, in 1874, a group of around 2000 young men and women abandoned their homes and universities to 'go to the people'. They aimed to win over the peasantry to their socialist ideas, by stirring up their resentment against their lack of land and their heavy tax burden. They believed that a new egalitarian reorganisation of society could grow out of the practices of the peasant commune and some even tried dressing and talking like peasants to persuade the villagers of their importance. This 'Populist' (*Narodniki*) movement had an almost religious zeal about it, but the romantic illusions of the young were soon shattered by scenes of peasant hostility, and the peasants' ignorance, superstition, prejudice and deep-rooted loyalty to the Tsar. By the autumn of 1874, 1,600 had been arrested.

In 1876, those who evaded capture set up 'Land and Liberty' (*Zemlya i volya*), a more radical organisation which split into two factions in 1879:

- **Black Partition** (*Chernyy Peredel*) which continued to work peacefully among the peasantry.
- **The People's Will** (*Narodnaya Volya*) which advocated violent methods, undermining government by assassinating officials.

It was The People's Will which scored its greatest triumph with the assassination of Tsar Alexander II.

Activity

Constructing a timeline

As you read this section make a timeline chart to show the development of opposition movements within Russia from c.1874. You can add to your chart after reading about the development of opposition after 1894 in Chapter 4.

Populism after 1881

The assassination in March 1881 proved a huge disappointment to the opposition. It yielded no practical benefits, and, on the contrary, led to a wave of arrests, greater police surveillance, the abandonment of Loris-Melikov's proposed constitutional reforms and the accession of a Tsar determined to enforce reactionary policies.

However, it did have some symbolic significance, showing the vulnerability of the autocracy, winning some support overseas and creating martyrs which helped popularise the revolutionary cause. Supporters of Populism continued to meet in secret and acts of terrorism with which it had become associated, continued despite the repression. In 1886, The People's Will was re-formed among students in St Petersburg and in March 1887, a group who made bombs with the intention of asassinating Alexander III, was arrested. Two months later, five including Alexander Ulyanov, Lenin's elder brother, were hanged.

■ **Key profile**

Alexander Ulyanov

Fig. 13 *Alexander and Vladimir Ulyanov (Lenin) as young men*

Alexander Ulyanov (1866–87) was the son of a government official from Simbirsk and part of Russia's small bourgeoisie. He (and his brother Vladimir) attended St Petersburg university, where he participated in radical student politics – attending illegal meetings and running propaganda campaigns. Alexander helped re-form The People's Will (*Narodnaya Volya*) in 1886, with a commitment to terrorism, but following his arrest for attempting to assassinate Alexander III, he was hanged.

Populism continued in the remnants of The People's Will, 'self-education' circles such as the Muscovite Society of Translators and Publishers, which translated and reproduced the writings of foreign socialists, and groups which made contact with radicals in the west. However, police activity, the execution, imprisonment and exile of leaders, a lack of funds and a lack of enthusiasm among the peasants all conspired to minimise incidences of violent revolutionary activity. Famine too played its part and some radicals turned their energies to relief work among the peasantry during the disastrous famine years of 1891–2. It was not until the Russian economy went through a massive transformation in the 1890s that revolutionary activity was reinvigorated and when that came about, its main thrust was in a direction very different from that adopted by the Populists.

The intelligentsia and the liberals

Opposition continued among the intelligentsia, but there still remained a Slavophile/Westerner division in attitudes.

The Slavophile tradition was strong in the work of the author Count Tolstoi, who turned from writing novels to moral tracts in the 1880s and 1890s. Tolstoi opposed Tsarist oppression and the injustice of the legal system, but he rejected violence and urged individuals to live pure and simple lives in order to bring about the moral regeneration of the country. His tract 'What I believe', written in 1883, was banned in 1884 but his work represented yet another assault on the authority of the autocratic government.

Other opposition voices, following the westernising tradition, were heard among the professional classes, which had grown considerably in number, thanks to Alexander II's reforms and the modernisation of the country. This new middle class of teachers, lawyers, doctors, merchants and government officials from the Zemstva sought greater freedom and participation in government. Their experience in the Zemstva, particularly in coordinating relief programmes during the 1891–2 famine, gave increased confidence and by the mid-1890s there were renewed calls for a national body to advise and petition the government.

Yet another strand of the intelligentsia, in the westernising tradition, was attracted by Marxism and they welcomed the spread of industrialisation in Russia as a precursor to socialist revolution.

Marxists

In the 1880–90s, Marxism also took root in Russia. Marxist ideas were not entirely new there. The writer and thinker Bakunin had provided the first translation of the *Communist Manifesto* in Russian in 1869, while the first volume of *Das Kapital* was published there in 1872.

 Question

Why did Populism decline in Russia in the 1890s?

Cross-reference

For more on the problems of 1891–2, turn to page 104.

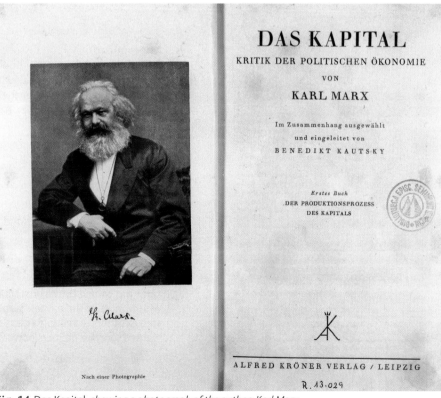

Fig. 14 Das Kapital, *showing a photograph of the author, Karl Marx*

Activity

Challenging your thinking

Using the diagram of Marxism below as a basis for discussion, find ways in which Marxist theories suited Russia in 1881 and think of obstacles to achieving a Marxist revolution there. In what ways did Russia differ from the Marxist model described? When you have studied the economic changes of Witte outlined in Chapter 4, return to your answer and debate the ways in which Witte's changes made the achievement of Marxist change more likely.

Key profile

Karl Marx

Karl Marx (1818–83) was a German Jew who studied law and worked as a journalist. He moved from Germany to France in the early 1840s, but his writings on the social and economic conditions of Paris led to his expulsion from the city and he settled in Belgium. He wrote *The Communist Manifesto* with his friend Friedrich Engels in 1848, immediately prior to the European revolutions of 1848–9. After moving to London, he wrote his major work *Das Kapital*. The first volume was published in 1867 and subsequent ones (after Marx's death) in 1885 and 1894.

Stage 1

Primitive Communism

Men performed the same economic function – hunter-gatherers. They worked together in order to survive. There was no private property and there were no classes. Eventually the most successful hunter-gatherer-warrior gained power and control over the others.

Stage 2

Imperialism

The strong man/Emperor ruled. He began by owning all the land but when threatened by outsiders, he would grant land to others in return for military services. A new land-owning aristocracy was therefore created.

Stage 3

Feudalism

Land was owned by the aristocracy who exploited the peasantry who worked it. There was a surplus of food which the aristocracy sold to others – creating a class of merchants and capitalists who wanted to share political power.

Fig. 15 *Marxist stage theory*

Marxist stage theory

In *The Communist Manifesto* (1848) and *Das Kapital* (1867), Karl Marx put forward a political theory based on 'economic determinism'. He suggested that all human history was driven by economic factors and that the economic position of a country determined its system of government. As different economic groups, or classes, competed to dominate economic life, they inevitably clashed with one another. This moved the country forward to the next stage of human history.

The Marxist stage theory is illustrated in Figure 15:

Stage 4

Capitalism

The wealthy merchants and factory owners (bourgeoisie) obtained political power and exploited the workers (proletariat). As the proletariat became politically aware they would rise up and overthrow the bourgeois government.

Stage 5

Socialism

There was a 'dictatorship of the proletariat' as workers' organisations redistributed food, goods and services fairly, according to need, and profits were shared by all. The middle classes came to understand that equality was superior to private ownership.

Stage 6

Communism

Everyone joined together for the common good. Money and governments were no longer needed and society was class-less. As all countries reached this stage the world would become state-less and competition (and wars) ceased.

Marxism, which derived from the theories of Karl Marx, provided a very specific interpretation of history based on class struggles. Some early thinkers had rejected this out of hand as of little relevance to the Russian experience, or had tried to adapt Marxist theory to suit a very different type of society. However, the coming of industrialisation and the growth of an urban proletariat began to change all this and during the reign of Alexander III, Marxist ideas began to take hold.

In Switzerland, Georgi Plekhanov, one of a group of Russian exiles, who had settled abroad to avoid persecution, established the Emancipation of Labour group in 1883. This group not only translated and arranged for Marxist tracts to be smuggled into Russia for the benefit of underground socialist groups, they also sought to demonstrate that all historical development followed Marxist laws and was fully applicable to Russia. In *Socialism and the Political Struggle* (1883) and *Our Differences* (1885), Plekhanov argued that Russian revolutionaries had to accept the inevitability of Marx's 'stages of development'. He stressed that Russia had to pass through the capitalist phase of development and that this was clearly underway. Revolutionaries, he believed, should concentrate their activities among the Russian workers in the cities, rather than wasting their energy on the peasantry, for it was from the Russian proletariat that the dynamism to drive a socialist revolution would emerge. Since the proletariat of Russia was still small and backward, he wanted revolutionary leaders to organise the workers so as to be ready for Marxism, but, he warned, their first task was to cooperate with the bourgeoisie to fight autocracy, in order to accelerate the capitalist stage.

■ **Key profile**

Georgi Plekhanov

Georgi Plekhanov (1856–1918) had been a Populist and a leader of Land and Liberty and Black Partition. He was exiled from Russia in 1880 and settled in Geneva where he made contact with western thinkers and studied the works of Marx and Engels. He co-founded Emancipation of Labour in 1883 (with Lev Deutsch and Vera Zasulich) and this was to merge with other socialist groups to form the Social Democratic Labour Party in 1898. In 1903, Plekhanov became a Menshevik and he remained an exile until 1917, when he briefly returned to Russia but despite his contribution to Russian Marxism, he disapproved of the Bolsheviks and died in Finland.

The immediate impact of Emancipation of Labour within Russia was quite small. Marxist teaching proved attractive intellectually, even if its message failed to oust entirely the appeal of Populism with its belief in the Russian peasantry. The group also received a setback in 1884 when its German contact, Deich, responsible for the smuggling of materials into Russia, was arrested by the German police. Certainly the Tsarist government was well aware of the movement and infiltrated it.

However, by the 1890s, Marxism was becoming more widely accepted in revolutionary circles as a commentary on what *had* happened in Western Europe, and what *was* happening in Russia at that very time. It was from these small beginnings that changes in thinking which were to have massive long term importance began to take root.

■ **Activity**

Class debate

Divide into two groups. One group should consider the ways in which the actions of Alexander III's government increased the likelihood of opposition to the Tsarist autocracy, while the other should consider the ways in which they strengthened the Tsardom. Each group should present its views to the rest of the class and you should then try to decide which is the more convincing view.

■ **Summary question**

How successful was Alexander III's government in preventing revolutionary activity within Russia?

4 Russia under Nicholas II, 1894–1914

Fig. 1 *Coronation of Tsar Nicholas II*

In this chapter you will learn about:

- Tsar Nicholas II and his style of government

- the growth of the reform/opposition movement and the government's reaction to this

- the causes, events and outcome of the 1905 revolution and the Dumas to 1914

- the impact of economic and social change in Russia between 1881 and 1914.

Cross-reference

Pobedonostev is profiled on page 63.

I rejoice to see gathered here representatives of all estates of the realm, who have come to express their sentiments of loyal allegiance. I believe in the sincerity of these feelings, which have been those of every Russian from time immemorial. But it has come to my knowledge that latterly, at some meetings of the Zemstva, voices have been heard from people who have allowed themselves to be carried away by senseless dreams about the participation of representatives of the Zemstva in the general administration of the internal affairs of the state. Let it be known to all that I devote all my strength to the good of my people, but that I shall uphold the principle of autocracy as firmly and unflinchingly as did my ever-lamented father.

1

Nicholas II's inaugural speech of 1894, probably written, as his father's had been, by his former tutor Pobedonostev, offered little hope to the liberal politicians of the Zemstva who had begun to renew their calls for a constitution, allowing some degree of broader participation in the government of Russia. Nor was it the only sign of what the new reign might bring. In May 1896, as the crowds celebrated Nicholas's coronation on the Khodynka Field on the outskirts of Moscow, hundreds were crushed to death, while Nicholas, and his new bride, Alexandra, enjoyed the evening dancing at a ball given by the French ambassador.

■ **Activity**

Research task

Undertake some further research into the life and personality of Nicholas II (to 1894) and write a short article on the new Tsar of Russia, as it might have appeared in a British newspaper at the time of his coronation.

Fig. 2 *Nicholas II standing before his throne*

■ **Cross-reference**

To learn more about the **Great Famine** of 1891–2, turn to page 104.

■ Domestic politics under Nicholas II, 1894–1914

Nicholas II was no bloodthirsty tyrant but, like his father, he had been brought up to take his duties as a ruler seriously and to believe that any concessions or signs of weakness would be indications of cowardice and failure on his part. No doubt such attitudes had been instilled in him by Pobedonostev who had worked with him as a tutor, although it was said that when Pobedonostev tried to instruct him in the workings of the state he became *'actively absorbed in picking his nose'*. Alexander III had never rated Nicholas very highly. He thought him a dunce and a weakling and referred to him as 'girlie'. Nicholas had excellent manners, a good memory and could speak good English, French and German, but he was not a practical man and politics bored him. When his father died, at the unexpectedly early age of 49, Nicholas is said to have said to his cousin:

> What is going to happen to me and to all of Russia? I am not prepared to be a Tsar. I never wanted to become one. I know nothing of the business of ruling. I have no idea of even how to talk to the ministers.

However, he accepted his inheritance as God-given and set out to rule in 'the Romanov way', asserting himself against the demands of the growing reform movement. As he declared shortly before his coronation, he was resolved:

> to maintain the principle of autocracy just as firmly and unflinchingly as it was preserved by my unforgettable dead father.

Changes in the reform movement and government reaction

The years after 1894 were a time of serious unrest in Russia. Although opposition movements were nothing new, Russian society had become more politicised in the years after the Great Famine of 1891–2. The failure of the over-bureaucratic Tsarist government to cope with the crisis, which had left voluntary organisations to provide the necessary relief work, had bred scorn and despair. As a result, there was not only greater public mistrust of the government's competence, but also a firmer belief in the power of ordinary members of society to play a role in the nation's affairs. Reformist groups had consequently become more clearly delineated and better organised and had developed a broader support base by 1900 than ever before.

There were three basic types of reformers pressing for change in Russia. Of these, the most moderate were the Liberals, who were to be found in the Zemstva and among the more educated members of society. The other two groups were more radical – the Social Revolutionaries, heirs to the Populists and the Marxist Social Democrats.

The Liberals

Liberals had long pressed for changes in the the governmental structure of the country and the experience of the Zemstva, together with factors such as the spread of education and the beginnings of a middle class as a result of industrialisation, offered them new opportunities to press their case. In 1903, the Union of Liberation (*Soyuz Osvobozhdeniya*) was founded under the inspiration of Pyotr Struve. Struve had defected from the Marxist movement, opposing its commitment to violent revolution, and had begun to publish a journal, *Osvobozhdenie* (Liberation), in Germany, to escape censorship. Struve believed that what Russia needed was a period of 'peaceful evolution' in which to adapt to its new industrialising status. He wanted to see a constitutional system put in place through which the urban workers could campaign legally to improve their conditions.

In 1904, the Union held a grand meeting to which representatives of the Zemstva and other professional societies were invited. Members declared their intention to work for the establishment of a constitutional government and arranged a series of about 50 society banquets during the winter of 1904, which were attended by members of the Liberal elite. However, little was achieved before the autocracy was put under pressure by the events of 1905. Indeed, the Liberals were fortunate to escape the closer attention of the police, which was only achieved because the latter were overworked coping with the activities of the Social Revolutionaries and the spreading agrarian and proletarian unrest.

LE MOUVEMENT LIBÉRAL EN RUSSIE
Graves bagarres à Saint-Pétersbourg

Fig. 3 *Suppression of the Liberal movement in Russia, 1904–5*

Cross-reference

The **events of 1905** are detailed on pages 89–95.

Key profile

Pyotr Berngardovich Struve

Pyotr Struve (1870–1944) was a lawyer, economist and philosopher who became interested in Marxism and was involved in Populist and Marxist activities in the 1890s. By 1900, Struve had become a leader of the moderate wing of Russian Marxists and when banished from St Petersburg travelled to Germany where he produced a magazine for the *Soyuz Osvobozhdeniya* (Union of Liberation) from 1904 which was smuggled into Russia, where it enjoyed considerable success. When German police, under pressure from the Okhrana, raided Struve's premises in October 1904, Struve moved his operations to Paris and continued publishing the magazine there until the October Manifesto proclaimed freedom of the press in Russia.

In October 1905, Struve returned to Russia and became a co-founder of the liberal Constitutional Democratic party. He represented the party in the Second State Duma in 1907, but after its dissolution, he concentrated on writing. With the outbreak of the First World War in 1914, Struve adopted a position of strong support for the government and after the Bolshevik revolution of 1917 joined the White movement.

The Social Revolutionaries

The Populist movement enjoyed a revival following the debates about the competence of the government at the time of the Great Famine which had highlighted the need to reform the rural economy. Populist ideas were particularly strong in the universities where there were several outbreaks of disorder from around 1899, culminating in the assassination in 1901 of the Minister of Education, N. P. Bogolepov, by a student named Pëtr Karpovich. The same year, a number of these new Populist groups came together to create the Socialist Revolutionary Party. Its most influential theorist was Viktor Chernov (1873–1952), a law graduate

Activity

Constructing a timeline

As you read this section, add the most important details to your timeline chart (as explained on page 75) on the development of opposition in Russia.

Cross-reference

R. A Stolypin is profiled on page 87.

Did you know?

Yevno Azef

Yevno Azef (1869–1918) came from a poor Jewish family. He became involved in Marxism and lived in exile in Germany, where he was recruited as a police informer by the Okhrana. In 1899, he returned to Russia and became a member of the Socialist Revolutionary Party. He took control of its 'combat organisation' (having organised the arrest of the previous head), used this position of influence to betray many comrades and organise the murder of V. P. Plehve in 1904. Some party sympathisers in the police ranks leaked information of Azef's activities to the party but at first the Socialist Revolutionaries refused to believe the reports. He was finally exposed in 1908 and fled to Germany where he died in 1918.

Cross-reference

Plekhanov is profiled on page 80.

Cross-reference

Pyotr Struve is profiled on page 83.

from Moscow and editor of the party journal, *Revolutsionnaya Rossiya* (Revolutionary Russia). This party accepted aspects of Marxist teaching but combined these with Populist ideas, to provide a specifically 'Russian' programme. They put forward the view that the interests of peasants and workers – the so-called 'labouring poor' – were identical. Therefore, they argued, they should work together to get rid of autocracy and bring about land redistribution. This set them apart from the pure Marxists, since they emphasised the importance of the peasantry as a revolutionary force and talked of 'land socialisation' rather than 'land nationalisation'.

The party played an active part in the 1905 revolution, developing a full programme in November 1905 and forming a separate combat organisation (*boevye otrady*) inciting students to carry out assassinations. Among their more spectacular 'successes' were the assassinations of V. P. Plehve, Minister for Internal Affairs in 1904, and the Prime Minister P. A. Stolypin in 1911, but the Social Revolutionaries were responsible for a spate of violence as the Tsarist regime was put under pressure in and after 1905. Between 1905 and 1909 there were 2,828 terrorist assassinations and 3,332 woundings, but the secret police foiled some activities and was successful in infiltrating the movement at its highest levels. There were 4,579 Socialist Revolutionaries sentenced to death between 1905 and 1909 and 2,365 were actually executed.

The Social Democrats

Although the 'Emancipation of Labour', founded in 1883 by Plekhanov was committed to bringing about a proletarian-socialist revolution in Russia and had tried to spread knowledge of Marxism more widely within Russia through propaganda and agitation, it had made slow headway before the industrial take-off of the 1890s. Censorship, the Okhrana and the limited development of an industrial proletariat had all hindered its activities. However, in the 1890s, as industrialisation speeded up, a number of workers' organisations, illegal trade unions, Marxist discussion circles, and other groups, sprang up. In an attempt to weld these groups together, in 1898, the First Congress of the Russian Social Democratic Workers' Party of the Soviet Union was held in Minsk.

Although this marks the launch of a new Marxist party, only nine delegates actually attended the Congress. It elected a three man Central Committee and produced a manifesto (drawn up by Pyotr Struve, who at this stage was a Marxist) but it was broken up by Okhrana agents who promptly arrested two of the newly elected Committee. It was not a promising start, but in the years that followed, Vladimir Ilyich Ulyanov (1870–1924), (Lenin), came to play a prominent part in the development of the party and in 1902 produced the pamphlet, *'What is to be done?'*, in which he argued that the party needed to redirect the workers away from trade unionism towards revolution which would destroy the Tsarist autocracy. Together with Plekhanov, Martov and others, he founded a new revolutionary newspaper *'The Spark'* (Iskra) and helped develop a strong underground party network.

Key profiles

Vladimir Ilyich Ulyanov (Lenin)

Vladimir Ilyich Ulyanov (1870–1924), known as Lenin from 1901 (after the river Lena in Siberia where he was exiled), came from a well-to-do professional family in Simbirsk. However, his brother's execution, following involvement in a plot to assassinate Tsar Alexander III, led to the family becoming ostracised which deeply affected Lenin. He was expelled from University in Kazan, for involvement in political rebellion, but he was able to take his exams and become a lawyer. In 1893 he moved to St Petersburg where he joined Marxist discussion groups and was arrested for inciting strikes. After four years in prison and Siberian exile, he went to London where he founded the Marxist newspaper '*Iskra*' and expressed his views in a pamphlet, '*What is to be done?*' in 1902. His uncompromising attitude led to a Marxist split in 1903 and Lenin remained in exile until 1917, save for a brief return to St Petersburg in October 1905.

Lev Bronstein (Trotsky)

Lev Bronstein (1879–1940) was the son of a well-off Jewish farmer from the Ukraine. He was an able writer and linguist and in his teens became involved in Marxist groups and strike activity. He was imprisoned and exiled to Siberia, but managed to escape using a disguise and false passport, from which he took the name Trotsky in 1902. He travelled to London and became a friend and associate of Lenin, although he failed to support Lenin in the 1903 dispute. In 1905 he became deputy chairman of the St Petersburg Soviet, and was arrested, but once more escaped abroad. He was in the USA when revolution broke in 1917 and he hurried back to help lead it.

Fig. 4 *Lenin worked hard to win supporters for the Marxist cause*

The second Social Democratic Party Congress took place in 1903, commencing in Brussels, but subsequently moving to a small congregational chapel in Shoreditch, London. The 51 voting delegates considered a variety of propositions as to how the party should move forward, and were divided on a number of these. While Lenin argued in favour of a strong disciplined organisation to lead the proletariat, others, led by Martov, believed that their task should be to develop a broad party with a mass working class membership which would thus be educated and encouraged to the point when it would spontaneously rise against its masters. While Martov saw members 'cooperating' with the party organisation, Lenin wanted every member to be a dedicated activist. Lenin certainly did not have the overwhelming support of the majority at the beginning of the conference and it was only when a

Exploring the detail

The split in the Social Democratic Party

The split in the Social Democratic Party was to have major consequences for the future of Marxism in Russia. In 1903–4, many members changed sides. Plekhanov abandoned the Bolsheviks, whom he had supported, while Trotsky left the Mensheviks in September 1904 over their insistence on an alliance with Russian Liberals. Between 1904 and 1917 Trotsky described himself as a 'non-factional Social Democrat' and spent much of his time trying to reconcile the different groups within the party. He clashed many times with Lenin and later conceded he had been wrong in opposing Lenin on the issue of party organisation.

number of representatives withdrew that Lenin won a vote in favour of a more centralised Party structure. Lenin then claimed that his supporters were the majority – in Russian 'the bolsheviki' while his opponents, led by Martov, were dubbed 'the mensheviki' (the minority) – even though, overall, the reverse was actually true. Over the next few years there continued argument and rivalry within the embryonic party about the nature, timing and organisation of the revolution which they were planning. The Bolshevik/Menshevik division hardened so that, by 1906, there were effectively two separate Social Democratic Parties.

Activity

Revision activity

Make a summary chart of the key groups pressing for change in Russia by 1905 – the Liberals, The Socialist Revolutionaries and the Social Democrats. You should give details of beliefs, aims and support for each group. You will probably need to subdivide the last of these groups.

Summary question

Explain why Marxism had only limited support in Russia before 1905.

The position by 1905

AQA Examiner's tip

It is impossible to understand the political changes that took place in 1905 without some appreciation of the economic transformation of Russia since the 1890s. You are advised to study the section on 'Economic and social change and its political impact' on page 103 before attempting the questions set on the causes of the 1905 revolution.

Fig. 5 *Railwaymen were among those who went on strike in favour of reform*

The years 1902 to 1907 were marked by widespread unrest in both towns and countryside. The famines of 1897, 1898, 1900 and 1902 cumulatively caused untold hardship, while Witte's policy, to squeeze yet more from the peasantry through taxation (to pay for the costs of industrialisation) had made the lives of the already down-trodden peasantry still more desperate. Risings in the provinces of Poltava and

Kharkov in 1902 were followed by so many instances of arson in rural communities, that the nickname 'the years of the Red Cockerel', referring to the leaping flames which resembled a rooster's comb, was coined. The unrest was at its worst in the central Russian provinces, where the landlord/peasant relationship was still at its most traditional, but it also spread into Georgia, the Ukraine and Poland. Peasants set fire to their landlords' barns, destroying grain or vented their anger by attacking landlords and officials or seizing their woodland and pasture.

The Tsar's minister, Stolypin, dealt with the disturbances with a ferocity which aggravated the situation further. Peasants were flogged, arrested and exiled or shot in their thousands. The gallows were in such constant use that they became referred to as 'Stolypin's necktie'.

■ Cross-reference

The work of **Pyotr Stolypin** is described in more detail later in this chapter, on pages 111–14.

■ Key profile

Pyotr Stolypin

Stolypin was a landowner who became Governor of Grodno, and then Saratov. He was an intelligent man, keen for progress and reform, but with a brutality and loyalty that earned him many enemies. When Saratov was badly hit by peasant disturbances in 1902, and again in 1904–6, he reacted with the utmost savagery, but he also headed a government commission on agriculture to consider practical reform. As Prime Minister from 1906 to 1911, he mercilessly stamped out terrorism so that the hangman's noose gained the nickname 'Stolypin's necktie' (*stolypinskii galstuk*). However, he combined this intolerance and ruthlessness with a belief in a radical reform of agriculture. He was assassinated at the Kiev opera house in September 1911 by Mordekhai Bogrov (1887–1911) a Jewish former law student – a Socialist Revolutionary terrorist and an agent of the Okhrana. His specific motive is unknown.

Even more disturbing was the unrest simmering in the rapidly expanding industrial cities. The influx of foreign capital and the growth of railways had transformed the Russian economy in the 1890s, producing an oppressed and discontented mass of more than two million factory workers in major cities such as St Petersburg and Moscow by the early years of the 20th century. Low wages, overcrowded lodging houses, long working days and an absence of job security provided an ideal recruiting ground for the newly-founded Social Democratic Party, particularly when, in 1902, an international slump added thousands of unemployed to the scene of urban misery. Although theoretically illegal, the number of industrial strikes escalated in the towns, from 17,000 in 1894 to around 90,000 in 1904. In 1901, the Obukhov factory in St Petersburg, for example, saw violent clashes between armed police and whip-carrying **Cossacks**.

In an attempt to control the proliferation of illegal unions, in 1900, the Moscow chief of the Okhrana, S. V. Zubatov, began organising his own police-sponsored trade unions with the approval of the Governor-General of Moscow, the Grand Duke Sergei. The idea was to provide 'official' channels through which complaints could be heard and aid provided, in an attempt to prevent workers being lured into joining the radical socialists. The experiment only lasted to 1903, when Zubatov was dismissed and exiled after one of his unions became involved in a general strike in Odessa. However, another union on the Zubatov model, the

■ Cross-reference

For more on the working classes in the cities, look ahead to pages 109–11.

■ Key term

Cossacks: tough cavalrymen from the valleys of the Steppe who had a strict code of honour and had become a separate and powerful social estate. They served the Tsarist autocracy and were border guards and bodyguards.

Assembly of St Petersburg Factory Workers, was formed in 1904 by Father Georgi Gapon. The Union was approved by Plehve, and had the support of the Orthodox Church. It soon had 12 branches and 8,000 members and Gapon tried to expand activities to Kiev and Moscow.

■ **Key profile**

Father Gapon

Father Georgi Gapon (1870–1906) studied at the St Petersburg Theological Academy and became an Orthodox priest and prison chaplain, working in the working class districts of St Petersburg. Believing he had a divine mission to help the workers, he began organising workers' unions from 1903 but remained intensely loyal and taught that the Tsar was obliged by God to respond to the workers' demands. He escaped with his life after the Bloody Sunday march of 1905, and briefly spent time in exile, supported by Socialist Revolutionaries. On returning to Russia in December 1905, he re-made contact with the Okhrana, but was found hanged in March 1906, possibly murdered by Socialist Revolutionary agents, angered by his double-dealing, or by the Okhrana.

The 1905 revolution

Russo-Japanese War and the events of 'Bloody Sunday' (9 January 1905)

■ Cross-reference

See page 136 for a map of this conflict.

■ Activity

Creative thinking

Write a short newspaper article for a Tsarist publication in which you describe and comment on Russia's decision to go to war against Japan in 1904.

Fig. 6 *Russo-Japanese War 1904–5: Japanese field battery in action during the attack on Port Arthur, 1904*

Plehve, Nicholas's Minister for Internal Affairs, is accredited with encouraging the Tsar to embark on a 'short swift victorious war' against the Japanese in January 1904 in order to stem the tide of unrest. The origins of the war lay in the Russian 'drive to the East' where Russian penetration had been bolstered by the building of the Trans-Siberian railway. Although the main line ended at Vladivostock, in 1896 the Chinese allowed an additional line to be constructed south from Vladivostok through Northern Manchuria to Harbin, and in 1898 a spur line was added to the naval base of Port Arthur on the Liaodong peninsula which Russia was granted on a 25-year lease. Since the expansionist Japanese had briefly held this peninsula in 1895, the two powers were almost bound to come into conflict and the Tsar, encouraged by his Ministers, showed no wish to compromise with the Japanese. Nicholas regarded himself as an expert on the area, since he had once toured there. He, like many Russians, regarded the Japanese with racial contempt, arrogantly referring to them as 'little monkeys' (*makaki*) and when the war opened with the Japanese capture of Port Arthur on 2 January 1904, there was a groundswell of patriotic sentiment for a war against the 'yellow danger'.

However, the Russians really had very little idea of their enemy, or the inadequacies of their own forces. Running a war 6,000 miles from the capital was never going to be easy and a series of defeats turned the initial surge of patriotism into one of opposition to the government. There was little mourning when Plehve was blown up by an Socialist Revolutionary bomb in July 1904 and in Warsaw crowds turned out to celebrate on the streets. There were renewed cries for a National Assembly, and the moderate Mirsky, who had replaced Plehve, reluctantly agreed to allow a meeting of Zemstva representatives in private quarters in St Petersburg in November 1904. However, when Mirsky presented the Tsar with an edited version of the Assembly's requests, Nicholas replied: *'I will never agree to the representative form of government because I consider it harmful to the people whom God has entrusted to me.'* All he was prepared to agree to was an expansion of the rights of the Zemstva.

On 20 December 1904, Port Arthur surrendered to the Japanese after a long siege. Such a humiliation did little to lower the growing discontent. War had only exacerbated the economic and social position of the peasantry and industrial workers by dislocating the supply of goods, creating shortages and raising the prices of essential commodities. On 3 January, a strike began at the Putilov Iron Works in St Petersburg which soon involved approximately 150,000 workers. Father Gapon, to whose union many of the strikers belonged, decided to try to diffuse the troubles by conducting a peaceful march to the Tsar's Winter Palace in the centre of St Petersburg in order to present a petition to Nicholas II outlining their case and demonstrating their loyalty. Their 'humble and loyal address to the Tsar' read:

Cross-reference

For more on the Putilov Works, see page 107.

> O Sire! We working men of St Petersburg, our wives and children, and our parents, helpless and aged men and women, have come to you, our ruler, in quest of justice and protection. We are beggars, we are oppressed and overburdened with work; we are insulted, we are not regarded as human beings but are treated as slaves who must suffer in silence.
>
> Our first wish was to discuss our needs with our employers, but this was refused us; we were told that we have no legal right to discuss our conditions. We asked that wages of casual labourers and women should be raised to one rouble a day, that overtime should be abolished and that more adequate medical attention should be provided for us with care and without humiliation. We asked that the factories should be rebuilt so that we could work in them without suffering from draughts, rain and snow,
>
> Your majesty! We are here, many thousands of us. We have the appearance of human beings but in fact we have no human rights at all, not even the right to speak or to think. We are turned into slaves by your officials. Any one of us who dares raise his voice in defence of the working class is thrown into prison, or sent into exile.

2

Activity

Source analysis

1 Having read this source, what impression do you gain of the attitude of the protestors a) to the Tsar, b) to the factory owners?

2 Do you think the sentiments expressed are genuine? Explain your views.

Although Gapon had been warned to call off the march, he naively went ahead and planned it for Sunday 9 January in the belief that the Tsar would take the workers' part. However, Nicholas himself chose to spend the weekend at Tsarskoe Selo, his summer palace, a little way from the city. The authorities had drafted 12,000 troops into the city as a precaution, so the situation was tense, even before the march began. On that Sunday morning, around 150,000 unarmed workers and their families, singing hymns and carrying icons, patriotic banners, crosses and pictures of former Tsars set out from various points around the city, to make their way towards the square outside the Winter Palace. However, at the Narva Gates, Gapon's column was charged by cavalry and shot at, leaving around 40 dead and hundreds wounded.

Bloody Sunday, 9 January 1905

Fig. 7 *Soldiers fire on rebel workers in front of the Winter Palace in St Petersburg, during 'Bloody Sunday', 1905*

At Troitskaya Square, not far from the Winter Palace, guards from the Pavlovski regiment fired into the crowds, leaving around 150 dead and wounded. The crowds fled in the direction of the Winter Palace Square where they met more Tsarist troops – Cossacks, cavalry and some heavy artillery. The inflamed crowds refused to disperse even when whips and the flat side of the sabres was used against them, but when troops with bayonets assumed a firing position, many fell to their knees and crossed themselves. The troops opened fire into the crowds and for the remainder of the afternoon and evening the confrontation continued. Workers fleeing the troops went on the rampage, attacking the homes of the nobility, looting shops and erecting barricades in the streets. The cavalry continued to charge through the lanes and alleys, shooting indiscriminately until all was quiet. According to one of the crowd:

> I observed the faces around me and I detected neither fear nor panic. No, the reverend and almost prayerful expressions were replaced by hostility and even hatred. I saw these looks of hatred and vengeance on literally every face – old and young, men and women. The revolution had been truly born, and it had been born in the very core, in the very bowels of the people.

3   *Quoted in Orlando Figes, **A People's Tragedy**, 1996*

The event (which became known as 'Bloody Sunday') was a turning point in the downfall of the autocracy. At the end of the day, the government put the number of dead at 76 and the wounded 233 but this would seem

Activity

Creative thinking

Write a letter, as though from one of the onlookers, describing the events of 'Bloody Sunday' and expressing your opinion of the march and its consequences.

to be a gross underestimate. A more realistic set of figures would probably be around 200 killed and 800 wounded. It sparked an outbreak of rebellion which spread through the peasantry and the military, among the national minorities and among other urban workers. Indeed people of all groups and classes began to express their pent-up frustrations – in words and actions. On 4 February, after the Grand Duke Sergei Alexandrovich, the Tsar's uncle, had been blown up by a Socialist Revolutionary bomb, Nicholas finally agreed to meet a few selected workers' representatives at Tsarskoe Selo. However, he seemed to have nothing new to offer and merely suggested they had been misled and should return to work. He also dismissed the moderate Mirsky and brought in two new officials who were prepared to follow a hard-line policy – A. G. Bulygin as his Minister for Internal Affairs and Major-General D. E. Trepov as the new military governor of St Petersburg.

The developments of 1904–5 can be seen in this time chart:

>
> **Did you know?**
>
> The months in this table are from the Russian Julian calendar, which was 13 days behind the Western Gregorian calendar in the early 20th century. The Russian calendar was eventually changed in 1918.

>
> **Question**
>
> How far was the political unrest of January–September 1905 the result of developments in the Russo-Japanese War of 1904–5?

Table 1 *Events of 1904–5*

1904–5 (Old style) Month	Events in Russo-Japanese War	Events in Russia
December	20 December: Russia's naval base at Port Arthur surrenders to the Japanese	
January		3 January: Strike at the Putilov Iron Works 9 January: 'Bloody Sunday'
February	9 February – 25 March: Battle of Mukden – Russian army defeated and 90,000 troops killed	4 February: Assassination of the Grand Duke Sergei Alexandrovich, the Tsar's uncle, killed by a Socialist Revolutionary bomb 18 February: Nicholas reaffirms his faith in autocratic rule but also promises an elected consultative assembly. He asks Bulygin to prepare draft proposals
March		Zemstva Liberals meet in Moscow
April		All Russian Union of Railway Workers established and everywhere workers begin forming illegal trade unions
May	14–15 May: The Russian Baltic fleet is sunk in the straits of Tsushima by the Japanese forces under Admiral Togo.	8–9 May: 'Union of Unions' is set up – a federation of liberal-left professional unions, demanding full civil and political rights, universal suffrage and nationwide elections to an assembly with full legislative powers Peasants' congress in Moscow calls for All Russian Union of Peasants
June		2 June: Congress of Union of Unions prepares for a general strike 14 June: Mutiny on the battleship Potemkin
July		Spread of peasant unrest 24 July: Bulygin publishes details of his plan for constitutional reform
August	23 August: Treaty of Portsmouth ended Russo-Japanese War. Russia concedes territory to Japan including the southern half of the island of Sakhalin (although less than Japanese had demanded)	
September		12–15 September: Zemstva Conference rejects Bulygin's draft proposal, known as 'Bulygin's Duma' and demands a Duma elected by universal suffrage 29 September: Printers' Strike sets off wave of strikes in Moscow

The sinking of the Baltic Fleet

As the situation in the Far East deteriorated, the Tsar agreed to send five divisions of the Baltic Fleet (moored on the Gulf of Finland). They set out on 2 October 1904, but sailing across the Dogger bank in the North Sea, the 'Suvorov' opened fire on two of their own ships, believing them to be patrolling Japanese torpedo boats. In the firing that ensued, a British trawler, one of a small fishing fleet off Hull, was sunk and two English fishermen drowned. There was an outcry in Britian and demands for war which were only allayed by the payment of a substantial fine by the Russians.

The fleet continued on a seven month voyage, around Africa, across the Indian Ocean, taking on coal from merchant vessels as few ports were prepared to allow the fleet to dock, and then northwards towards Manchuria. By the time it reached the Straits of Tsushima, where it encountered the Japanese fleet, it was in poor shape. Apart from the four new battleships, the Russian ships were old and the long voyage and the lack of opportunity for maintenance, meant their hulls were badly fouled, reducing their speed. While the Japanese ships could travel at 16 knots (30km/h), the Russian fleet could reach only 9 knots (17km/h) making them far less manoeuvrable. Furthermore, the Japanese had more modern range-finders and superior gunners and shells. These soon wrecked the Russian superstructures and fatefully ignited the large quantities of coal stored on the Russian decks. The battle which began at 10.00am on 14 May was over by 11.00am the next day. Nearly the entire Russian Baltic fleet was lost while the Japanese lost only three torpedo boats.

The mutiny on the battleship Potemkin

The Potemkin was one of the Black Sea Fleet moored in the Crimea. This had been unable to take part in the Russo-Japanese War since the Straits Convention of 1871 had forbidden Russian warships to sail out into the Mediterranean while Turkey was at peace. Protest began over a meat ration which was considered inedible by the sailors. When one of the sailors' spokesmen was shot, a full scale mutiny ensued in which seven officers were killed. Sailing under a red flag, the sailors took the ship into the port of Odessa where they placed the dead sailor's body at the bottom of the 'Potemkin steps' between the city and the harbour. The next day, thousands of townsfolk, who had their own grievances against the local authorities, arrived to pay respects and show solidarity with the sailors. When these crowds refused to disperse, troops were ordered to fire at random into their midst. Many jumped into the sea – more than 2,000 were killed and around 3,000 wounded. This was an even worse massacre than that of Bloody Sunday in St Petersburg. The boat eventually sailed off to Romania where the mutineers surrendered in return for a safe passage home.

Cross-reference

The Convention of 1871 regarding the Black Sea is further discussed on page 119.

October Manifesto

By October 1905, the Russian Empire seemed to be near to total collapse. There were strikes and demonstrations in all the major cities, peasant uprisings throughout the countryside and demands for independence from the Poles, Finns, Latvians and other minority groups. To oppose

Fig. 8 *Battleship Potemkin*

such activity a radical right wing organisation was formed, the Union of the Russian People, which organised gangs known as the **Black Hundreds** to beat up protestors and Jews. Nicholas, who allowed his name to be associated with the Union of the Russian People, continued to spend his days giving tea parties and hunting. He had complete trust in Trepov as military governor of St Petersburg and assumed he would soon be able to reassert control.

However, the dismal end to the Russo-Japanese War did not create a mood for compromise. On the contrary, the rebels grew more confident and the strikes became better organised and more militant. A St Petersburg Soviet (Council), inspired by the Union of Unions, and dominated by Mensheviks, was set up to direct a General Strike, and this began in Moscow at the beginning of October 1905.

It took until 17 October for the Tsar to agree to sign a decree promising constitutional reform and only after he was pressed to do so by all around him. Sergei Witte, the Chairman of the Tsar's Council of Ministers, warned that the country was on the verge of a revolution that would 'sweep away a thousand years of history', while Trepov declared the need for some moderate reform and the Grand Duke Nicolai, the Tsar's uncle, reputedly threatened to shoot himself unless reforms were instituted. The Tsar's 'October Manifesto' promised:

■ to grant the population the unshakeable foundations of civic freedom based on the principles of personal rights, freedom of conscience, speech, assembly and union

■ to admit to participation in the **Duma** those classes of the population which at present are altogether deprived of the franchise

■ to establish it as an unbreakable rule that no law can become effective without the approval of the state Duma and that the representatives of the people should be guaranteed the supervision of the legality of the actions of authorities appointed by Us.

4

Sergei Witte

Sergei Witte (1849–1915) came from a Georgian family, enobled by state service, with Dutch blood on his father's side. He attended Odessa University and worked for the Odessa Railway from 1871–7 where he became an expert on railway administration and wrote a book on rail tariffs in 1883. In 1889, he joined the Ministry of Finance in order to develop a new railways department and in 1892, was promoted, firstly to Minister of Communications, and then, Minister of Finance, a post he held until 1903. Although an able and forward-thinking administrator, the results of his measures invited controversy. He was the author of the 1905 October Manifesto and became Russia's first Prime Minister that year, but was forced to resign after six months. He opposed the entry of Russia to the First World War on economic grounds, and died shortly afterwards, in 1915.

There were celebrations on the streets of St Petersburg, as crowds gathered to wave red flags and sing the French revolutionary anthem, the Marseillaise. The General Strike was called off and there was talk of the birth of a new Russia. However, the real radicals, like Trotsky and Lenin were far from convinced and tried desperately to get the workers to fight on. Lenin's Bolsheviks wrote in their workers' bulletin *'We have been granted a constitution, yet autocracy remains. We have been granted everything, and yet we have been granted nothing'*. In some ways their view accorded with that of the Tsar himself. Nicholas had no intention of becoming a 'constitutional monarch' and few of his Ministers had a real commitment to the manifesto promises.

On 19 October, Nicholas was to write to his mother, the Empress Maria about the issue of the October Manifesto:

> You can't imagine what I went through before that moment. From all over Russia they cried for it, they begged for it, and around me many, very many, held the same views. There was no other way out than to cross oneself and give what everyone was asking for.

5

Counter-revolution

Unrest and violence continued and counter-revolution set in. Despite the Manifesto promise of 'full civil rights', Trepov ordered troops to 'fire no blanks and spare no bullets' in forcing striking workers back to their factories. Furthermore, in the final months of 1905, the Jews, whom the right wing associated with 'socialists and revolutionaries' suffered in terrible pogroms while gangs were sent to round up and flog the peasants in a bid to restore order.

On 3 December, the Headquarters of the St Petersburg Soviet was surrounded and its leaders, including Trotsky, arrested, tried and subsequently exiled to Siberia. This weakened the revolutionary movement in the capital and gradually the authorities regained control. However, there was still a further month of street warfare in Moscow and troops from St Petersburg and heavy artillery were brought in to restore order. An artillery bombardment of the working class Presnaya district eventually ended the unrest as workers' homes were reduced to rubble. Even then, there were outbreaks of trouble in the countryside for a further two years.

The major events of October–December 1905 are as detailed below:

Table 2 *Events of October–December 1905*

October	**6 October:** Railway strike begins.
	10 October: Moscow railways brought to a halt – General Strike in the city.
	12 October: General Strike in St Petersburg.
	Liberal Kadet party established by the Union of Unions and Zemstva groups.
	13 October: St Petersburg Soviet set up to direct strikes.
	17 October: Manifesto issued, pledging a constitution, extending franchise and civil liberties. Witte becomes Prime Minister and issues an amnesty for political prisoners. The General Strike in St Petersburg is called off.
	18 October: Demonstrations for and against the Manifesto – Trotsky publicly denounces it; right wing violence is led by the Black Hundreds and strikers begin to return to work. Pobedonostev is dismissed but the reactionary Durnovo replaces Bulygin as Minister for Internal Affairs.
	Military mutinies continue.
November	**3 November:** Peasants' redemption payments halved amidst heightened rural unrest.
	4–7 November: Second General Strike in St Petersburg ends and demand for 8-hour day abandoned.
	8 November: Lenin arrives in St Petersburg.
	6–12 November: Second Congress of Peasants' Union demands nationalisation of land.
	14 November: Peasant union leaders are arrested.
	Press censorship ends.
	26 November: Head of St Petersburg Soviet is arrested – Trotsky takes over.
December	**3 December:** Government arrests 250 members of the St Petersburrg Soviet, including Trotsky.
	7 December: General Strike in Moscow paralyses the city.
	11 December: New electoral law is passed, granting wide, but indirect male suffrage.
	Ruthless suppression of rural unrest using the army begins.
	16 December: Durnovo orders mass dismissal of all 'politically unreliable' local government employees.
	Full-scale artillery barrage of working class district (Presnya) of Moscow by government.
	19 December: Last remnants of Moscow revolt crushed.

The aftermath of revolution and the era of the Dumas

Fig. 9 *The Duma opened amidst great expectation in April 1906*

Activity

Group activity

By the end of 1905, the Tsarist regime was still intact. Can you suggest reasons why the 1905 revolution failed to topple the Tsar? Consider the opposition's aims, methods and support, and make a list of the strengths and weaknesses of the opposition forces and the Tsarist autocracy in order to arrive at a conclusion.

The new constitution

Although the October Manifesto had provided no precise detail as to what the election arrangements for, or powers of, the promised Duma would be, over the following months, a new constitutional arrangement was drawn up as follows:

There were to be two legislative houses:

Lower Chamber (The State Duma)	Upper Chamber (The State Council)
■ Lower Chamber –The State Duma – members elected under a system of **indirect voting** by estates – heavily weighted in favour of the nobility and peasants (who were assumed to be the crown's natural allies). ■ Deputies were to be elected for a five year term. 	■ Upper Chamber –The State Council – half elected by Zemstvos, half appointed by the Tsar – noble representatives from the major social, religious, educational and financial institutions. 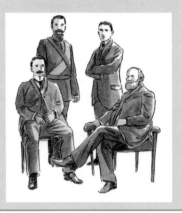

The two houses had equal legislative power and all legislation also had to receive the approval of the Tsar. Any one of the three bodies could veto legislation.

Government (Council of Ministers under the Prime Minister)	
■ The government (Council of Ministers under the Prime Minister) was to be appointed exclusively by the Tsar. The government was responsible to the Crown, not the Duma. 	

Fig. 10 *The new Russian constitution*

The Fundamental Laws

Five days before the first Duma met, Nicholas issued a series of Fundamental Laws (23 April 1906) defining his view of power:

Article 4: To the All-Russian Emperor belongs supreme autocratic power. It is ordained by God himself that his authority should be submitted to, not only out of fear but out of a genuine sense of duty.

Article 9: No legislative act may come into force without the Emperor's ratification.

Article 87: The Emperor may rule by decree in emergency circumstances when the Duma is not in session.

Article 105: The Emperor may dissolve the Duma as he wishes.

6

The Tsar also claimed:

- the sole power to declare war, conclude peace and negotiate treaties with foreign states and to have control over all foreign relations
- supreme command over all land and sea forces of the Russian state
- complete contol over military expenditure and household expenses
- the sole power to appoint and dismiss government ministers
- the right to overturn verdicts and sentences given in a court of law
- control over the Orthodox Church.

Political groupings

There were to be four Dumas between 1905 and 1917. The main political parties which contested the elections (in addition to the independent candidates and fringe groupings) are detailed below:

Table 3 *The main political parties between 1905 and 1917*

Party	Details
Social Democratic Workers' Party (SD) – divided between the Bolsheviks and Mensheviks	Founded in 1898. Committed to Marxism. Split, in 1903, into: **Bolsheviks**: Led by Vladimir Lenin. Believed in discipline, centralisation, organisation and the role of the proletariat under party guidance. From 1905, favoured a peasant/proletariat alliance. **Mensheviks**: Led by Yulii Martov. Believed in cooperation with bourgeoisie/liberals rather than peasantry and the use of legal channels of opposition.
Socialist Revolutionaries (SR)	Founded in 1901. Led by Viktor Chernov. Favoured Populist ideas of redistribution of land and nationalisation. Left of party favoured terrorism to achieve aims.
Trudoviks (Labour group)	Non-revolutionary break-away from SR party of moderate liberal views but with no formal programme. Favoured nationalisation of non-peasant land, democratic representation, a minimum wage and 8-hour working day. Supported by peasants and intelligentsia.
Kadets (Constitutional Democrats)	Led by Pavel Milyukov (1859–1943). A central liberal party which favoured a constitutional monarchy with parliamentary government; full civil rights; compulsory redistribution of large private estates with compensation and legal settlement of workers' disputes.
Octobrists (Union of 17 October)	Leaders included Alexander Guchkov (1862–1936). A moderate conservative party which accepted the October Manifesto and opposed further concessions to workers or peasants. Supported by wealthy landowners and industrialists.
Progressives	A loose grouping of businessmen who favoured moderate reform.
Rightists – including the Union of the Russian People	Leaders included Vladimir Purishkevich (1870–1920). The Union of Russian People was extremely right wing favouring monarchism, chauvinism, Orthodoxy, Pan-Slavism and anti-Semitism. Promoted violent attacks on the left wing and pogroms through its street-fighting gangs, the Black Hundreds. Other rightists shared conservative views but were less extreme.
Nationalist groupings	Ukraininans, Polish, Georgian, Muslims – all seeking rights and greater independence.

The results were as follows:

Table 4 *Duma election results, 1906–17*

Party	1st Duma: 1906	2nd Duma: 1907	3rd Duma: 1907–12	4th Duma: 1912–17
SDs (Bolshevik)			19	15
SDs (Menshevik)	18	47		
SRs		37		
Trudoviks	136	104	13	10
Kadets	182	91	54	53
Octobrists	17	42	154	95
Progressives	27	28	28	41
Rightists	8	10	147	154
National grouings	60	93	26	22
Others		50		42

Activity

Thinking and analysis

Before reading further, study these results. What changes can you observe in the make-up of these four Dumas?

The four Dumas

The first Duma: May–July 1906

A national election campaign took place through the winter of 1905–6. The Bolsheviks and SRs refused to participate, as did the extreme right wing Union of Russian People. This meant that the first state Duma, optimistically referred to as the 'Duma of National Hopes', was overwhelmingly radical-liberal in composition. The Kadets fought a skilful campaign and won the largest number of seats of any grouping. More than a third of the new deputies were peasants, and peasant farmers made up the single biggest professional group. There were also far more deputies to the left, than to the right of the Kadets, and the deputies formed a group that was strongly critical of the Tsar and his ministers.

They met at the Tauride Palace in St Petersburg on 1 May 1906.

Maurice Baring, the English journalist writing for the *Morning Post* attended one of its first sessions:

I had the good fortune to gain admission to the Duma yesterday afternoon. I think it is the most interesting sight I have ever seen.

One saw peasants in their long black coats, some of them wearing military medals and crosses; priests; tartars; Poles; men in every kind of dress except uniform. When the sitting began I went up into the gallery. The members go to their appointed places, on which their cards are fixed and the impression of diversity of dress and type becomes still stronger and more picturesque.

You see dignified old men in frock coats; aggressively democratic-looking intellectuals with long hair and pince nez; a Polish Bishop dressed in purple; men without collars; members of the proletariat; men in loose Russian shorts with belts and men dressed in the costume of two centuries ago.

Fig. 11 *A cartoonist depicts the Tsar's attitude to the Duma – 'Oh how these deputies stink!'*

They were a motley band and commentators commented on the 'uncivilised' manners of some of the peasant deputies, who threw their smoke ash onto the polished floors and and spat out the husks of the sunflower seeds they liked to chew. It was said that the Tsar's mother was upset for several days after witnessing all these commoners in the Palace.

No sooner had the elections taken place than Sergei Witte, the architect of the October Manifesto and head of Nicholas's Council of Ministers resigned, under pressure from reactionary influences at Court.

This was a blow to the hopes of the liberals who no doubt hoped that, under his guidance, a form of government would evolve whereby Ministers would take note of the Duma's views and work together with it in the formulation of policies. Witte was replaced by Ivan Goremykin, an old-fashioned conservative. Since the government had been able to negotiate a large loan of 2,250 million gold francs from France in April 1906 to keep it solvent, there was no need for it to rely on the Duma for the approval of the budget.

Key profile

Goremykin

Ivan Goremykin (1839–1917) was a lawyer with strongly conservative political views. He had served as Minister for Internal Affairs between 1895 and 1899, before becoming Prime Minister in 1906. He was soon forced to resign in July 1906, after disagreements with the first Duma and was replaced by Peter Stolypin. Goremykin was a close ally of Rasputin and again became Prime Minister in 1914. He retired in February 1916 but was recognised as an ex-Tsarist and murdered by mobs in December 1917.

Cross-reference

Rasputin is profiled on page 102.

From the outset, Nicholas found the first Duma too radical. Almost its first act was to pass an 'Address to the throne' in which it requested a political amnesty; the abolition of the State Council; the transfer of ministerial responsibility to the Duma; the compulsory seizure of the lands of the gentry, without compensation; universal and direct male suffrage; the abandonment of the emergency laws; the abolition of the death penalty; and a reform of the civil service. Nicholas ordered Goremykin to inform the Duma that their demands were 'totally inadmissible', whereupon, the Duma passed a vote of 'no confidence' in the government and demanded the resignation of the Tsar's ministers. Uncertain what to do, the resolution was simply ignored until, ten weeks later, the Duma was dissolved and Goremykin replaced as Prime Minister by Stolypin, who had a reputation as a hard-liner for his resolute measures when faced with unrest in his Province of Saratov.

Cross-reference

Stolypin is profiled on page 87.

At this, around 200 delegates (including 120 Kadets, of which Lvov was one) travelled to the Finnish town of Vyborg and issued an appeal to citizens to refuse to pay taxes or do military service. It met with no popular response and the government punished those that had signed the appeal by disenfranchising and giving them a three month prison sentence. This deprived the Kadets of their most active leaders, although since the most prominent Kadet, Milyukov, was neither a deputy nor a signatory he was not involved.

Prince Lvov

Prince Georgy Yevgenyevich Lvov (1861–1925) began his career as a lawyer and worked in the Civil Service until 1893. In 1905 he joined the Constitutional Democratic Party (*Kadets*) and won election to the first Duma. He became chairman of the All-Russian Union of Zemstva in 1914 and was the head of the Provisional government of Russia, after the Tsar's abdication in 1917. Although later arrested by the Bolsheviks, he escaped and lived out his days in Paris.

The second Duma: February–June 1907

Stolypin's government tried to influence the elections to the next Duma, supporting the Octobrists, who more than doubled their representation. However, partly because of the disenfranchisement of the leading Kadets, the more moderate-liberal centre was reduced in size and the more extreme left wing increased enormously because the Bolsheviks, Mensheviks and SRs decided to paticipate. Only around 30 representatives from the first Duma were returned and the second Duma soon received the nickname, the 'Duma of National Anger' because it was even more oppositional than its predecessor. Neither the left nor the right wanted the Duma experiment to succeed and they succeeded in crippling it as a political force.

Stolypin struggled to find any support for the agrarian reform programme he had drawn up and resorted to passing legislation under the emergency powers granted by Article 87, while the Duma was not in session. When the Duma refused to ratify this, he spread a story about a Social Democrat plot to assassinate the Tsar. When the Duma deputies refused to waive the SDs' immunity from arrest (a right of all Duma delegates), Stolypin simply dissolved the Duma. The SD delegates were immediately arrested and exiled and and an (illegal) emergency law brought in to alter the franchise. The weight of the peasants, workers and national minorities was drastically reduced and the representation of the gentry increased.

Explain why Stolypin changed the electoral law in 1907.

The third Duma: November 1907–June 1912

Not surprisingly, the groups which favoured the government, the Octobrists and Rightists, won the majority of seats, while the Kadets and Socialists were much reduced in size as well as being divided in principles. This time the Duma's nickname in radical circles was the 'Duma of Lords and Lackeys'. Generally, this Duma was far more submissive and it agreed 2,200 of around 2,500 government proposals. However, it is a sign of how unpopular the Tsarist regime had become that even this Duma proved confrontational. There were disputes over naval staff, Stolypin's proposals to extend primary education and his local government reform. By 1911, the Octobrists had turned into government opponents and the Duma had to be suspended twice, while the government forced through legislation under emergency provisions. Although the Duma ran its course, by 1912 it was clear that the Duma system was not working.

The fourth Duma: November 1912–17

The party groupings were broadly similar in the final Duma, although the Octobrists did considerably less well, creating a greater rift between right and left. However, it was a relatively docile body and the new Prime Minister, Kokovtsov (who replaced Stolypin after his assassination in 1911 and remained in the post until 1914) proclaimed, *'Thank God we still have no parliament.'* He simply ignored the Duma and its influence declined. It was too divided to fight back, and in any case, the workers again seized the initiative with a revival of direct action and strike activity in the years leading to the outbreak of war.

Developments, 1912–14

By 1912 it would seem as though the autocracy had recovered from the bruising of 1905. Thanks largely to the work of Stolypin, the agrarian situation was improving, and with the Dumas weakened to the point of meaninglessness, the future looked brighter for the traditional governing classes. The revolutionary groups which had led the opposition were much weakened, partly because of police activity, and partly because of their own internal quarrels. The Marxists were particularly divided, with the hardening of the Bolshevik/Menshevik divide and the attack, in 1909, by Pyotr Struve, one of the original founders of the SD, on the whole idea of revolution. The revival of Pan-Slavism and a new focus for Russia's imperial ambitions in the Balkans also offered opportunities for a revival of patriotism which might deflect public attention from the troubles at home.

Nevertheless, there were some more ominous developments taking place.

From April 1912, the workers' movement revived, following the massacre of 500 striking miners from the Lena goldfields in northern Siberia. Between 1912 and 1914, there were around 9,000 strikes involving 3 million workers, and many of these were organised and encouraged by the Bolsheviks who dominated the largest trade unions in Moscow and St Petersburg. The Bolshevik newspaper *Pravda*, established in 1912, sold approximately 40,000 copies a day.

While labour troubles resurfaced, the Court became increasingly detached. 1913 was the tercentenary year of the Romanov dynasty and Nicholas and Alexandra revelled in the jubilee rituals organised to celebrate the permanency of the Romanovs. In St Petersburg, the Emperor and his family left the Winter Palace to drive through the streets in open carriages, for the first time since the events of 1905, and crowds flocked to cheer, wave banners, wonder at the decorated streets and thank God for their Tsar. At Kazan Cathedral, where an elaborate thanksgiving service took place, a pair of doves briefly flew from the rafters and hovered over the heads of the Tsar and his son, which the former interpreted as a sign of God's blessing on his dynasty. After a round of balls and dinners in the capital, the royal family embarked on a three month tour of 'old Muscovy', the original heartland of Russia where they enjoyed a triumphal entry into Moscow. Nicholas led the way on a white horse, to the adulation of the confetti-throwing crowds who had gathered beneath the Romanov flags that filled the streets.

It is little wonder that Nicholas was to return convinced that 'my people love me' and that his wife, Alexandra was to complain, *'Now you can see for yourself what cowards those state ministers are. They are constantly frightening the Emperor with threats of revolution and here – you see it for yourself – we need merely to show ourselves and at once their hearts are ours.'* While Nicholas was flattering himself with the belief that the Romanovs could do no wrong, there was a sense of political and social

Activity

Source analysis

Consider this quotation from the modern historian, Alan Wood:

'A tragic drama it certainly was; a revolution it was not. After 1905, there was no real devolution of political power, which still rested in the hands of an irresolute Emperor and his appointed ministers. There was no radical redistribution of property and no realignment of the hierarchical class structure of society. The principles of Orthodoxy, autocracy and nationalism still provided the regime with its ideological bedrock. The traditional institutions of the state – bureaucracy, church, military and police – continued to function unaltered. And the Romanov Empire remained – bruised but unbroken.'

In the light of what Wood has written, would you agree or disagree that the events of 1905 deserve to be called a 'revolution'? Explain your answer.

Cross-reference

For more on the **agrarian situation**, and Stolypin's work, look at pages 108–9 and 111–14.

Russia's imperial ambitions in the Balkans are detailed on page 120.

Summary question

How successful were the Dumas in restoring stability to Russia in the years 1906–12?

Cross-reference

For more on the **Lena goldfields**, look ahead to page 115.

Fig. 12 *Nicholas II with his son Alexei*

■ **Exploring the detail**

Tsarevich Alexei and haemophilia

Haemophilia is an incurable and sometimes fatal medical condition in which the blood lacks an enzyme essential for clotting. It is a hereditary disease, carried by women but usually only found in males. Alexei's haemophilia had been transmitted by his mother from his great-grandmother, Queen Victoria. Within a few months of his birth, there had been some unexpected bleeding from his navel, which had stopped after a few days. However, the dark swellings which appeared each time he bumped himself and the crippling of his joints accompanied by excruciating pain, were clear signs of the disease. As the boy grew older, he had to spend weeks in bed and to wear a heavy iron brace when he walked.

crisis all around. None of the issues that had sparked the 1905 troubles had been resolved, yet the court simply turned its back and seemed to believe that all could continue as it always had. The only party with which Nicholas showed any sympathy was the 'Union of Russian People' which reinforced his mystical belief in the unassailable bond that existed between himself and his people.

The court's distance from reality was, perhaps, epitomised by the rise of Rasputin, a self-styled clairvoyant and 'faith-healer'. His nickname came from the Russian word for dissolute – *rasputnyi*. Rasputin was of peasant origins, but he had spent time with pilgrims, orthodox monks and a mystical sect, the Khlysty, and by the time he drifted to St Petersburg in 1903, he was able to claim special spiritual powers. He had arrived at a time when an interest in spiritualism, astrology and the occult was strong among those of high society who preferred to turn their backs on the political problems and social deprivation around them. Consequently, despite his filthy appearance and peasant behaviour, Rasputin soon made his mark on society and in November 1905, he was introduced to the Royal family.

Nicholas and Alexandra had borne five children – the grand-duchesses Olga, Tatiana, Maria and Anastasia and the eldest son and heir, or *Tsarevich*, Alexei. Alexei, who had been born in 1904, suffered from the disease of haemophilia, whereby the blood fails to clot and even a small knock causes internal bleeding, bringing swellings and crippled joints. Alexandra, who was an intensely religious woman, was in despair in her desire to help her son and when Rasputin appeared to be able to lessen Alexei's pain, she was persuaded that he was indeed a 'man of God' sent in answer to her prayers. That he was a peasant made him all the more attractive. It had long been the Tsarist belief that only men of the soil were the true Russians.

■ **Key profile**

Rasputin

Rasputin (1869–1916) was a peasant from Tobolsk province in Western Siberia. He had spent three months at Verkhoturye monastery as a young man, although he never became a monk due to his lack of education. He also spent time with a mystical sect called the Khlysty, so called after a Russian word for a whip as a reference to their practice of holding nocturnal meetings at which members danced naked and whipped one another. They believed redemption came through sin, particularly sexual sin. Rasputin wandered through Russia, living off charity and showed a gift for preaching and faith healing. Above all he had brilliant penetrating eyes, which some suggest exerted a hypnotic power. In St Petersubrg he found immense power and prestige and an opportunity to indulge his lewd fantasies. Prince Yusopov arranged his murder in December 1916. He and his accomplices are said to have fed him poisoned cakes, shot him three times (in the heart, back and head) and finally battered his head, wrapped his bleeding body in a curtain and dumped it through a hole in the ice in the river Neva.

Rasputin gained such a hold over the Tsar and his wife that he became a source of enormous influence at court. Since he was more than happy to accept bribes, gifts and sexual favours, he was soon being approached by anyone who wished to advance themselves. His power seemed unassailable and this naturally brought him many enemies – within political circles, in the Church and even in the army, where his influence over appointments was resented. Rumours of his behaviour, and in particular his sexual behaviour, abounded, and while it seems quite probable that he was actually homosexual and impotent, it was even suggested (with no foundation in fact) that he was the lover of the Empress, or one of her daughters.

Nicholas refused to take action against him, despite Rasputin's obvious misdeeds and the damage caused to the royal family by the allegations. When both Stolypin and the President of the Duma tried, on separate occasions, to present the Tsar with a dossier of evidence against him, Nicholas replied, *'there is nothing I can do'* and, after stressing that this was a family matter, *'I will allow no one to meddle in my affairs'*.

Rasputin's status was thus able to damage the reputation of the Tsar with those very people on whom he relied to prop up the monarchy – politicans inside and outside the Court, civil servants, Orthodox bishops and Army officers. The Rasputin scandal was probably more a symptom than a cause of the weakened position the monarchy found itself in by 1914, but it certainly showed that whatever the 1905 revolution had achieved, it had failed to alter the outlook of Tsar Nicholas.

By 1914, it would be fair to say that the Tsarist regime had, in some respects, 'modernised' along western lines. The introduction of the Dumas together with the economic policies of Witte and Stolypin all marked major advances. However, neither Alexander III nor Nicholas II fully appreciated the social and political consequences of economic modernisation. While they wanted Russia to be a 20th century power which could compete with the west, they were too rooted in Russia's past to be effective leaders at a time of change. The Tsarist autocracy was reactionary, oppressive and perhaps worse still, inefficient. While the people of Russia became more urban, more educated and more politicised, the last two Russian Tsars tried to maintain the 17th century autocracy of the dynasty's founder, Mikhail Romanov.

Cross-reference

The economic policies of **Witte** and **Stolypin** are described in the section below, pages 104–8 and 111–14.

AQA Examiner's tip

The key words, 'totally inadequate' should provoke some debate in your answer. You may, for example, suggest that Nicholas's immediate response was weak, but in the longer term, he responded sensibly – by setting up the Dumas. On the other hand, you may agree that he was faced with a crisis he could not cope with and made innumerable errors of judgement.

Summary questions

1 How important was the part played by Rasputin in weakening the Tsarist autocracy between 1906 and 1914?

2 How far was Nicholas II's response to the crisis of 1905 'totally inadequate'?

Economic and social change and its political impact

Economic development, 1881–1914

The transformation of the Russian economy had begun in the reign of Alexander II in response to the humiliation of defeat in the Crimean War (1854–6). A railway building programme had started and there was some small-scale development of factories – some state-owned and geared to the manufacture of armaments and others in the hands of foreigners. However, by 1881, Russia's economic development still lagged far behind that of western Europe and there was a huge gulf between Russia's potential, given its vast supplies of natural resources and manpower, and the country's actual levels of achievement.

It was not until the reign of Alexander III that a real 'industrial revolution' took off and its development owed much to Alexander's and Nicholas II's Finance Ministers, Ivan Vyshnegradsky (1887–92) and Sergei Witte (1892–1903).

Vyshnegradsky and Witte adopted similar policies – improving the Russian economy by increasing indirect taxes, negotiating loans, reducing imports and expanding exports, particularly of grain. Through the Tariff Act of 1891 Russian iron, industrial machinery and raw cotton became heavily protected against outside competition.

It was put about that Vyshnegradsky said:

> We ourselves shall not eat, but we shall export

and one of the results of this policy was witnessed in 1891 when a bad harvest brought famine, in which many thousands died, in 17 of Russia's 39 provinces. Vyshnegradsky was sacked in 1892 over the clear link between national disaster and government policy, although by 1892, the Russian budget was in surplus.

Sergei Witte was totally committed to economic modernisation, seeing it as the only way of preserving Russia's 'great power' status. Economic development would, he believed, provide employment and raise standards of living, so curbing unrest and revolutionary activity. Given the lack of an entrepreneurial class in Russia, he believed industrialisation had to be directed 'from above', an arrangement sometimes referred to as 'state capitalism'.

Witte brought in engineers and managers from France, Belgium, Germany, Britain and Sweden to advise on planning and techniques and to encourage investment, and a new rouble was introduced in January 1897, backed by the value of gold.

The result can be seeen in the table below:

Table 5 *Foreign investment, 1880–1914*

Year	Foreign investment in millions of roubles
1880	98
1890	215
1895	911
1914	2,000

Much of this investment went into the mining and metal trades, while a substantial amount supported the oil industry and banking. France proved the biggest investor supplying a third of all the foreign capital, but Britain provided 23 per cent, Germany 20 per cent, Belgium 14 per cent and the USA 5 per cent.

Exploring the detail

The Famine of 1891–2

The 1891–2 famine affected 17 of Russia's 39 provinces. In 1891, there had been an early winter and a long hot dry summer which ruined crops. A population weakened by hunger became susceptible to disease, so that when food began growing again, cholera and typhoid killed still more. This was a double tragedy as the able-bodied workers who succumbed to disease left families destitute without the main bread-winner. Over 350,000 died from starvation or disease. The government failed to organise adequate relief and it was left to volunteer groups to help the stricken peasants.

Activity

Thinking point

What problems might be encountered in trying to carry out a policy of economic modernisation in Russia?

Industrial growth

Railways

Fig. 13 *The expansion of railways in the 1880s and 1890s was an important factor in Russia's economy*

The state began to buy up private companies and begin the construction of state railways in the 1880s. By the mid 1890s, 60 per cent of the whole Russian railway system was state-owned and by 1905 this proportion had increased to nearly 66 per cent.

Table 6 *Annual average railway construction, 1861–95*

Years	Kilometres
1861–5	443
1866–70	1,378
1871–5	1,660
1876–80	767
1881–5	632
1886–90	914
1891–5	1,292

By 1905, Russia had 59,616 kilometres of railways, which, although still small in comparison with the size of the country, nevertheless showed an impressive rate of growth. This had many implications. The railways helped open up the Russian interior and allowed more extensive exploitation of Russia's raw materials. They also linked grain-growing areas to the Black Sea ports, therefore reinforcing the export drive.

The very building of the railway lines themselves was also a stimulus to the development of the iron and coal industries and permitted the development of new industries along the length of the expanding rail network. Transport costs fell, bringing down the price of goods, while the government made money from freight charges and passenger fares.

The Trans-Siberian Railway

At Witte's instigation, a railway was constructed between 1891 and 1902 (with additions continuing to 1914), linking central European Russia and Moscow with the Pacific Ocean. It ran to Vladivostok through an arrangement with the Chinese Eastern Railway in Manchuria – a distance of 7,000 kilometres. It brought economic benefits – through its construction and by opening up Western Siberia for emigration and farming. It also had strategic benefits, but it promised more than it delivered.

The most acclaimed development was the impressive construction of the Trans-Siberian Railway, which crossed Russia from west to east. Its building provided a huge industrial stimulus while the psychological boost it provided, both at home and abroad, was perhaps even greater.

From 1908–13, the rate of railway building somewhat slowed. By 1913 Russia had the second largest railway network in the world, with 62,200 kilometres, but this fell well short of the USA's 411,000 kilometres.

Heavy industry

Fig. 14 *A train of tankers carrying oil from oil wells at Baku in which the Nobel Brothers invested*

In the early stages of industrial growth, the lighter industries, particularly textiles, led the way. By the time Witte came to power, textile manufacture was one and a half times that of coal mining, oil, minerals, and the metal trades put together. Witte believed that, by concentrating production in key areas and by developing large factory units of over 1,000 or so workers, big increases in heavy goods production could be achieved.

Table 7 *Factories and factory workers, 1887–1908*

Year	Number of factories	Number of factory workers
1887	30,888	1.3 million
1908	39,856	2.6 million

The main areas of industrial development were around St Petersburg and the Baltic coast, Moscow and the provinces of Vladimir, Nizhni Novgorod and the Urals to the east, the Donbas (Donets basin) and Krivoi Rog ironfields of the south-eastern Ukraine and south-western Russia, the Baku coalfields on the Caspian Sea and in Poland.

The Donbas region, an area of 23,300 sq km, for example, was supplying 87 per cent of all Russian coal by 1913. Adjacent were the rich ironfields of the Krivoi Rog where an ironworks had been set up in Donetsk in 1872. By 1913, this region was predominant in heavy industry and was making 74 per cent of all Russian pig iron.

The Caspian sea port of Baku, which had begun pumping in 1871, also grew tremendously. Russian oil production increased between 1885 and 1913 from 153 million '**puds**' to almost 570 million and Russia became, not only internally self-sufficient, but also able to compete with the USA on the international market.

Moscow overtook St Petersburg as an industrial centre, because of its position as the hub of the entire rail network and the main link between Europe and the East. However, St Petersburg grew too, particularly in the engineering sector with the expansion of the Putilov Works.

Key term

Pud: a Russian measure of weight (equivalent to about 2.6 stone).

A closer look

The Putilov Works

The Putilov Works was first established as a state-run iron foundry in 1789, but moved to the southern side of St Petersburg in 1801 and passed through state and private hands several times before Nikolai Ivanovich Putilov, a retired official from the Naval Ministry, purchased the plant in 1867 as a rail factory. The company provided nearly a quarter of all state orders for locomotives, wagons, and rails. Putilov died in 1880, but between 1885 and 1900 the Putilov Works expanded enormously by shifting production away from mass production of rails, with its high costs of raw materials and production, towards goods that could be produced in smaller quantities but with greater profitability, e.g. machinery, artillery and products made of high-quality steel. The result was that the factory's workforce grew by two thousand in a mere three years (1891–4). Its artillery designs competed successfully with Krupp's in Germany and by 1903, the firm was able to take on a massive expansion of armaments production that ensured the company's survival through the First World War.

Textiles still dominated, accounting for 40 per cent of the total industrial output in 1910, but there was still some impressive growth in heavy industry:

Table 8 *Production (millions of metric tons)*

	1880	1890	1900	1910
Coal	3.2	5.9	16.1	25.4
Pig iron	0.42	0.89	2.66	3.0
Crude oil	0.5	3.9	10.2	12.1

Russia's rate of annual growth, at more than 8 per cent per annum between 1894 and 1904, was the highest of any industrial country in the last decade of the 19th century, although it had begun from a very low base compared with other countries. As a result, Russia moved up the league table of industrialised nations from 1887 to 1897, to become the world's fourth largest industrial economy. This growth helped bolster an increase in Russian exports and foreign trade, although the bulk of the export trade was in grain rather than industrial goods and the increase in grain exports fell short of Witte's predictions.

■ Cross-reference

For the social cost of **industrial expansion**, look ahead to the next section in this chapter, pages 109–11.

However, all this relentless drive for industrial expansion came at an economic as well as a social cost. Russia's expansionist foreign policy proved a huge drain on finances and under Witte, the state budget more than doubled, eating into the profits of the country's economic growth. Other economic downsides were the country's dependence on foreign loans, the neglect of domestic and lighter industry and the relative neglect of agriculture.

■ Summary question

Using the information and statistics provided, discuss how successful the Tsarist state was in promoting industrial growth in Russia between 1881 and 1913.

Agriculture

Fig. 15 *A peasant's day was long and hard*

■ Exploring the detail

Land Banks

The Peasants' Land Bank held funds and reserves of land with which to assist peasants who wished to acquire land directly or through purchase from nobles. The Nobles' Land Bank was designed to help nobles with the legal costs involved in land transfer and in land improvement schemes. Interest rates on loans from these banks were kept deliberately low. They helped increase peasant ownership and between 1877 and 1905, over 26 million hectares passed into peasant hands. However, they also helped prop up some inefficient farms which continued in their traditional ways.

While much attention was given by Vyshnegradsky and Witte to the development of an industrial economy, the same was not true of agriculture. Although the rural economy provided a livelihood for 80–90 per cent of the Russian population, it was largely ignored or sacrificed in the interests of industrialisation until around 1906. Most farming was small-scale and in the hands of former serfs and state peasants, tied to their local mir by the redemption dues they were repaying. In the years of good harvest, farmers' incomes remained low because bread prices were kept down – while in the bad years, peasants faced starvation, as in 1891–2 and again in 1897, 1898, 1900 and 1902.

The Russian population grew from approximately 60 million in 1861 to 125 million in 1897, but the amount of land available to farm did not, and the subdivision of estates caused the average holding to fall from 35 acres to 28 in the years 1877 to 1905. Although the government introduced the Nobles' (1882), and Peasants' (1883) Land Banks to enable the purchase and development of larger farms, they sometimes merely increased debts which, together with high levels of taxation and the competition posed by cheap American grain, made modern farming impossible.

Quite apart from ignorance, and the suspicion in which some western farming practices were held, until 1905, agricultural output was hampered by the system of the mir, in which farmers were bound to work together. The *solcha* or wooden plough was still widely used and medieval rotation systems which wastefully left fallow land each year were practised. A lack of husbandry also deprived the soil of manure so that the grain output from American farms was on average one and a half times that of the Russian farms, while that from British farms was four times as great.

The beginnings of important changes in agriculture took place as a result of the reforms of Pyotr Stolypin but the degree of change by 1914 was still limited.

Another government initiative from 1896 was to sponsor emigration to new agricultural settlements in Siberia, opened up by the Trans-Siberian Railway. However, such emigration was insufficient to alleviate the pressure of a growing population on resources.

Social change

Upper and middle classes

Some major social changes were establishing themselves in the period between 1871 and 1914 and yet perhaps the most marked feature of Russian society before the First World War was the way in which it was still strongly divided between a small upper strata of nobility and the broad mass of peasantry. There were still huge social and economic inequalities. While change in the countryside affected some nobles adversely, others thrived on the favourable arrangements for land distribution or involvment in industrial enterprises, and financial speculation. As a class, the landowners retained much of their previous wealth and status.

The small middle strata of society also benefited from the economic changes and grew as some crossed the threshold into 'middle management' as small workshop owners and traders, and perhaps in time, larger factory owners and professionals, such as bankers, doctors and teachers. The middle class of professional men and merchants had always been small in Russia. It was estimated at no more than half a million in 1897. However, government contracts, for example to build railways and state loans to build factories, provided tremendous opportunities for the enterprising. The growth of education and the demand for more administrators also fuelled a growing middle class.

Urban working class

In Russia's major cities, the arrival of new large factories, in addition to the growing numbers of smaller workshops, swelled the urban population. The 2 million factory workers in Russia in 1900 had become 6 million by 1913. Between 1867 and 1917, the Empire's urban population quadrupled from 7 to 28 million, and this was mainly the result of the influx of peasants looking for work in the cities.

Some only settled temporarily, retaining their land and returning to their villages to help out their families for the harvest. Some joined the bands of migrants who might stay in one place for a few years before moving on, while others put down roots and produced children who grew up to think of themselves as urban workers. By 1914, three out of every four people living in St Petersburg were peasants by birth, compared with just one in three, 50 years earlier. What is more, half the city's population had arrived in the previous 20 years. The situation in Moscow was much the same and here an even more 'peasant' atmosphere surrounded the workers' quarters in the city. Livestock roamed the streets and there were numerous outdoor 'peasant' markets, including one on Red Square.

■ Cross-reference

The **reforms of Pyotr Stolypin** are detailed later in the next section, pages 111–14.

The facilities needed to provide for this growing urban class were grossly inadequate. Workers often found themselves living in barrack-like buildings, owned by the factory owners that were dangerously overcrowded and lacking in adequate sanitation. These workers had to eat in canteens and wash in communal bath-houses. Even those who managed to find 'private' city accommodation fared little better. In St Petersburg at the turn of the century, for example, about 40 per cent of houses had no running water or sewage system. Excrement was simply set in piles in the back yards and collected by wooden carts at night. It is hardly surprising that 30,000 inhabitants died of cholera in 1908–9.

Yet the demand for work and accommodation was such that rents remained high, often taking half a worker's wages. Those who could not afford rents simply lay down in the factory alongside their machines or lived rough on the streets.

Workers' wages varied tremendously according to whether they were skilled or unskilled. Women, who comprised a fifth of the industrial workforce in 1885, but a third by 1914, were amongst the lowest paid, earning less than half the average industrial wage. According to a female doctor, Kostroma L. Katenina, working for the Zemstva in 1913:

> One cannot but note the premature decrepitude of the factory woman. A woman of 50 who has worked at the factory thirty or more years, frequently looks ancient. She sees and hears poorly, her head trembles, her shoulders are sharply hunched over. She looks about 70 years old. While in the west, elderly workers have pensions, our women workers, having given decades to the factory so that they are prematurely enfeebled, can expect nothing better than to live out their last days as latrine attendants.

8

Conditions were, perhaps, at their worst during the industrial depression of 1900–8. However, even when industry began to revive, the wages of industrial workers failed to keep pace with inflation. The average industrial wage increased from just 24.5 to 264 roubles per month in the years to 1914, while inflation was running at 40 per cent.

There were some attempts to alleviate the workers' lot as seen in the table below:

Table 9 *Workers' legislation, 1885–1912*

Date	Law
1885	Prohibited night-time employment of women and children
1886	Decreed that workers had to be employed according to contracts overseen by factory boards
1892	Employment of children under 12 forbidden and female labour banned in mines
1897	Hours of work reduced to 11 and a half
1903	More efficient system of factory inspection
1912	Health insurance for workers

After the 1905 revolution, hours were cut further and in regulated factories (although not workshops, which were far more common) had reached ten hours by 1914. Education also spread with government promotion of technical schools and universities although the investment in education was far less than that in the railways and much was only reluctantly conceded.

The peasantry, and the work of Pyotr Stolypin

There was also social change in the countryside which was home to more than 80 per cent of the population and where, for the majority, conditions were equally harsh, albeit in slightly different ways from in the towns.

Pyotr Stolypin strongly believed that the future of Russia depended on building a prosperous peasantry. Despite the widespread rural poverty, a significant number of peasants had manged to improve themselves since the emancipation decree by buying up land and farming more efficiently. They had come to form a 'rural upper class' of better-off peasants known as the kulaks. Stolypin described them as the 'sturdy and strong' and believed the future of Russian agriculture could be assured if men like these were able to flourish, making a surplus to spend on consumer goods which would stimulate industry, as well as supporting the Tsar who had made them wealthy!

Stolypin's programme of reform began in 1903, when the mir's responsibility to pay taxes on behalf of all the peasants in the village was removed. However, it was not until after the unrest and violence of 1905 and Stolypin's appointment as Minister for Internal Affairs in July 1906, that major changes were undertaken which had a profound impact on the peasants. The main changes are shown in the key chronology on page 112.

The legislation encouraged land transfers and the development of larger farms as poorer peasants were encouraged to sell out to the more prosperous ones. Peasant ownership grew and the hereditary ownership of land by peasants increased from 20 per cent in 1905 to nearly 50 per cent by 1915. However, it was a slow business and by 1913, only 1.3 million out of 5 million applications for the consolidation and hereditary tenure of individual farms had been dealt with. Emigration also took 3.5 million peasants to Siberia between 1905 and 1915, turning the region into one of the Empire's major agricultural regions, particularly for dairy farming, eggs and butter and cereal production.

There was some improvement in farming methods as larger farms increased in number and machinery and artificial fertilisers were more widely used. However, strip farming persisted, particularly in the central districts of Russia, where conservative peasants were reluctant to give up the security the mir afforded them. By 1914, there were still only around 10 per cent of peasant holdings that had moved beyond strip farming.

Fig. 16 *Pyotr Stolypin*

Cross-reference

The **unrest of 1905** is detailed earlier in this chapter, on pages 86–7.

Key chronology

September 1906 The amount of State and Crown land available for peasants to buy was increased.

October 1906 Peasants were granted equal rights in their local administration.

November 1906 Peasants were given the right to leave the commune and the collective ownership of land by a family was officially abolished. This made the land the personal property of an individual (usually the eldest male) who was given the right to withdraw it from the commune and consolidate the scattered strips into one compact farm.

Land organisation commissions were set up containing representatives elected by the peasants, to supervise this procedure.

A special Land Bank was also established to help peasants fund their land ownership. (These reforms did not actually become fully operative until approved by the third Duma in 1910.)

1907 Redemption payments were ended – as promised in 1905.

June 1910 All communes which had not redistributed land since 1861 were dissolved.

An increase in government subsidies to encourage migration and settlement in Siberia.

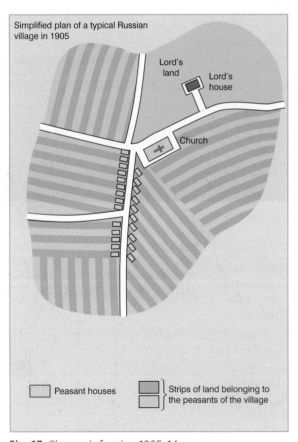

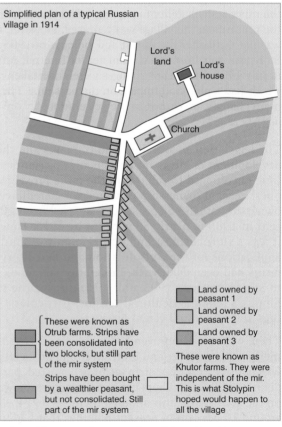

Fig. 17 *Changes in farming, 1905–14*

*Adapted from R. Radway, **Russia and the USSR**, 1996*

Stolypin is said to have claimed that he needed 20 years for his reforms to have an effect and the coming of the war obviously prevented this. However, his policies had certain important limitations. By encouraging the kulak class, he actually made the poorer peasants poorer. While some peasants rose in rank and joined the kulaks, others fell into deeper hardship as they were forced to sell up and to rely on renting land, paid for with money or their own labour. Furthermore, the 50 per cent of land which remained the private property of the tiny minority of noble landowners was unaffected.

Probably fewer than 1 per cent achieved kulak status. Many of the rest were forced to leave their farms and join the bands of migrant labourers looking for either seasonal farming work or industrial employment. This was not simply the result of government policy or Russia's industrial revolution. Living standards varied in different parts of the country, with more prosperous commercial farming in the peripheral regions in parts of the Baltic, the Western Ukraine, the Kuban and Northern Caucasus to the south and in Western Siberia. Areas of former state peasants tended to be better off than those of the emancipated serfs, because they had been granted more land.

Despite improvements in health care, provided through the Zemstva, a large proportion of the peasantry were turned down as unfit for military service and mortality rates were higher than those in any other European country – four times as high as the German rates. In the 1890s the infant mortality rate was 57.4 per cent of all deaths throughout the country and in some provinces, considerably higher. Average life expectancy at the end of the 19th century was 27.25 for males, 29.83 for women while in England the average age of death was 45.25. It would therefore be fair to say then that economic change affected the majority of the peasantry for the worse.

Fig. 18 *The peasants were still the mainstay of the Russian economy in 1910*

1 How far did Stolypin transform the lives of the rural peasantry in Russia between 1906 and 1914?

2 Which social group gained most from economic change in Russia between 1890–1914? Explain your answer.

Political impact of economic and social change

It is no coincidence that Russia's rapid industrialisation in the last decade of the 19th century was to be followed by the explosive political atmosphere of 1905, which nearly brought the autocracy down. Economic change had created both leaders and 'followers' to challenge Russia's outdated political system.

The small but growing middle classes found their natural home on the councils of the Zemstva. Their opportunity to influence local decision making, naturally led to criticism of central directives and further demands for a part in national government. This was not satisfied until the creation of the Duma in 1905, and the government's preference to ignore them as a group drove some into the revolutionary camp. While in most western states the moderate liberal-minded middle class became a backbone of the establishment, in Russia the reverse was the case and many revolutionary leaders came from this very background.

Furthermore, developments in town and countryside created a discontented mass, ready to follow a lead. This was, perhaps, more true in urban areas (where the 'proletariat' lived and worked in close proximity, sharing grievances) than the countryside, although even here the social adjustments caused by Stolypin's reforms together with the spread of education, began the slow process of awakening the peasantry from its inertia and acceptance of conditions. Nevertheless, peasant protest was more usually directed at the 'traditional' – a failed harvest, or unfair land allocation – than the expressly political, for example a demand for constitutional government.

However, the towns and cities were breeding places for political discontent although activism was comparatively rare before 1905 – partly because strike activity was illegal and the secret police efficient – and, more likely, because workers were used to a hard life as peasants and feared the loss of their job, at a time when many were clamouring for work. However, it was in the industrial centres that socialist ideas took root and provided the impetus to the troubles of 1905.

■ Cross-reference

For **the troubles of 1905**, look back to pages 88–95.

Strike activity, which fell in the aftermath of the troubles of 1905, escalated again from 1912 and in 1914, there were 3,574 stoppages. The government's only response to such activity was repression. When workers at the Lena goldfields in Siberia went on strike for better wages and conditions in 1912, for example, troops were sent in and 270 workers were killed and 250 injured.

A closer look

The Lena goldfields massacre

The gold miners of the Lena river banks in northern Siberia worked long hours for low pay in an inhospitable climate. In 1912, a group of miners went on strike over some inedible horsemeat and the Bolsheviks helped spread dissent. When their ring-leaders were arrested, several thousand miners converged on one mine to present petitions. (They may have been encouraged to do so by the authorities in order to get them together.) As they approached, they were fired on and around 500 were killed. This set off a wave of sympathetic strikes throughout Siberia and beyond.

It would not be an exaggeration to say that one of the gravest mistakes of the Tsarist governments was to fail to respond effectively to the effects of economic and social change, for it was from the large and discontented working class in the cities that the impetus to overthrow the regime would eventually come in 1917.

Learning outcomes

Through your study of this section, you should have a good grasp of the key political, economic and social developments in Russia between 1881 and 1914 and should be aware of how they relate one to another. You will understand how the assassination of Alexander II largely ended efforts to reform an outdated autocracy and ushered in a period of reaction under Tsar Alexander III. You have learnt how Alexander's conservative government failed to stem the tide of the growing opposition movement, and how it was swelled by the exploited workers of Russia's expanding industries as well as by the non-Russian nationalities and Jews, who were the victims of persecution during that reign.

You should also understand the basic dilemma faced by Alexander III, and even more acutely by Nicholas II, of how to reconcile industrial growth and economic modernisation with a static political system. You have seen how Nicholas's failure to respond to the pressure of the middle and working classes led both to rise against him in 1905. Furthermore, you have learnt how the setting up of the Dumas proved a bitter disappointment to the rebels of 1905 and how, by 1914, a sense of impending gloom was pervading all levels of Russian society, as reflected in the scandals at court connected with Rasputin.

The future of the Russia that went to war in 1914 already looked grim. Although the outcome of this foreboding is beyond the scope of this book, it should come as no surprise to learn that the Tsarist autocracy was ultimately to be overthrown in 1917.

AQA Examination-style questions

(a) Why did Stolypin carry through a series of agricultural reforms between
1906 and 1911? *(12 marks)*

You will need to consider the reasons behind Stolypin's decisions to release
peasants from the mir, end redemption payments and provide new forms of
landholding. You will need to explain what Stolypin was hoping to achieve and
should try to link his aims to other aspects of economic policy and change, so as
to provide a conclusion which shows your understanding of context. Remember
you are not required to assess his achievements or consider the wisdom of his
reasoning.

(b) How successful were the Russian governments in promoting economic change and
modernisation between 1891 and 1914? *(24 marks)*

You will need to make a judgement by balancing examples of success against
examples of failure. Obviously you will want to consider the railway building
boom and the work of Witte and Stolypin in expanding the economy and
carrying through some social reforms. However, these will need to be balanced
against Russia's indebtedness to other countries, the limited overall extent of
development and the weaknesses of the agricultural position.

Kaiser Wilhelm II during military manoeuvres

In this chapter you will learn about:

- the reason why a network of alliances developed in the period 1871–1914

- how the German policy of Weltpolitik affected diplomacy

- how rivalry and tension grew before 1908 as a result of colonial clashes

- the impact of arms escalation, the growth of the military and preparations for war.

We don't want to fight, but by jingo if we do,
We've got the ships, we've got the men, we've got the money too.
We've fought the Bear before, and while Britons will be true,
The Russians shall not have Constantinople!

1

The lines of a popular British music hall song of 1878 reinforce the view that, in the 1870s, most of Europe would have been more fearful of the ambitions of Russia than of Germany. 'The Bear' had been expanding and advancing its ambitions for the last century and more. (It has been calculated that the Russian Empire expanded at the rate of 55 square miles per day between 1683 and 1914.) By the 1870s, Russia's desire to win land and an outlet to the Mediterranean sea at the expense of Turkey (Constantinople) caused concern throughout Europe and frightened more than the British musical hall audience. Germany, on the other hand, was still a 'new' country, and, it would seem, a pacifist one now that the state had been unified. There seemed little to fear there, despite Bismarck's earlier talk of 'blood and iron' in forging the German nation. In the late 1870s, it was the British who were ready for war, fired by a national pride and confidence that bred jingoism – an intense sense of patriotism. However, by 1914 much had changed. While Nationalism was strong everywhere, it was in Germany, above all, that cries for 'world domination' and the power of the military were most felt. Russia had been weakened by defeat from Japan and internal revolution in 1905, and while still immense in size and human resources, it had been forced to become more reactive than proactive. What is more, when it came to 1914, the British were hesitant and reluctant to go to war. Yet, when they did so, it was in support of Russia (and France).

The state of Europe c.1871

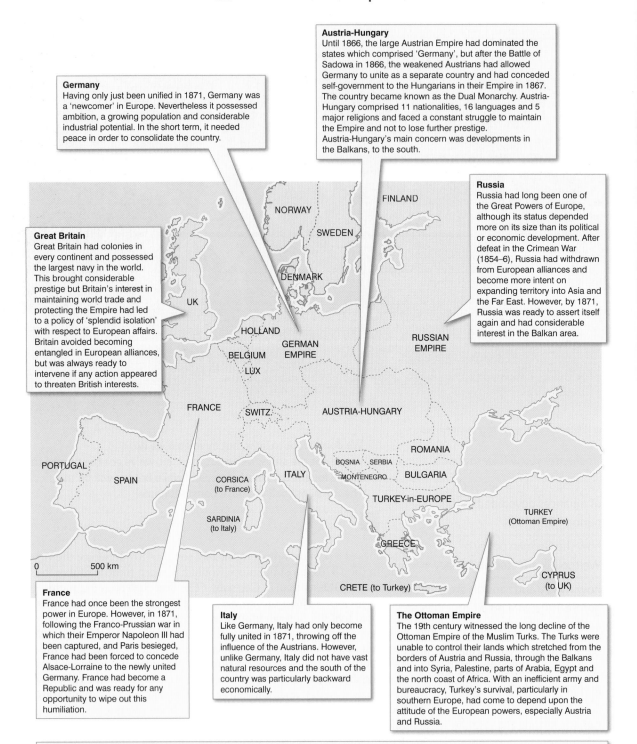

Germany
Having only just been unified in 1871, Germany was a 'newcomer' in Europe. Nevertheless it possessed ambition, a growing population and considerable industrial potential. In the short term, it needed peace in order to consolidate the country.

Austria-Hungary
Until 1866, the large Austrian Empire had dominated the states which comprised 'Germany', but after the Battle of Sadowa in 1866, the weakened Austrians had allowed Germany to unite as a separate country and had conceded self-government to the Hungarians in their Empire in 1867. The country became known as the Dual Monarchy. Austria-Hungary comprised 11 nationalities, 16 languages and 5 major religions and faced a constant struggle to maintain the Empire and not to lose further prestige. Austria-Hungary's main concern was developments in the Balkans, to the south.

Russia
Russia had long been one of the Great Powers of Europe, although its status depended more on its size than its political or economic development. After defeat in the Crimean War (1854–6), Russia had withdrawn from European alliances and become more intent on expanding territory into Asia and the Far East. However, by 1871, Russia was ready to assert itself again and had considerable interest in the Balkan area.

Great Britain
Great Britain had colonies in every continent and possessed the largest navy in the world. This brought considerable prestige but Britain's interest in maintaining world trade and protecting the Empire had led to a policy of 'splendid isolation' with respect to European affairs. Britain avoided becoming entangled in European alliances, but was always ready to intervene if any action appeared to threaten British interests.

France
France had once been the strongest power in Europe. However, in 1871, following the Franco-Prussian war in which their Emperor Napoleon III had been captured, and Paris besieged, France had been forced to concede Alsace-Lorraine to the newly united Germany. France had become a Republic and was ready for any opportunity to wipe out this humiliation.

Italy
Like Germany, Italy had only become fully united in 1871, throwing off the influence of the Austrians. However, unlike Germany, Italy did not have vast natural resources and the south of the country was particularly backward economically.

The Ottoman Empire
The 19th century witnessed the long decline of the Ottoman Empire of the Muslim Turks. The Turks were unable to control their lands which stretched from the borders of Austria and Russia, through the Balkans and into Syria, Palestine, parts of Arabia, Egypt and the north coast of Africa. With an inefficient army and bureaucracy, Turkey's survival, particularly in southern Europe, had come to depend upon the attitude of the European powers, especially Austria and Russia.

The collapse of the Concert of Europe
The concept of maintaining peace and stability through the cooperation of the Great Powers had given rise to the idea of a 'Concert of Europe' in the first half of the 19th century. Following more than 20 years of fighting during the period of the French Revolutionary and Napoleonic Wars (1793–1815), the European powers had tried to ensure a 'balance of power' to keep the peace. The conservative and backward-looking Eastern powers (Russia, Prussia and Austria) had sometimes found themselves to have little in common with the more liberal western states of Britain and France, but the 'Concert' had survived until the Crimean War of 1854–6 had brought renewed fighting between Britain and France (with support, in 1855, of Austria) against Russia. Therefore, it broke down and the withdrawal of Russia and unification of Italy and Germany changed the face of the continent.

Fig. 1 *Europe c.1871*

The year 1871 marked a turning point in the history of European relations. Of course, those living at the time were not aware of this, but it is possible, with hindsight, to see that the 'Concert of Europe', which had brought the European powers together after the defeat of Napoleon in 1815 had, by 1871, well and truly broken down. The Concert's commitment to peace and stability had never been continuous, nor easy to maintain, but in the years up to 1854 at least, the Great Powers of Europe – France, Britain, Austria, Prussia and Russia – had shown a reasonably healthy respect for international treaties and the European 'balance of power'. However, the Crimean War (1854–6) had destroyed some of that trust and brought to the fore men whose attitude to politics was rather different from that of the great diplomatists of the past. Gorchakov, the Russian Foreign Minister from 1856, and Bismarck, Prussia's Minister-President from 1862, shared a similar adherence to 'Realpolitik' – literally, 'real politics'. Essentially this meant they were prepared to do whatever was necessary to achieve their own ends.

Key profile

Prince Gorchakov

Prince Alexander Gorchakov (1798–1883) was Foreign Minister of Russia from 1856 to 1882. Prior to becoming Foreign Minister he had served as Ambassador to Vienna. At first, he welcomed Prussia's victory over Austria in 1866 but the subsequent growth in Prussian/German strength alarmed him. At the London Conference in 1871, Gorchakov successfully negotiated international agreement for Russian naval forces to operate in the Black Sea. Gorchakov's personal jealousy of Bismarck encouraged him to humiliate Bismarck by making a personal visit to Berlin during the 'War in Sight' Crisis (see pages 122–3) to warn him to curb anti-French feeling.

Exploring the detail

The Black Sea Straits

In 1841, it had been agreed that the straits of the Bosphorus and Dardanelles, leading from the Black Sea into the Mediterranean, would be closed to warships while Turkey was at peace. In 1871, this had been revised, to allow warships through if Turkey's independence was under threat, but the Russians, who maintained a Black Sea Fleet on the Crimea, were anxious to get a further revision. During the Russo-Japanese War of 1904–5, Russia was unable to use the Black Sea Fleet as permission to use the Straits was not granted. After failure in that war, attention was once more focused on the Balkans as Russia became even more anxious to open up the route out of the Crimea.

Influences on Germany from 1871

Fig. 2 *The Prussian victory over Austria at Sadowa in 1866 opened the way for German unification*

■ **Cross-reference**

Bismarck's unification of Germany, including the Austrian defeat at **Sadowa** and the German seizure of Alsace-Lorraine as a result of the Franco-Prussian War, is discussed in the Introduction on pages 5–6.

By 1871, the results of 'Realpolitik' were clearly visible in Germany. Bismarck had used his skill and diplomacy to engineer wars that had enabled Prussia to absorb the separate states of Germany. His treaties were aggressive, not defensive, and his success was built on the military might of the Prussian army. Austria was forced out of a position of dominance in Germany and the formerly powerful Austrian state was humiliated by a crushing defeat in a six-week war. France, for 300 years the dominant power of Europe, was similarly disposed of, and two key provinces, the mineral-laden Alsace and Lorraine, were seized from France as the prize of German victory. This was the greatest upheaval since the French Revolution and through it the balance of power in Europe had been transformed. The dangers of a Europe torn by war now seemed possible. Yet, having forged the German Empire in 1871, Bismarck had declared that his military ambitions in Europe had been fulfilled. He wanted to 'cultivate and hold what we have won' and prevent any disruption to the settlement he had fought so hard to obtain. To him, 1871 was the beginning of a new era, but to achieve his full ambitions for Germany, it suited him to preserve peace.

Influences on Russia from 1871

The Russians were less inclined to sit back after 1871. Russia had ambitions for expansion – in Central Asia, the Far East and in the Balkans, where the power of Turkey was in decline. The Russians bore lingering resentment for the defeat (by Britain and France) experienced in the Crimean War of 1854–6 and remembered Austria's failure to support Russia in that contest. They had welcomed Bismarck's defeat of the French in 1870. With France in no position to oppose, and Germany anxious to retain Russia's goodwill, it provided them with the perfect opportunity to announce their intention to abandon the Black Sea clauses of the Treaty of Paris of 1856. These clauses had said that no warships could use the Black Sea in peace time and had put paid to Russian ideas of creating a grand naval fleet there. Such was the position of the other powers, that in 1871 they were prepared to revise the treaty in Russia's favour.

1871 marked a turning point, not to a period of war but to one of 'armed peace' in Europe. The successes of the Prussian armies, the defeat of the French, the weakness of the Austrians (who had been excluded from both Germany and the newly forged nation of Italy), the ambitions of the Russians and the anxiety of the British were to form the basis for rather different relations between the powers from those experienced in the 1815–71 era.

European developments and the beginnings of the alliance network, 1871–90

Having manoeuvred to permit the unification of Germany, Bismarck was anxious that his creation should not be torn apart by European war. However, he faced a major problem, given that both Austria and Russia had interests in the Balkans and France remained a hostile, although weakened state on the German border. The annexation of Alsace-Lorraine had turned France into a permanent enemy and Bismarck was determined that France should be kept isolated at all costs, as an ally might provide the strength it needed for a war of revenge. However, this policy proved less easy to uphold than Bismarck had anticipated. He had expected it would take years for France to recover from the defeat experienced in the Franco-Prussian War, but he was rapidly proved wrong.

■ **Key term**

Alliance: an agreement between two or more countries to support each other.

The French indemnity, 1871–2

In addition to seizing Alsace-Lorraine in 1871, the Germans had also set the French the massive task of paying an indemnity (fine) of 5,000 million gold Francs (£200m) and had placed an army of occupation in France. This was set to remain until the indemnity was paid. Bismarck had expected the indemnity to keep France weak for some years, but the new Republican French Government, under Adolphe Thiers (President 1871–3), used the presence of the German occupying army to mobilise French public opinion. Playing on patriotic sentiment and offering the lure of a 5 per cent interest payment, the government persuaded those with cash to spare, to come forward and save the Republic. By late 1872, the French were able to announce that enough money had been raised to pay off the German indemnity and in 1873 the German army of occupation was forced to leave. The women of Paris swept the streets as the Germans departed, symbolically scrubbing them clean from foreign contamination. Thiers was regarded as a hero and deemed the 'liberator of French territory'. Furthermore, Bismarck had to look on as the French army was reorganised and compulsory military service introduced. Nor was Bismarck any more pleased when Thiers was replaced by President MacMahon in 1873. MacMahon's right wing, pro-Catholic government was formed just as Bismarck began his anti-Catholic Kulturkampf in Germany.

Cross-reference

Bismarck's **Kulturkampf** is described on pages 15–19.

'Dreikaiserbund' of 1872

Bismarck needed to construct a system that would protect Germany from French revenge and between June and October 1873, he

PUNCH, OR THE LONDON CHARIVARI.—MAY 22, 1875.

"O, LOVELY PEACE."
HANDEL.

B—SM—RCK *(the Bear-Leader).* "MY BEAR ALWAYS DANCES TO THE GENTEELEST OF TUNES."
GOLDSMITH.

Fig. 3 *Bismarck plays a penny whistle alongside Emperor Franz Joseph of Austria-Hungary, while the Russian Bear dances*

Cross-reference

The **reign of Alexander II** is looked at in the Introduction on page 4, and **Kaiser Wilhelm I** is profiled on page 11.

Key chronology

Alliances, 1872–90

1872	*Dreikaiserbund* – Germany, Austria-Hungary and Russia.
1879	Germany signed Dual Alliance with Austria-Hungary.
1881	Dreikaiserbund renewed.
1882	Italy joined Germany and Austria-Hungary to form the Triple Alliance.
1887	Germany signed Reinsurance Treaty with Russia.
1890	Germany allowed Reinsurance Treaty with Russia to lapse.

Cross-reference

Prince Gorchakov is profiled on page 119.

forged the *Dreikaiserbund* or Three Emperors' League between Emperor Franz Joseph of Austria-Hungary, Alexander II of Russia and Kaiser Wilhelm I. The opportunity for such an agreement had been provided by a visit by both the Austrian and Russian rulers to Berlin in September 1872 and although it did not address any of the issues which divided these powers – particularly Austria and Russia's conflicting attitude to the Balkans – it stressed the common interest of these three conservative Emperors to fight against the forces of 'revolution' at a time when socialism was beginning to spread. For Bismarck, the informal agreement was also seen as a way of maintaining the isolation of France and of securing Germany's own southern and eastern borders. Furthermore, it held out the expectation that Austria and Russia would not get involved in war together, which was something Bismarck was keen to avoid. However, in practice the agreement meant little and merely provided a deceptive veil of unity which was not to last.

Key profile

Emperor Franz Joseph

Emperor Franz Joseph (1848–1916) came to power during the revolution of 1848. His long reign saw Austria decline from one of Europe's leading powers. His narrow conservative approach led him to appoint incompetent commanders such as General Benedek, who lost the war of 1866 against Prussia. In 1914, Franz Joseph made the fateful decision to involve Austria in a war against Serbia, which precipitated the First World War.

'War in Sight' Crisis, 1875

The advent of MacMahon's government had strained relations between Germany and France even further and when, in January 1875, the French government began discussing further army reforms, creating a new regiment and ordering an extension of the cavalry and armaments divisions, Bismarck was alarmed. He demanded an increase in the size of the army budget from the Reichstag and, from April, used the German press to stir up anti-French sentiment, deliberately creating a clamour for a defensive war from the Germans by accusing the French of preparing to attack Germany. Both sides threw accusations at one another. The Germans claimed the Pope was urging France to attack while the French suggested the Germans were preparing an unprovoked war against France. Rumours ran riot, particularly after the French headlines picked up on some injudicious comments from Bismarck's envoy to Paris, Radowitz, who talked too much one evening after a good meal and plenty of wine. Bismarck had probably never intended the 'crisis' to turn into a war, but it was viewed seriously enough by Tsar Alexander II and his foreign minister Gorchakov for both to visit Berlin in May 1875 to warn Bismarck to control the German media.

The British were also anxious to preserve peace and a balance of power and Queen Victoria sent a personal letter to Emperor Wilhelm I ordering him to put an end to Bismarck's 'game'. Bismarck was forced to back-track and the incident passed, but it did have a deeper significance.

The opposition of both Russia and Britain had shown Bismarck that only Austria was prepared to stand by him in times of trouble and the meaninglessness of the Dreikaiserbund was made apparent. While it had been easy to obtain a pledge from Russia to oppose 'revolutionary forces', this did not mean that Russia had abandoned its suspicions about the new Germany. In some respects, Bismarck was the victim of his own success. Since he had exploited circumstances to create a strong new European power, he had left other nations suspicious of his future intentions. It is hardly surprising that few were ready to trust him.

The Eastern Question

The first three quarters of the 19th century had witnessed the long decline of the Ottoman Empire (Turkey). With further decline likely, both Austria and Russia were determined to profit from Turkey's problems. Austria also feared the rise of nationalistic Balkan peoples, such as the Serbs and Bulgarians, who were anxious to secure total independence and enlarge their territories. Since Austria-Hungary was made up of mainly ethnic groups such as Serbs, Croats and Poles there was always the fear that the Serbs might want to break away and join Serbia.

For the Russians, the concern was less about races than about the geographical and strategic advantages of having some control over the area. Access to the Mediterranean from the Black Sea was only possible if the Balkan area remained in friendly hands. Although the Russians had fought several wars against Turkey, they believed a weak Turkey was preferable to Austro-Hungarian expansion into this key area. However, there was also some concern, real or convenient, for the many **Orthodox Christians** living in the Balkan area and this gave the Russians a moral reason for involvement. Certainly, the Pan-Slav movement in Russia believed their country had a right, and even a duty, to protect these people.

> ### Key terms
>
> **The Eastern Question** concerned both the efforts of various subject nationalities in the Balkans to secure independence from Turkey, and the policies of states such as Russia, Austria and Britain in controlling these ambitions and taking advantage of Turkey's weakened state. Sometimes it suited them to prop Turkey up, at other times to support the subject races. By 1870, all the main Balkan peoples except the Bulgarians had acquired some independence.
>
> **Orthodox Christians:** Christians who followed the Eastern rite after the split in the Catholic Church in the 11th century. While Catholics in Austria-Hungary looked to the Pope, Orthodox Russians and Serbs looked to the Patriach of Constantinople, as the Spiritual Head of the Church. Since the capture of Constantinople in 1453, the Patriarch of Moscow was the senior Orthodox Patriach outside Turkish control.

PUNCH, OR THE LONDON CHARIVARI.—MARCH 24, 1877.

"PONS ASINORUM!"

Fig. 4 *The cartoonist shows the Russian Bear looking to advance Russian interests in Turkey while the British, Germans and Austrians were preoccupied by their own affairs*

France had some sympathy with nationalist movements in the Balkans but, as the area was of little relevance to France, the country was generally happy to prop up Turkish power in the interests of peace. However, to make this more acceptable to public opinion, France encouraged Turkey to reform and to allow more self-government within the Turkish Empire.

Britain was less tolerant. Britain feared Russian expansion into the Balkans leading to a Russian presence in the Eastern Mediterranean which would threaten British trade routes and increase the likelihood of Russian expansion in the Middle East. They also feared Russian expansion towards India. Britain's traditional policy was therefore to preserve the Ottoman Empire.

German concerns were different again. The rival territorial ambitions of Russia and Austria left Bismarck with a dilemma. While declaring that the Balkans were 'not worth the bones of a single Pomeranian grenadier', he was conscious that if it came to a war between Russia and Austria-Hungary, Germany would be forced to take sides.

Balkan Crisis, 1878

In 1875, there was a revolt by the mainly Christian Serbs in Herzegovina against the severity of Turkish rule. The Turks had imposed heavy

Fig. 5 *The Balkans from 1878*

taxes on the area and resentment had bred a revolt which spread to neighbouring Bosnia. Serbia and Montenegro also joined in to help their fellow Serbs, demonstrating their Pan-Slav sentiment. They declared war on Turkey in 1876 and this provoked a Bulgarian rising which the Turks put down with utmost ferocity. Whole villages were wiped out and men, women and children hacked to death or burned alive. There was tension throughout Europe and the new Turkish Sultan, Abdul Hamid II, tried to prevent intervention by announcing a new democratic constitution for all the subject peoples of his Empire. However, he refused to agree to Turkish disarmament and in 1877, Russia, in alliance with Montenegro, Romania and Serbia, declared war on Turkey.

The Russian army enjoyed huge success against Turkey. They marched to Adrianople and by January 1878 looked poised to take Constantinople. However, Britain and Austria intervened. Although the British Prime Minister, Disraeli, had initially made light of the Turkish atrocities, Russia's rapid advance frightened him and he ordered the British fleet to the Dardanelles in pursuit of the traditional British policy of propping up the declining Turkish Empire. Austria, who had secured a secret agreement with Russia in 1876 to occupy Bosnia and Herzegovina, was alarmed lest the war increase the power of Serbia and Russia to a point where both would be able to resist such Austrian ambitions. Consequently the Austrians demanded an armistice and Russia, having no substantial fleet since its decimation in the Crimean War, could not afford to continue and risk the opposition of the combined forces of Austria, Turkey and Great Britain. Nevertheless, Russia was in a strong position to dictate peace terms to the Turks and the ensuing Treaty of San Stefano in March 1878 was highly favourable to the Russians. Under the terms of this treaty:

◼ an enlarged Serbia and Montenegro gained complete independence
◼ Russia gained territory in Asia and Bessarabia (at the mouth of the Danube). (This was taken from its ally Romania, who received a strip of Turkish territory in return.)
◼ Bosnia and Herzegovina were granted home rule
◼ a '**Big Bulgaria**' was created, including the district of Macedonia – which cut Turkey off from its remaining possessions in the Balkans. It included many Greeks and Serbs as well as Bulgarians and was to be 'advised' by Russia for two years. (This 'Big Bulgaria' would help protect Russia's access to the Mediterranean.)

Congress of Berlin, 1878

The Treaty of San Stefano caused considerable alarm among the Great Powers, who feared that if they did not intervene, Russia would dominate the Balkans. Disraeli was horrified to see what he could only imagine to be a Russian 'puppet state' being created out of Bulgaria and he was supported by Austria (who had secured a British promise that there would be no objection to the Austrian occupation of Bosnia and Herzegovina) in demanding a European Conference. In Germany, Bismarck was also alarmed at the prospect of trouble between Austria and Russia over the latter's gains and, faced by the possibility of war with Great Britain, Russia accepted the proposal for a Great Power conference in Berlin in June–July 1878, held under the chairmanship of Bismarck.

At Berlin it suited Bismarck to play the 'honest broker', standing aside from personal gain and working in the interests of peace. The main aim of all attendees, except the Russian delegates, was to limit Russia's gains from her success in the Russo-Turkish War and to achieve a more acceptable resolution to the Eastern question. At the resulting Treaty of Berlin in July 1878:

◼ the complete independence of Serbia, Montenegro and Romania and the Bessarabia arrangement was upheld

◼ **Key term**

'**Big Bulgaria**': the creation of a Big Bulgaria would give Bulgaria the maximum territory it could hope to lay claim to, mainly at the expense of Serbia.

- the Big Bulgaria was split into three – one part became a new state of Bulgaria (with no access to the Mediterranean); one part was a semi-independent district known as Eastern Rumelia; one part returned to Turkey
- Russia was allowed to keep her Asian conquests – but only because Disraeli had persuaded the Turkish Sultan to give Cyprus to Britain to offset the growth in Russian power
- Austria-Hungary was allowed to occupy, but not annex, Bosnia and Herzegovina and a further strip of territory separating Serbia from Montenegro
- the Sultan promised reforms to improve the position of his Christian subjects.

Bismarck took satisfaction from having chaired a conference which appeared to restore European peace. It was the high point of his career as a diplomatist and he reflected in the glory, portraying Germany as a peace-loving power, seeking to control its more aggressive companions. However, Bismarck was only too aware that the Russians held Germany responsible for this pro-Austrian peace settlement and the reintroduction of tariffs in 1879 (which hit at Russian agriculture) only confirmed this opinion. The League of the Three Emperors could no longer be seen to have any meaning and Bismarck was driven to strengthen his links with Austria-Hungary, lest the Russians seize a future opportunity to take revenge on Germany.

Dual Alliance, 1879

Bismarck was aware that his involvement at Berlin risked the possibility that Russia might turn to France for an alliance and he felt that it was important for Germany to have a clear understanding with Austria-Hungary to strengthen Germany's position. There were other reasons for this too. An alliance with Austria would be popular with the southern German states which had been antagonised by Bismarck's Kulturkampf. It would ensure the safety of Germany's southern borders and offer the prospect of increasing trade along the Danube. Bismarck was anxious to avoid isolation and the anti-German campaign in the Russian press, mainly centred on the new German tariffs on Russian exports, increased his concerns. Consequently, the Dual Alliance was signed in October 1879. In this, Germany and Austria-Hungary agreed that:

- Germany and Austria-Hungary would help each other in the event of an attack by Russia
- each would remain neutral if their ally was attacked by another European power (not Russia) – this was known as 'benevolent neutrality'.

The clauses only referred to Germany and Austria being 'attacked', not provoking a war. Thus, in the event of war, it would be important for the parties to demonstrate that they were the aggrieved nation. Furthermore, the second clause meant that Austria would not support Germany if the latter were to be attacked by France alone, only if it were France in alliance with Russia. Nevertheless, the Dual Alliance was to remain central to German security and was constantly renewed to 1914.

Whether Bismarck had planned the Alliance to be of such importance is debatable. The historian William Carr has suggested that it was made to deal with a temporary situation and was never intended to suggest that

Cross-reference

Bismarck's reintroduction of **tariffs** on imports of grain in 1879 is discussed on pages 20–1.

Activity

Group activity

Split into two groups. One group should act as Russia, the other as Germany. Each group should devise a short statement to release to the press regarding their success at the Berlin Conference.

Question

How successful was the Congress of Berlin in fulfilling Bismarck's aims in foreign policy?

Bismarck was making a choice between Austria and Russia as an ally. Indeed, it is possible that Bismarck believed an agreement with Austria might, by isolating Russia, drive that country back into alliance.

On the other hand, the alliance does seem to have been based on the personal respect that Kaiser Wilhem I had for Emperor Franz Joseph, on Germany's support for Austria-Hungary at the congress of Berlin in 1878 and on their shared hostility towards France. Nevertheless, in making an alliance with Austria-Hungary, Bismarck had tied Germany to the weakest of the Great Powers.

Article IV of the Dual Alliance stated:

> This Treaty, in conformity with its pacific character and to prevent any misconstruction, shall be kept secret by both High Contracting parties, and it will be communicated to a Third Power only with the consent of both Parties, and strictly according to a special agreement.

2

Questions

1 Why do you think the treaty was kept secret?

2 What danger did this Treaty pose for the future peace of Europe?

Dreikaiserbund of 1881

Despite the supposed secrecy, the Russians felt acutely aware of their isolation. Negotiations began in 1880 for a new Dreikaiserbund.

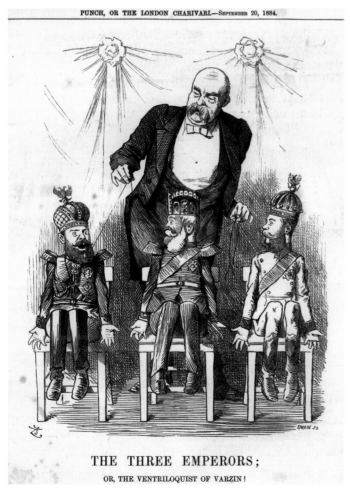

PUNCH, OR THE LONDON CHARIVARI.—September 20, 1884.

THE THREE EMPERORS;

OR, THE VENTRILOQUIST OF VARZIN!

Fig. 6 *The cartoonist shows Bismarck's control over the Emperors of Austria, Germany and Russia (Varzin was Bismarck's country estate)*

■ Cross-reference

To recap on the **assassination of Alexander II**, return to pages 57–8.

Pobedonostev is profiled on page 63.

However, in March 1881, three months before the signing of the agreement in June, Alexander II was assassinated and succeeded by Alexander III. Although the treaty temporarily helped defuse some of the tension in the Balkans, the advent of new Pan-Slav ministers like Pobedonostev in Russia boded ill for future harmony there. The treaty, which was renewable every three years, remained in force until 1887 but was not subsequently renewed.

Under the 1881 Dreikaiserbund it was agreed that:

■ each power would remain neutral if one of the three was involved in a war with a fourth power

■ there would be mutual consultation in Balkan affairs (and Bismarck accepted in principle that a 'Big Bulgaria' could be recreated. In return, Russia agreed that Austria-Hungary could take complete control of Bosnia-Herzegovina when ready to do so)

■ other agreements made at the Congress of Berlin should be upheld.

The alliance had different implications for the various parties:

■ Russia felt it offered some security from a British naval attack in the North or Black Sea areas as neither Germany nor Austria-Hungary would back Britain in such a case, while the Austrian navy would deter any British naval attack via the Mediterranean, and Germany bordered the Baltic Sea leading to St Petersburg.

■ Bismarck believed that he had made a war between Russia and Austria-Hungary much less likely and this made him more secure in relation to France, because any conflict in Eastern Europe would have given France an opportunity to attack Germany to get Alsace-Lorraine back.

■ Austria-Hungary was reassured by the display of German support and this was made clear when Bismarck signed an agreement two weeks later which said that the Dreikaiserbund did not override the Austro-German Alliance.

Triple Alliance, 1882

In 1881, the French seized Tunis in North Africa. Their action had actually been encouraged by the British and Germans at the Congress of Berlin in 1878. While the British wanted French support to block Russian ambitions, Bismarck wanted France to look away from Alsace and Lorraine. Consequently, after some wranglings about costs, in 1881, amidst fears that the Italians were preparing to take the area for themselves, the French acted.

The Italian government was angered and alarmed and so turned to Bismark. The Italians accepted an agreement to drop their claims to the Trentino and Trieste (areas peopled by Italians but ruled by Austria) as the price of an alliance to protect themselves from the French. Thus in May 1882, Italy joined Germany and Austria-Hungary in the Triple Alliance. This stated that:

■ Germany and Austria-Hungary would defend Italy if Italy was attacked by France

■ Italy would to support Germany and/or Austria-Hungary if either were attacked by two Great Powers

■ Italy was not required to fight against Great Britain.

In 1883, the alliance was extended to include Romania, which had the effect of sealing off Russia's western borders. The Triple Alliance had increased Germany's security and was a major diplomatic

■ Did you know?

Italy's involvement

Despite the Triple Alliance, in 1914, when the First World War broke out, Italy did not feel bound to ally herself with Germany and Austria-Hungary. This was because it would have meant fighting against Great Britain – a scenario specifically excluded in the alliance. Therefore Italy could safely remain neutral.

achievement. However, the system Bismarck had engineered was very complex and these alliances alone could hardly be regarded as a guarantee of peace. Indeed, in the years between 1887 and 1890, new developments in the Balkans threatened the uneasy peace which had hitherto prevailed.

Balkan troubles, 1885–7

At the Congress of Berlin in 1878, the creation of a Big Bulgaria had been rejected by the Great Powers. On 5 October 1885, however, Prince Alexander of Bulgaria had gone ahead and united Eastern Rumelia with Bulgaria to create the 'Big Bulgaria' rejected seven years earlier. In 1886, at the Treaty of Bucharest, following a failed Serbian attack, the union was recognised. The Russians, who had acted as 'protectors' of Bulgaria, were angered by Alexander's independent action and forced his abdication. In 1887, Prince Ferdinand of Saxe-Coburg-Gotha was elected as the new Prince of Bulgaria and he made a formal acceptance of Russian influence as the natural leader of the Slav peoples. However, the following years showed a marked cooling in the relationship, leaving Russia anxious for other client states. Serbia, which officially had Austrian 'protection', looked increasingly to Russia, creating new tensions both within the Balkans and between the European powers.

Cross-reference

The proposal for a '**Big Bulgaria**' in 1878 is discussed on page 125.

Reinsurance Treaty, 1887

By 1887, there were concerns within both Russia and Germany about the future of the Dreikaiserbund which was due for renewal that year. Some Russians, led by Katkov, argued that the treaty was incompatible with Russia's interests in the Balkans where Austria was the main stumbling block to Russian expansion. Within the German government, voices were raised that the Dreikaiserbund undermined Germany's promises to Austria-Hungary in the Dual Alliance. However, Bismarck could not afford to allow a situation to develop which ranged France and Russia against Germany and Austria-Hungary, so he began negotiations, in secret, with the Russian government, even though this involved agreements that were actually prejudicial to his Austrian ally. He also held back German investments in Russia, in order to pressurise the Russians to sign. The resulting 'Reinsurance Treaty', so-called because it was Bismarck's way of trying to avoid war with Russia, promised that:

- Russia should be allowed to be the prevailing influence in the Balkans
- both Germany and Russia would each remain neutral if the other became involved in a war with a third Great Power
- the above clause was not to apply if Germany attacked France, or Russia attacked Austria-Hungary.

The secret Treaty, which was to be renewed every three years, was a mark of Bismarck's desperation. Its very secrecy showed how difficult it had become to control the competing interests of the powers and avoid war.

The accession of Wilhelm II and the departure of Bismarck

Although Bismarck's resignation in 1890 was mainly brought about by his differences with the new Kaiser, Wilhelm II, and clashes over domestic policy, Bismarck preferred their disagreements over foreign policy to be cited as the cause of his departure. The ambitious and military-minded Kaiser wanted to expand Germany's colonies, build a great navy and exert German–Austrian control in the Balkans, even at the expense of Russian hostility. Against Bismarck's better judgement,

Cross-reference

To revise the **accession of Wilhelm II** in 1888, the **differences between Kaiser Wilhelm II and Bismarck**, and **Bismarck's resignation in 1890**, revisit Chapter 1.

Activity

Revision activity

Copy the map of Europe in c.1871 on page 118, omitting the surrounding text boxes. Use it to indicate the development of the alliance network using different colour shading, and write an accompanying timeline.

Key chronology

Developments in international relations, 1893–1907

1893 Russia signed secret Military Convention with France.

1894 Chancellor Caprivi of Germany was forced to resign; he had tried to build a better trade relationship with Russia.

1894 Russia ratified treaty with France.

1894 General Schlieffen completed his plan to meet the threat of a Russo-French alliance.

1896 Anglo-French Agreement on South-East Asia.

1897 Admiral Tirpitz appointed head of German Naval Ministry and von Bülow became German Foreign Minister – both supported Weltpolitik.

1898 First German Naval Law.

1904 Anglo-French Entente.

1905 First Moroccan Crisis.

1905 Russia defeated by Japan in Far East; 'Bloody Sunday'.

1906 Conference at Algeçiras; Great Britain backed France over Morocco.

1907 Russia and Great Britain signed a treaty resolving their colonial differences.

Cross-reference

The engagement of Wilhelm II and his chancellors in **Weltpolitik** is covered on pages 36 and 45–6.

in March 1890, the Reinsurance Treaty with Russia was allowed to lapse, on the grounds of its incompatibility with the Austrian alliance. Germany was once more dependent on Austrian friendship alone and Russia was left without allies.

A closer look

Assessing Bismarck's foreign policy

The traditional picture of Bismarck as expressed in W. L. Langer's *European Alliances and Alignments, 1871–1890*, has been that of the 'expert juggler', so aptly characterised in the Punch cartoon seen on page 127 who spent his years as chancellor deftly managing the states of Europe and avoiding conflict and war. However, according to A. J. P. Taylor in *The Struggle for Mastery in Europe: 1848–1918*, Bismarck was more concerned about a 'balance of tension' than peace and was quite happy for aggression to be channelled into colonial conquests and war that did not threaten central Europe. Two underlying themes seemed to have remained constant: the permanent isolation of France and peaceful co-existence with Austria-Hungary and Russia. Beyond that, it is difficult to know whether Bismarck's policies were guided by principle or pragmatism. Furthermore, his 'success' can be questioned. His commitment to Austria after 1878 was, according to John Murray (*Essays in Modern European History*) a political disaster. However, it should not be forgotten that Bismarck did try to keep the Reinsurance Treaty with Russia and, had he not been forced to resign, it would almost certainly have been renewed in 1890. Perhaps the two most damning comments that can be made of Bismarck are that he assumed so much control it was hard for anyone to follow him and that his preference for conducting foreign policy in secret made it difficult for others to understand or trust his motives.

Summary questions

1 Explain why Bismarck signed the Dual Alliance with Austria in 1878.

2 How far had Bismarck increased Germany's security within Europe by 1890?

Diplomacy and the alliance system, 1890–1914

German foreign policy in the 1890s – the impact of Weltpolitik

The accession of the young, headstrong and angst-ridden Kaiser Wilhelm II in 1888 and the departure of Bismarck in 1890 brought important new influences to bear on the development of international relations. While Germany prospered economically, Wilhelm maintained the belief that enemies were ganging up against him from both within and without Germany, and his decision to engage in *Weltpolitik* or 'world policy' and build a vast battlefleet (though it was undertaken in the interests of greater security) severely limited the prospects for peace and stability in Europe.

From 1897, in particular, under von Bülow, and later Bethmann Hollweg, Wilhelm II sought an increasingly prominent 'world role' for Germany. This involved acquiring colonies, creating economic spheres of influence

Fig. 7 *The* Kaiser Wilhelm der Grosse *battleship: Wilhelm's Weltpolitik included building up a strong German navy*

and building a powerful navy to complement the strength of the German army. Associated with this idea was a fear of 'encirclement' by other powers, which would damage Germany's international standing.

To its supporters among the right wing Conservatives and big businessmen, Weltpolitik was merely fulfilling Germany's natural destiny. Germany was already a powerful country but as industrialisation created new economic demands, the acquisition of raw materials and markets beyond Europe was regarded as imperative. Germany needed to share in the scramble for colonies and this, its proponents argued, was essential for the survival of Germany as a leading nation. The Pan-German League promoted German expansionism and militarism, encouraging patriotism and extreme nationalism known as jingoism, to increase support for the Kaiser. This right wing pressure group succeeded in generating mass support for Weltpolitik and with the support of the middle and upper classes and their political representatives in the Reichstag, exerted considerable political pressure on the imperial government to pursue the policy to the full.

Von Bülow summed up some of the arguments for Weltpolitik in his speech to the Reichstag in December 1897:

> The times when the German left the land to one of his neighbours, the sea to the other, and reserved heaven, where pure doctrine is enthroned, for himself, have passed. We regard it as one of our foremost duties, specifically in East Asia, to further and cultivate our shipping, our trade and our industry.
>
> We must demand that the German missionary and the German trader, German goods, the German flag and German ships in China are just as much respected as those of others. In short, we don't want to put anyone in the shade, but we demand our place in the sun too. In East Asia, as in the West Indies, we will endeavour to safeguard our rights and our interests, true to the tradition of German policy, without unnecessary severity, but also without weakness.

3

Cross-reference

The **Pan-German League** is introduced on page 54.

Questions

1 Von Bülow's speech in Source 3 brought much laughter and cries of 'bravo' and applause in the Reichstag. Can you suggest from whom and why?

2 Explain why Germany wanted to establish a colonial Empire in the 1890s.

A British Foreign Office official commented:

> The dream of an Empire had taken a deep hold on the German imagination. All declare with one voice. We must have colonies and we must have a fleet. A healthy country like Germany with its 60 million inhabitants must expand to have territories to which its overflowing inhabitants can emigrate. When told the world is now parcelled up, the reply is, 'The world belongs to the strong'.

4

A closer look

German Imperialism

German Imperialism had actually begun in the Bismarckian period, encouraged by the establishment of the German Colonial Union (formed 1882) and the Society for German Colonisation (1884). Germans established control in areas where trading interests had already developed – south-west Africa, Togoland and the Cameroons and German East Africa (now Tanzania) and New Guinea. Under Wilhelm II, Germany not only sought colonial expansion, it interfered in the colonies of others, as for example, when the Kruger telegram was sent in support of the Boers in their fight against the British. Germany was part of the delegation which made Japan modify its gains after war with China in 1897 and so acquired a 99-year lease of Kiaochow. In 1898, the Caroline and Mariana Pacific Islands were bought from Spain while in 1899, Germany took control of the Samaoan Islands in the Pacific. Germany also engaged in the Berlin–Baghdad railway project from 1888, in agreement with the Turkish government, despite its implications for relations with Britain and Russia. Although Germany's colonial empire only reached a million square miles by 1914, it nevertheless exerted an importance beyond its size. The development of interests in Africa and the Far and Middle East, together with the Kaiser's policy of naval expansion, bred mistrust and suspicion and contributed to the breakdown of relations in Europe.

Russian foreign policy in the 1890s – Russian expansionism

In the 19th century, Russia had been continually expanding its territory in Asia. However, expansion into southern Asia largely ceased in the 1890s, although the legacy of British suspicion regarding Russian intentions towards Persia and Afghanistan remained.

Russian imperialism in the Far East, however, continued and this was to bring Russia into conflict with Japan by 1904. Russia had two ambitions in the area – to gain part of Chinese Manchuria which jutted into Russian territory (and prevented a direct railway line to Vladivostok – see Figure 10 on page 136) and to obtain an ice-free port to the south of Vladivostok, in territory belonging to the Chinese.

The Japanese had ambitions to take a similar area from China and in 1894 successfully defeated the Chinese in Korea. The Russians used the opportunity to press their own demands on China and an agreement was made whereby the Chinese allowed the Russians to continue the

Exploring the detail

Russian expansion in Afghanistan and Persia

During the 19th century, the Russians had expanded into southern Asia. They reached the border with Afghanistan at Penjdeh in 1885 and although forced to withdraw, the British feared a Russian push towards (British) India and the Indian Ocean. When, in 1898, a railway line from Merv to Khushk on the Afghan border was started, Anglo-Russian tensions increased. Although, given the distances involved and the mountainous terrain, a Russian assault on British possessions was unlikely, the British remained watchful and suspicious.

Cross-reference

This area can be seen on the map on page 136.

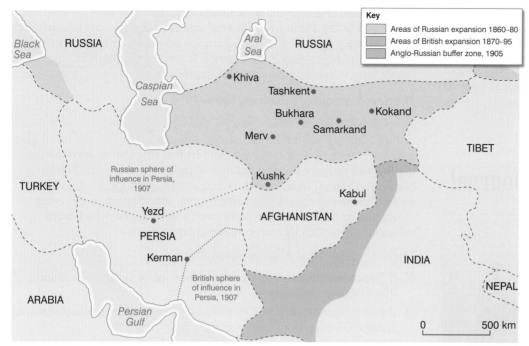

Fig. 8 *Russian expansion in central Asia*

Trans-Siberian railway across its territory. In 1898, Russia went on to obtain a 25-year lease of the Liaotung peninsula and Port Arthur – an ice-free port. Consequently, Russia's position in Manchuria made that country the dominant colonial authority in China, although the Japanese controlled Korea.

After the Boxer Rising, when violent Chinese nationalists rose in protest against foreigners in China between 1898 and 1900, a joint force of all the interested colonial powers – British, French, Japanese, Russian and German – moved in to crush the movement. The affair swelled the number of Russian troops in Manchuria to 100,000 by 1901. Russia had effectively established a protectorate there.

Russia's other interests lay in Europe, and particularly in the Eastern Mediterranean, where Russia hoped to be able to extend its influence in the Balkans and force a revision of the Straits Agreement.

Such ambitions had brought Russia into conflict with Austria-Hungary, which had its own agenda for the area, and Britain, which had constantly opposed Russian ambitions to expand towards the Mediterranean lest it block the British trade route to India.

Although Russia had been drawn into the Dreikaiserbund, lingering suspicions of German behaviour at the Congress of Berlin and Wilhelm II's refusal to renew the Reinsurance Treaty had weakened its ties with Germany. However, in compensation, Russia's relations with France had been steadily improving since the 1880s. This may seem odd, given that France was a republic and Russia an autocracy. However, France had stepped into the gap left by the Germans when Bismarck had introduced tariffs on the import of Russian wheat from 1879 and had refused to support Russian industry with German loans. They had given Russia loans and also entered a deal whereby the Russians were buying French armaments.

France looked favourably on Russia as a potential ally in Europe. Since the French had clashed with Italy in Africa, they wanted support lest the Germans supported the Italians. In 1887, Britain had signed the

■ Cross-reference

The Trans-Siberian Railway

Russian influence in the **Balkans** is discussed on page 123.

The Straits Agreement is introduced on page 119, and will be further discussed in Chapter 6, page 154.

For the **Reinsurance Treaty**, refer back to page 129.

For Bismarck's introduction of **tariffs** on the import of Russian wheat, see pages 19–20.

Key term

Status quo: keeping land possessions as they are. In 1887, this included keeping the Balkan states as they were and the Ottoman Empire free from foreign domination.

VOYAGE DU PRÉSIDENT DE LA RÉPUBLIQUE EN RUSSIE
La revue de Krasnoë-Selo

Fig. 9 *The French president visits Russia*

Cross-reference

The accession of **Tsar Nicholas II** is discussed on page 81.

Caprivi and Hohenlohe are covered on pages 32 and 35.

The Schlieffen Plan is discussed on pages 33, 46 and 143–4.

Exploring the detail

Armenian Massacres

The Turks began a large scale persecution of Armenians in its territories in 1896, killing 6,000 in Constantinople alone. This broke Turkey's promises of good behaviour and reform given at the 1878 Congress of Berlin. Gladstone came out of retirement to lead a moral crusade, demanding joint European action but he received no support. This was humiliating and suggested that Britain had lost its authority within Europe.

Mediterranean Agreements with Austria-Hungary and Italy (to keep the **status quo** in the Meditarranean area) and appeared friendly towards the Triple Alliance and in 1891 that alliance – between Germany, Austria-Hungary and Italy – had been renewed. It seemed that both France and Russia were isolated and secret talks began.

The development of alliances, 1894–1914

Russia and the Dual Alliance, 1894

In July 1891, a French fleet had visited Kronstadt, the Russian naval base near St Petersburg, and Tsar Alexander III had stood up to acknowledge the Russian military band's rendition of the Marseillaise (the French National Anthem) imbued with revolutionary spirit! On 27 August, an agreement was signed promising mutual consultation in the event of war and in August 1892, specific details were agreed, which were subsequently ratified by each country in January 1894.

The consequent Dual Alliance stated that:

- if France was attacked by Germany alone, or by Germany and Italy, Russia would give support
- if Russia was attacked by Germany alone, or by Germany and Austria-Hungary, France would give support.

The terms were officially kept secret but by 1895, the rest of Europe was well aware that agreements had been reached.

The results of the Dual Alliance

Russian-German relations did not collapse immediately. The accession of Nicholas II in 1894 (the same year that Caprivi was replaced by the conservative Hohenlohe as chancellor in Germany) actually suggested that relations might improve. The Emperors of Russia and Germany appeared to get on well together and the two countries cooperated in action in the Far East. In October 1904, the Kaiser suggested a Franco-German alliance against Britain. Tsar Nicholas was in favour but wanted to consult the French first. The following year, when the Kaiser entertained the Tsar on board his yacht, he persuaded him to sign the treaty of Björko, in which they agreed to give each other support in the event of war. Neither von Bülow in Germany, nor Russian or French ministers liked the agreement and it was dropped, whereupon Russo-German relations worsened.

Germany's military generals, believing no agreement with Russia was likely, set about revising their strategies to face the possibility of a simultaneous war with both Russia and France. The result was the drawing up of the Schlieffen Plan, which was to have immense repercussions for German policies over the next decade.

The Dual Alliance also had another important result. It left Britain more isolated than before and encouraged politicians to consider whether Britain's traditional isolation was, in fact, dangerous. Britain's isolation was reinforced when the Prime Minister, Gladstone, failed to persuade other countries of Europe to support action against the Turks over the Armenian Massacres of 1896 and again, during the Boer War of 1899–1902, when Britain found the climate of opinion in Europe was overwhelmingly hostile to the British action.

The British were deeply suspicious of the intentions of the Dual Alliance. Relations between Britain and France had been tense since 1882, when Britain had occupied Egypt, and Britain had also come into conflict with Russia in the Far East over Persia and Afghanistan. This anxiety increased as French hostility grew when an Anglo-Egyptian army under Lord Kitchener clashed with the French Captain Marchand at Fashoda in East Africa (modern-day Sudan) in 1898.

However, although the French expressed their indignation over the Boer War, it was Kaiser Wilhelm II who sent a telegram to the Boer President, Kruger, congratulating him on repelling Britain's Jameson raid in 1896. Although Kruger did not officially accept German aid in the war, Anglo-German relations were soured when some German ships, intercepted by the British navy, were found to be carrying supplies for the Boers.

So while the signing of the Dual Alliance helped impel the British government to consider abandoning its long cherished policy of 'splendid isolation', it was not altogether clear to whom Britain should turn.

The end of British isolation

The quest for an alliance partner at first led British statesmen to consider a German alliance. Although there had been disagreements between Britain and Germany, those between Britain and France and Britain and Russia had been greater and Queen Victoria liked the idea of an alliance with her grandson, Wilhelm II. In 1898, 1899 and 1901, Joseph Chamberlain, the Colonial Secretary, with the support of Lord Salisbury who was both Prime Minister and Foreign Secretary, proposed an alliance to Germany. However, Germany's response was less than encouraging. Britain was not prepared to ally herself to Austria-Hungary as well as Germany and so risk war with Russia in the Balkans. As these negotiations got underway in the spring of 1898, Germany began its naval building programme and pushed forward its plans for the Berlin–Baghdad railway. Both were outright challenges to Britain, which feared for its dominance at sea and was suspicious that the Germans had designs on Egypt and India.

In October 1900, the Marquess of Lansdowne succeeded Salisbury as Foreign Secretary. In the same year, the Boxer Rebellion had broken out in China. Britain had accepted that an international force led by Germany should be sent to suppress it, but had expected, in return, that Germany would negotiate with Russia to halt its plans for expansion in the Far East. However, Germany had made no attempt to do so. British suspicions were roused that the Germans were actually planning to combine with Russia against Britain in the Far East and Lansdowne was determined to secure an alliance, of at least a limited nature, to forestall the possibility of acting alone in a war with Russia and Germany.

In January 1902, Britain signed the Anglo-Japanese alliance. The treaty said:

- Britain and Japan would support one another if either were attacked by two or more powers in the Far East
- if either were attacked by one power, the other would remain neutral.

Entente Cordiale, 1904

British negotiations for an '**entente**' with France also began. Queen Victoria had died in 1901 and Edward VII, who was personally suspicious of the Kaiser's intentions, proved quite popular with the French. Lord Lansdowne and the French Minister, Delcassé, finally reached an understanding in 1904:

- Britain and France settled their old disputes and the French recognised the British occupation of Egypt, while Britain agreed not to oppose the French in Morocco (the latter being kept as a secret term, since, by an agreement of the Great Powers made in 1880, France had no right to assume control here).

Key chronology

Alliances, 1894–1907

1894 Dual Alliance between France and Russia.

1902 Anglo-Japanese Alliance.

1904 Entente Cordiale between Britain and France.

1907 Anglo-Russian Convention.

Cross-reference

The **Boxer Rebellion** is outlined on page 133.

Key term

Entente: An 'entente' is an understanding. It is not an alliance and does not bind either party to support the other in the event of a general war.

Cross-reference

The **Moroccan Crisis arising between 1905 and 1906** is detailed in the next section, pages 136–40.

Activity

Thinking point

Imagine you had been asked to advise the British Prime Minister in 1904 whether Britain should pursue an alliance with Germany or Russia/France. What would you have written?

Cross-reference

The impact of the **Russo-Japanese War** on Russia is discussed on pages 88–92.

- Both countries agreed to help the other against outside powers in the event of any disputes over Egypt or Morocco.

- Regular consultation on naval and military matters was arranged and it was agreed that there would be further consultation if an attack on either seemed imminent.

The Entente Cordiale was to grow into a stronger alliance in the years up to 1914 as a result of clashes in those years. Following the first Moroccan Crisis of 1905–6, France, Britain and Russia found themselves ranged together against Germany and this led the French to put pressure on their Russian allies to enter into agreement with the British.

Russo-Japanese War

Fig. 10 *Russia and the Far East*

Russia's expansion in the Far East brought it into conflict with Japan. In 1898, and again in 1903, the Japanese had tried to get the Russians to agree to a deal whereby Japan would retain influence over Korea in return for Russia's influence over Manchuria. Russia's refusal to make such a deal provoked the Japanese attack on Port Arthur in February 1904.

The War was ended by the treaty of Portsmouth (USA) by which Russia handed over South Sakhalin and the lease of Port Arthur to Japan, evacuated Manchuria and recognised Korea as a Japanese sphere of influence.

Russia's military weaknesses worried France, especially in view of the growing strength of Germany, while Britian became less anxious about Russian expansion in the Far East. In 1907, the Russian Foreign Minister,

Izvolsky, made an agreement with Britain's ally, Japan, to guarantee the independence of China, and settle their differences over Korea and Manchuria, so it seemed as though the issues which had divided the two countries in the Far East were no longer of relevance. Consequently, Britain, France and Russia grew closer together.

Fig. 11 *Tsar Nicholas II reviews his forces, 1904*

The Anglo-Russian Agreement, 1907

- Agreement was reached on the Afghanistan/Indian border; Britain was given control over the foreign policy of Afghanistan while Britain and Russia were given equal trading rights.

- Russia was given control over Northern Persia while Britain controlled the south and the Persian Gulf. The central section remained neutral.

From 1907, Britain was firmly in the Russo-French camp, but their agreements only amounted to a 'Triple Entente' rather than a definite alliance. When war finally came in 1914, it was by no means certain that Britain would fight on the Franco-Russian side and it was under no legal obligation to do so. Furthermore, Germany was given assurances that the Anglo-Russian Convention was not intended to damage them and, on the whole, with the exception of the Bosnian Crisis, Russo-German relations showed some (at least superficial)

> **Cross-reference**
>
> See map on page 133.

improvement in the years up to 1914, although, beneath the surface, both countries ensured that they were prepared for war if it came.

The importance of the alliances

It is difficult to assess the part played by the alliances in the outbreak of war. Certainly, the alliances were quite limited by themselves. They were not openly 'offensive' and their main purpose was to prevent isolation and offer protection in the event of an attack. In some respects, it could even be said that they played a part in preserving the peace, as the division of Europe into two power blocks helped to ensure a balance of power and prevented any one nation pushing its ambitions too far. All the various alliances contained limitations and provisos and there was no reason why they had to lead to war – even in the circumstances of 1914. The terms of the Triple Alliance, for example, only obliged Germany to assist its ally, if Austria was attacked – and Austria was not. Furthermore, Italy's involvment in the Triple Alliance was never more than lukewarm and this was proven by its failure to join the war in 1914 – and its decision to 'change sides' in 1915. The Triple Entente was an even looser grouping. Britain was not formally obliged to go to war on behalf of either France or Russia and none of these powers were allied to Serbia, where eventually opposition to Austria provided the excuse for war. The diplomatic system that had been constructed left considerable room for manoeuvre – it was simply that, in 1914, the powers concerned chose not to take advantage of this.

However, these treaties did pose a danger to peace. They created loyalties, they reinforced economic links and they led to military talks between the generals of the participating nations. Their existence encouraged the preparation of mobilisation and campaign plans which assumed the 'teams' were settled. As a result, the preparations which they brought about, placed the politicians of 1914 in a position in which they felt obliged to act with haste in order to fulfil the generals' intentions. It was these plans, and a 'will to war', which ultimately turned the peacetime alliances into alliances of aggression.

■ Growing rivalry and tension

The fluid alliance system which had come into being by 1905 only became more firmly defined as a result of the colonial clashes over Morocco which occurred in 1905 and 1908–11. In 1905, the newly found friendship of Britain and France was still to be tested and there was an abortive attempt by the Emperors of Russia and Germany to reconcile their differences and make the Treaty of Björkö the same year. Had this been ratified, the Björkö Treaty would have made a promise of mutual assistance in the event of an attack. However, Nicholas II's Ministers vetoed it, as they were concerned about the loss of French revenue that was likely to result.

Colonial clashes

First Moroccan Crisis, 1905

Morocco was a state, subject to the rule of the Turkish Sultan, in North Africa. Both French and German traders were active there and under the terms of the Entente Cordiale of 1904, Delcassé, Prime Minister of France, had received a British pledge of support for France to take control of the area.

Question

Explain why a Triple Entente of Britain, France and Russia developed in the years 1904–14.

Fig. 12 *Wilhelm II's telegram to von Bülow on his visit to Tangiers in 1905*

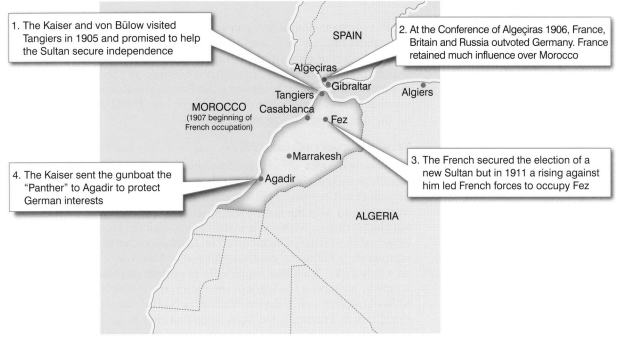

1. The Kaiser and von Bülow visited Tangiers in 1905 and promised to help the Sultan secure independence

2. At the Conference of Algeçiras 1906, France, Britain and Russia outvoted Germany. France retained much influence over Morocco

3. The French secured the election of a new Sultan but in 1911 a rising against him led French forces to occupy Fez

4. The Kaiser sent the gunboat the "Panther" to Agadir to protect German interests

Fig. 13 *The Moroccan crisis, 1905–11*

While on a Mediterranean cruise, Kaiser Wilhelm II sailed into the Moroccan capital, Tangiers, on 31 March 1905, supposedly in support of German business interests in the area. Here, he gave outspoken speeches in which he recognised the Sultan of Morocco as an independent ruler and questioned the (originally secret) agreements between France and Britain which had been subsequently 'leaked'. He may have hoped that his outspokenness would persuade the French to back down and show the British the weakness of their new ally, or he may simply have wanted to place the Germans at the forefront of European affairs by demanding an international conference on the Moroccan question.

According to the Memoirs of von Bülow:

> It was not only the extent of our economic and political interest in and about Morocco which persuaded me to advise the Kaiser to set his face against France. In the interests of peace, we must no longer permit such provocations. I do not desire war with France, but I did not hesitate to confront France with the possiblity of war. I felt that I could prevent matters coming to a head, cause Delcassé's fall, break the continuity of aggressive French policy, knock the continental dagger out of the hands of Edward VII and the war group in England, and simultaneously ensure peace, preserve German honour and improve German prestige.

5

Delcassé, who tried to resist German pressure, failed to win support and was forced to resign and Germany's 'coup' seemed to have succeeded. The conference met at Algeçiras in Spain between January and March 1906 but the Germans found the British, Russians, Italians, Spanish and even the Americans all supporting the French claims. Germany's only ally was Austria-Hungary and the country suffered a major diplomatic defeat.

Whether the event was as important as is sometimes suggested has been questioned by the historian A. J. P. Taylor. He has pointed out that

■ Question

How successful was von Bülow's handling of the First Moroccan Crisis of 1905–6?

■ Cross-reference

The **Pan-German League** is described on page 54.

For details of the **Naval Race**, see pages 114–18.

■ Key terms

Revanchist: revanchism was the desire of France to recover the lost provinces of Alsace and Lorraine taken by Germany in 1871 after France was defeated. These provinces were rich in natural resources of coal and iron ore.

Autonomous: able to do what you want without reference to other authorities – in this case the Reichstag and civilian authorities.

■ Summary question

Explain why the Moroccan Crises of 1905–6 and 1911 led to increased tension between the Great Powers.

■ Cross-reference

The role of the **Reichstag** and the German civilian authorities is detailed in Chapters 1 and 2.

the British made no military preparations to back the French and that subsequent military talks were ineffectual. Nevertheless the rebuff did have the effect of increasing Wilhelm II's fears and leading Germany to abandon the idea of the international conference as a means of settling disputes. Furthermore, by allowing the British and Russians to come together to iron out some of their problems over Persia, it opened the way for the Anglo-Russian Agreement of 1907.

Second Moroccan Crisis, 1911

Morocco was again the centre of European tension in 1911 when the French provoked a renewed crisis by sending troops to the Moroccan capital, Fez. The official reason given by France was that the troops were there to help the Sultan defeat some local rebel tribesmen but the Germans, with some justification, claimed that France had breached the earlier agreements. The Germans reacted in an extreme manner by sending the gunboat *Panther* to Morocco which docked on 1 July 1911. This was supposedly to protect German interests and seems to have been the work of the nationalistic German Foreign Minister, Alfred von Kiderlen-Wächter, who had connections with the Pan-German League. It has been suggested that he and his associates had hopes of establishing a greater German presence in North Africa.

The British were immediately alarmed by the potential threat to Gibraltar, at the entrance to the Mediterranean. On 21 July, Britain's Chancellor of the Exchequer, Lloyd George, gave a speech at the Mansion House pointing to Britain's desire for stability in Morocco and expressing a determination to support France. Faced with such resolution, Germany backed down and a compromise was agreed whereby Germany received some territory in the French Congo by way of compensation. The French were able to establish a formal French protectorate in Morocco in March 1912 and all the crisis seemed to have achieved was a further weakening of Anglo-German relations and a strengthening of Anglo-French ones. It was no coincidence that the Naval Race was stepped up in the next two years. In France, those elements favourable to a compromise settlement with Germany lost out to the more nationalistic politicians and Poincaré, a **revanchist**, came to power. Furthermore, from 1912, Britain and France undertook a series of military conventions, beginning with a naval agreement in March 1912 whereby Britain undertook to allow the French navy to dominate the Mediterranean, while Britain would confine itself to Gibraltar and the North Sea.

The second Moroccan crisis did not affect Russia. Indeed, the Russian foreign minister Izvolsky claimed, *'Russian public opinion could not see in a colonial dispute, the cause for a general conflict'*. However, the crisis had created a new level of tension in Europe and it was to have a direct link to the outbreak of war. In 1911, Italy chose to copy the French example with an unprovoked attack on Turkish Tripoli. This, in turn, encouraged the Balkan States to renew their quest for greater power and it was out of this turmoil that the First World War erupted.

Arms escalation and the growth of military strength

From around 1907, there was an increase in military influence on policy making, particularly in Germany and Russia. The German army was virtually **autonomous**, while in Russia, Generals became sufficiently powerful that in 1914, they were able to threaten the Tsar with defeat if he did not allow their orders for a mobilisation to go ahead. This growing

Fig. 14 *German artillery testing the new anti-aircraft cannon designed by Krupps to 'shoot down airships'*

militarism was reflected in the amassing of weapons, an increase in the size of armies and navies, an increase in military spending and the development of elaborate military planning.

Weaponry

The growth of industry in the 19th century was also associated with the growth of weaponry. By the 1880s, the development of modern machines and chemicals had permitted the advent of high explosives, the machine gun and long range **artillery**. Such weapons promised to transform war, as did the growing railway network that could be harnessed to carry troops to the front line.

The increasing production of weapons concerned Tsar Nicholas II sufficiently for him to suggest a conference at The Hague in 1899 to consider disarmament, but although the Great Powers met for discussions, nothing was achieved. Germany argued that Britian's demand to stabilise arms production at existing levels was simply a ploy to keep German armaments permanently inferior to Britain's own. The only achievement was the setting up of a tribunal at The Hague for arbitration

> ### Key term
>
> **Artillery:** large guns which accompany infantry units. Field Artillery is used to support infantry on the battlefield while heavy artillery was designed to defend or attack fortified towns or fortresses.

in a dispute. A second conference in 1907 achieved similarly little. International rivalry caused the arms race to continue to feed on itself.

Germany, home to the powerful Krupp Empire, led the way in the production of weapons, but in the years from 1908, both France and Russia strove to equal or outpace the German advances. In 1908, a bill was passed to strengthen the French artillery while in Russia, Sukhomlinov pressed for increased military spending to build up the Russian artillery. By 1914, Russian army expenditure was equivalent to 1,577 million marks compared to the German army expenditure of 1,496 million marks.

Armies

Not only did the numbers of weapons increase, but so did the size of armies. All the continental European powers relied on compulsory military service. France had introduced it during the Revolutionary Wars at the end of the 18th century, Austria-Hungary in 1868, Germany from 1870, Italy from 1873 and Russia from 1874. Only Britain was without a conscripted army.

In Germany, although the length of military conscription was reduced from three to two years in 1893, the total size of the army was increased, particularly after 1907, to provide for an army of 5 million men in wartime. Between 1913 and July 1914, Germany increased its forces by 170,000 men. Austria was less prepared but in March 1914, Austria increased the annual levy of recruits from 175,000 to 200,000 men.

France enacted the 'Three Year Service Law' in 1913 to extend the service of conscripted soldiers from two to three years to match the size of the German army. By the time war broke out in 1914, the French army had a mobilised strength of 3.5 million, nearly matching Germany's 3.8 million, despite the fact that the population of France was only 40 million as opposed to Germany's population of 60 million people. Producing an army of this size turned France into the most militarised society in Europe. Eighty per cent of young men of the appropriate age were in military service in France, compared with only 50 per cent in Germany.

Russia also increased service from three to three and a half years and launched a further 'Great Programme' in 1913 whereby over half a million Russians per annum would be conscripted. Russia never had time to fulfil the programme before war broke out, but by 1914, it could mobilise the biggest army of all – 4.4 million soldiers.

Even Britain organised a small but strong British Expeditionary Force for service on the continent and a Territorial Army for home defence. The BEF originated from Haldane's army reforms of 1907 and was developed on the military advice of Douglas Gaig. On mobilisation in 1914, it consisted of a general headquarters, three army corps, each of two infantry divisions, a large cavalry division of four brigades, and a fifth independent cavalry brigade.

Military spending

Supporting the arms race was a huge rise in military spending. The total defence expenditure of Germany, Russia, Austria-Hungary, Italy, France and Britain combined rose, as indicated in Table 1.

Table 1 *Defence expenditure of the Powers in £ million*

1870	1880	1890	1900	1910	1914
94	130	154	268	289	398

While France increased defence spending by 10 per cent, Britain increased military expenditure by 13 per cent, Russia by 39 per cent and Germany by 73 per cent in the years 1870–1914.

Table 2 *Russian military expenditure 1908–12 (mn roubles)*

	Army	Navy	Other military expenditure	Total
1908	462.5	93.5	52.0	608.0
1909	473.4	92.2	64.9	630.5
1910	484.9	112.7	50.0	647.6
1911	497.8	121.0	50.6	669.4
1912	527.9	176.1	110.5	814.5
1913	581.0	245.0	382.0	1208.0

Military planning

Conscription and large reserves were accompanied by detailed planning for both war and mobilisation. Technological and organisational developments led to the formation of general staffs with precise plans that often could not be reversed once they were begun. The German Schlieffen Plan and Russian Plan 19 laid down precise mobilisation orders and campaign strategies. The Schlieffen Plan depended on fast action against France, if it was to succeed in knocking out that enemy before dealing with the assumed slower mobilisation of Russia. However, the development of the Russian railway system threatened the success of the plan before it was even launched. Had the Russian 'Great Programme' been carried out in full, it has been projected that, by 1917, French-financed improvements to the Russian railway system would have enabled the Russians to reduce the time required to mobilise the entire army from 30 to 18 days.

The Schlieffen Plan

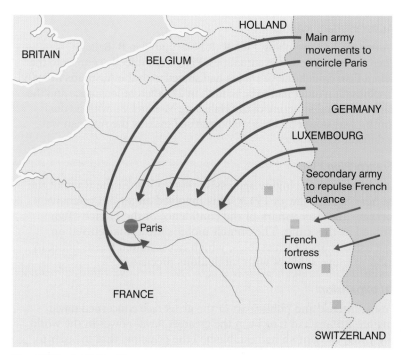

Fig. 15 *The Schlieffen Plan*

The Schlieffen Plan had been drawn up in outline as early as 1892 by Count Alfred von Schlieffen, Chief of the German General Staff from 1891 to 1906, but was only formally adopted in 1904. It was based on the premise that if, as a result of a Franco-Russian alliance, Germany faced the prospect of a war on two fronts, France would have to be defeated before the Russians had time to mobilise. This was to be achieved by a massive invasion of France through Luxembourg and Belgium, so avoiding the French defences on the Franco-German border. The attack would encircle Paris in a pincer movement and the Germans would attack the French army from the side and the rear. Another German army would repulse the likely French advance through Alsace-Lorraine. This plan had three significant repercussions:

■ It threatened Belgian neutrality, guaranteed by most European powers, but especially by Britain.

■ It was Germany's only plan for war and it encouraged the German High Command to favour a war on two fronts.

■ The plan necessitated massive armies in the west of Germany and it led to a huge increase in army forces after 1900, and especially in 1913.

The Russian 'Plan 19'

After Germany offered Austria-Hungary support against Russia, in 1908–9, the Russian War Ministry drew up a new war plan – Plan No. 19. This provided for a speedy attack on East Prussia during the critical opening phase of war, so diverting German troops from France, and the French provided capital for railway building to implement it. However, in May 1912, Russian traditionalists, more concerned about Russian expansion in the Balkans, forced an alteration by which Russian forces were to be divided and half sent to the Southern Front, to attack Austria-Hungary through Galicia. This was to prove to Germany's advantage in 1914.

The Austrian 'Plans R and B'

The Austrians had two plans, Plan R (Russia) and Plan B (Balkans) – designed to cover different eventualities. Plan B ran directly counter to the Schlieffen Plan (which the Germans had shared with the Austrians in 1909). The mobilisation order had to be written in 27 different languages and the military command structure of the Habsburg Monarchy – with its dual authority – was slower and less well organised making the Austrian war plans difficult to institute.

The French 'Plan XVII'

France developed the highly aggressive 'Plan XVII' in the wake of the Three Year Service law of 1913. This involved an all-out offensive in Lorraine and was a mark of the confidence of the French High Command at this time. The French mobilisation was centred on precise use of railway timetables, which necessitated trains being in position to move soldiers with meticulous precision.

Naval expansion

The most intense and public part of the arms race concerned naval expansion. Britain had long been the greatest naval power in the world and by 1889, the British had established the principle that in order to maintain naval superiority in the event of war they would have to have a navy two and a half times as large as the second-largest navy. In 1891, there was an increase in the German navy, but expenditure was only

Activity

Thinking point

In what ways might mobilisation plans affect the outbreak of war?

Fig. 16 *The dockyards were expanded to support the growing navy*

around £4m, which was a fraction of that spent by Britain and France. However, from 1897, the appointment of Admiral von Tirpitz as Naval Secretary led to an aggressive campaign for the creation of a larger and more powerful German fleet. Such a course was fully supported by the Kaiser who declared, *'the trident must be in our hands'*. There were a variety of factors behind the German decision:

■ The Kaiser himself was strongly in favour of building a fleet. Wilhelm II had always been a keen sailor and a fervent admirer of the British navy, whose uniform he was proud to wear.

■ A navy was essential to the realisation of Weltpolitik – the achievement and protection of a 'place in the sun'.

■ There were good economic reasons to build a fleet. Construction would bolster ports and shipping interests and export industries.

■ An influential book on naval strategy (which the Kaiser had read) – *The Influence of Sea Power on History* by Admiral Mahan – suggested that a large fleet was essential if a state was to gain admission to the ranks of Great Powers at the end of the 19th century.

■ Demands for a strong navy came from a number of power interests including merchants engaged in overseas trade, colonialists and powerful voices in the iron and shipbuilding industries.

> ■ For Germany, the most dangerous naval enemy at the present time is England. It is also the enemy against which we urgently require a certain force as a political power factor.
>
> ■ Commerce raiding and transatlantic war against England is hopeless, because of the shortage of bases on our side and the superfluity on England's side.
>
> ■ The military situation against England demands battleships in as great a number as possible.

6   *From a memorandum by von Tirpitz to Wilhelm II, 1897*

■ **Cross-reference**

To recap on **Weltpolitik**, revisit pages 45–6.

■ **Activity**

Source analysis

Read Source 6.

1 What motives are suggested for naval expansion in Source 6?

2 Prioritise the reasons for the building of a strong navy. Compare your list with that of a partner and discuss any differences.

■ Exploring the detail

Von Tirpitz

Although Tirpitz admired the British and sent his two daughters to The Cheltenham Ladies' College, he regarded Britain as the biggest threat to Germany's independence and believed that naval construction would encourage the British to seek closer relations with Germany. In fact, it had the exact opposite effect. In the autumn of 1897, he launched a huge and successful campaign in favour of naval expansion. His programme crippled Germany financially and, in his obsession with battleships, Tirpitz ignored other types of technology such as U-boats (submarines). Yet, in the event, Germany came closest to winning the war against Britain through unrestricted submarine warfare, and not through open battle in the North Sea.

■ Exploring the detail

The Navy League

The Navy League was set up in 1898 by the Reich Naval Office to act as a pressure group, demanding further increases in naval strength. The League sent out magazines to its members explaining the arguments for higher naval expenditure. The League was funded by industrialists who hoped to benefit from the programme of shipbuilding. By 1900, it had a membership of 270,000 and it went on to reach a membership of over one million, most of them from the middle classes.

Fig. 17 *Admiral von Tirpitz*

The Navy Law of 1898 set out plans for the expansion of the German navy to match that of Britain. It aimed to bring the German Imperial Navy up to the strength of 14 battleships (from 7) and 4 cruisers and also to increase the number of smaller vessels. (Britain had 54 battleships and 34 cruisers.) Von Tirpitz gained support for his naval building campaign by funding the Navy League. The campaign was hugely popular with the public but, of course, played a crucial role in worsening Anglo-German relations.

In 1900, the second Navy Law was passed, which provided for a 20-year building programme and the construction of a high seas fleet of 38 battleships, 8 battle cruisers and 24 cruisers. The race was on! Britain responded with a new naval base at Rosyth in 1903 and Parliament approved plans for the formation of a North Sea Fleet. Sir John Fisher was appointed First Sea Lord in May 1904, and was determined to meet the threat from Germany. It was also decided to adopt the revolutionary design for a new dreadnought class of battleships, with ten 12-inch guns rather than the usual four. These ships, which would also be faster than earlier models, would cost £1m each but they would make the German fleet obsolete. The first was launched in February 1906.

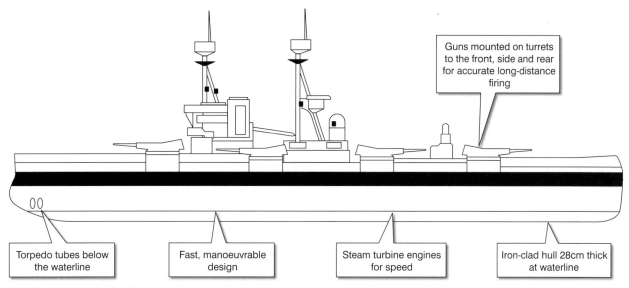

Guns mounted on turrets to the front, side and rear for accurate long-distance firing

Torpedo tubes below the waterline

Fast, manoeuvrable design

Steam turbine engines for speed

Iron-clad hull 28cm thick at waterline

Fig. 18 *Diagram of a dreadnought*

The British believed they had secured superiority because the Germans could not manufacture an equivalent ship without first widening and deepening the Kiel Canal. However, in May 1906, the German government laid down plans to extend the number of German ships under construction, add six cruisers, and widen and deepen the canal. In 1909, Britain then increased the planned number of dreadnoughts.

By March 1912, Germany was planning further shipping increases to create a third fleet. The Kiel Canal was widened in 1913 and the new ships could make their way from the Baltic to the North Sea. This spurred on the Franco-Russian Naval Convention in July and the Anglo-French Naval Agreement whereby British ships were moved to the North Sea and French ships from Brest to the Mediterranean.

Although the British suggested an agreement whereby a German fleet of 60 per cent the size of the British would be allowed, the Kaiser would accept no compromise.

The naval race left Britain feeling deeply threatened. Churchill expressed some of the British feeling when he said:

> The purpose of the British navy is defensive. There is a difference between British naval power and that of the German Empire. Our Empire is existence to us – it is expansion to them. The whole fortunes of our race and Empire would perish if our naval supremacy was impaired. It is our navy which makes Britain a great power. Germany was one before she had a ship.

7

Cross-reference

The **Franco-Russian Naval Convention** and the **Anglo-French Naval Agreement** are outlined on page 140.

Activity

Thinking point

Write a reply to Churchill's comments from a German member of the Navy League.

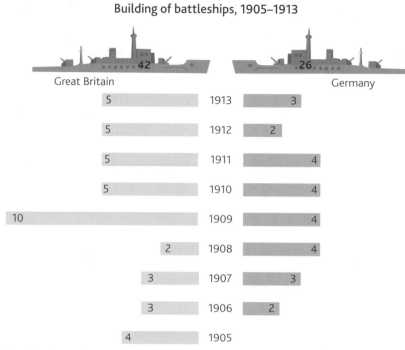

Fig. 19 *The naval race*

The importance of the arms race

Once underway it was very difficult to halt the arms race. All sides distrusted the others' intentions and national pride prevented any climb-down. A huge vested interest in the arms industry was created, ranging from arms manufacturers and their share holders to newspaper proprietors who made money from the stories. Increased military and naval rivalry also led to a belief that war must come soon and the increase in military control in civilian government increased cooperation among military staff within each of the 'armed camps'. All powers held secret talks. Britain and France cooperated over the navy and Germany and Austria made military agreements. The armaments race certainly helped prepare Europe for war by 1914.

However, the link between this arms race – on both land and sea – and the final outbreak of war is, of course, unproven. Stockpiling weapons or building ships does not necessarily create war, even if it does create conditions which favour war. Some have argued that the build up of weapons and military capacity should have been a deterrent to war, for the risks involved were enormous. However, it may have been that the powers of Europe were anxiously awaiting a moment to try out their strength and no doubt the accumulation of arms gave the generals confidence, perhaps an over-confidence, in their country's power.

Germany, Russia and their preparedness for war

In many respects, the German military commanders were ready for war in 1914. Indeed, they had been expressing their concern since 1911–12, lest the balance of power tip away from Germany. They were aware that Russia was industrialising fast and its population was growing, railways had been built, right up to the German border and the Great Programme, launched in 1913, looked set to expand Russia's military beyond the size of Germany's. The German

■ **Cross-reference**

To revisit the **1912 war council** in Germany, see page 46.

For Russia's **Great Programme**, refer back to page 142.

The Schlieffen Plan is covered on pages 143–4.

General Staff, who held so much power in the military-minded Reich, were understandably alarmed that their only war plan, the Schlieffen Plan, would fail to work once the Russian railways were completed. Furthermore, with French power reviving under the leadership of Poincaré in 1912–13, Germany's fears of encirclement had grown. Maybe not all, but certainly some generals were more than ready for a 'preventive war' – as popularised by the book *Hour of Destiny* published in 1914 by Colonel Frobenius. As Moltke said in June 1914, Germany should:

> wage a preventive war in order to beat the enemy while we still have some chance of winning.

Russia was clearly less prepared for war. The Great Programme had only just been launched in 1913 and although Russia was strong in manpower, it remained economically backward and notoriously inefficient compared to the might of Germany. However, Russia had developed considerably in the years since 1890 and its ally, France, was supremely confident of its own military ability. The case for French militarism had been made in *La Fin de la Prusse and le Démembrement de L'Allemagne* by Gaulois Franc in 1913. Although the chances of Russia's ambitious plans being carried out in full were slim, nevertheless, the military preparations being made by French/Russian alliance partners heightened Germany's sense of vulnerability.

Austria-Hungary was not ready for war either and the chances of the Austrian 'Plan R' succeeding were limited, given the growth in Russian strength. Conrad von Hötzendorf, the Austrian Chief of Staff, later wrote:

> After the Treaty of Bucharest (1913), I ceased to urge war and indeed attempted to postpone it until our military preparations – the only chance of saving Austria – improved.

However, whatever their state, all countries had prepared mobilisation plans and when the Sarajevo Crisis broke in 1914, these took over.

Summary questions

1. Explain why there was an arms race in Europe between 1890 and 1914.
2. How important was the lapsing of the Reinsurance Treaty in 1890 in creating the Triple Entente?

Cross-reference
Poincaré's leadership is addressed on page 140.

Cross-reference
The Sarajevo Crisis is covered on pages 150 and 157–60.

The Balkans and the outbreak of the First World War, 1908–14

Fig. 1 *The arrest of Gavrilo Princip, Franz Ferdinand's assassin*

In this chapter you will learn about:

- why the Balkans were politically unstable

- the circumstances and results of the Bosnian Crisis of 1908–9

- the reasons for, and impact of, the Balkan Wars of 1912–13

- why the assassination of Archduke Franz Ferdinand at Sarajevo led to a war between the European powers

- different interpretations of the reasons for the First World War.

On Sunday morning, 28 June 1914, Archduke Franz Ferdinand, heir to the throne of the Austro-Hungarian Empire, and his wife, Sophie, were visiting Sarajevo, the main town in the Austrian province of Bosnia. Franz Ferdinand was well aware of the risk of visiting this part of the Empire. There were many Serbs living in the area and terrorists were known to be stirring up support for a union of Bosnia with nearby Serbia. Franz Ferdinand had dismissed the risks, but, as he was being driven through the town, a bomb was thrown. It either bounced off the car or was deflected by the Archduke. Twenty people were killed, but the royal party was uninjured and able to proceed to the Town Hall. Franz Ferdinand was outraged. The rest of his tour was cancelled. However, he insisted that, after lunch, he be taken to the hospital to see those injured in the morning's bomb attack. Sophie also demanded that she accompany him and their request was agreed, although, for his own safety, it was felt best that he take a route that avoided the city centre.

Strangely enough, no one seemed to have told the driver of this decision, and as the car approached Appel Quay, the driver began to turn right. The Bosnian governor called out to tell him that they were going the wrong way. As the chauffeur slowly reversed, shots were fired and Sophie, struck by the first, fell between the Archduke's knees. The driver sped away towards the hospital and the Archduke, with blood pouring from his mouth, sobbed as he held the body of his beloved wife. The gunman was seized by the crowd, but by 11.30pm, the royal couple were dead. A month later, on 28 July, Austria declared war on Serbia and the First World War began.

Problems in the Balkans, 1908–14

The Balkan situation pre-1908

For much of the last quarter of the 19th century, Austria-Hungary and Russia had vied with one another to maintain and increase their influence in the Balkans. However, in 1897, at a time when the Turks seemed relatively strong, the two powers had signed an agreement to maintain the status quo there.

The agreement stated that:

■ neither power would attempt to alter the balance of power within the Balkans

■ both powers would oppose any other power which tried to gain territory in the Balkans

■ both accepted that the Black Sea Straits were closed to warships when Turkey was at peace

■ if the Ottoman Empire (Turkey) collapsed, Austria-Hungary could annex the provinces of Bosnia and Herzegovina, as formerly agreed in 1881.

However, in the early 20th century, a number of new pressures brought the two powers into conflict with one another again.

Growth of Serbian nationalism

In 1903, King Alexander of Serbia was assassinated in a military coup and a new and more aggressive dynasty – the Karageorgevics – came to power with Paul I as King. Paul was not only strongly pro-Russian; he also encouraged Serbian nationalism. The Serbs saw themselves as champions of the Southern Slavs and wanted to form a united Slav state, incorporating Croats, Slovenes and Slavs. Their ambitions extended to incorporating Bosnia, Herzegovina and Montenegro into a Greater Serbia and while not all the inhabitants of these territories favoured such a move, all contained active nationalist groups.

Russian concerns

Russia had long posed as a champion of the Slavs and this 'Pan-Slavism' became a powerful influence within Russia, particularly after Russia's defeat in the Russo-Japanese war. The Karageorgevic dynasty in Serbia was strongly pro-Russian, as was Prince Boris of Bulgaria, who signed a military agreement with Russia in 1902. Russia appeared to be in a strong position in the area, although, after defeat in the Far East, Russia's credibility as a military power had suffered a blow. There was some discussion within Russia, in 1907, of reaching a new agreement with Austria-Hungary, but the Bosnian Crisis of 1908 promptly ended such ideas. The year before, Russia had, in any case, come to an understanding with Britain over Persia and Afghanistan and this was to form the basis of the Triple Entente of Russia, Britain and France.

Austro-Hungarian concerns

The Austro-Hungarians saw the growth of Serbian nationalism as a threat to the integrity of their Empire which contained around 7 million Serbs and Croats. They were particularly concerned about Serbia's ambitions for the two provinces of Bosnia and Herzegovina, which the Empire itself was hoping to incorporate.

Count Aehrenthal became Foreign Minister in 1906 and, in an attempt to curb Serbian ambitions, the tariff arrangements between the two countries were not renewed that year. This led to the so-called 'Pig War' of 1906–8. Austria-Hungary tried to strangle the Serbian economy by banning imports of meat from Serbia and depriving that country of an important source of revenue but the Serbs survived by selling elsewhere. However, in 1908, Serbia was forced to accept a new commercial treaty committing Serbia to higher imports from the Austro-Hungarian Empire.

Exploring the detail

The Sarajevo assassination

Many conspiracy theories have grown up around the Sarajevo assassination. Pictures of Sarajevo at the time of the Archduke's visit show thin crowds and few policemen in the streets. Consequently, it has been suggested that the Austrian officials who managed the province deliberately allowed Serb terrorists to assassinate Franz Ferdinand. It is known that some officials disliked the Archduke because he had quite liberal ideas about dividing up the Empire to give the Serbs (Slavs) within it more control over their own affairs. Furthermore, the Head of Security in Bosnia had a personal grudge against the Archduke because he had been passed over for promotion. However, none of this can be proven and it is perhaps more likely that the absence of policemen was because the visit was organised by the military. All that can be said is that since the opportunity for the assassin to shoot the Archduke and his wife was presented by a slowly reversing car, the likelihood of the chauffeur being 'in the know' seems quite possible.

Key chronology

Events of 1908–14

1908 October	Austria-Hungary annexed Bosnia-Herzegovina in defiance of the 1878 Congress of Berlin.
1912 March	Balkan League formed by Greece, Serbia, Montenegro and Bulgaria.
1912 October	Balkan League defeated Turkey in the First Balkan War.
1913 May	Treaty of London ended First Balkan War.
1913 June–July	Second Balkan War: Serbia and Greece attacked Bulgaria.
1913 August	Treaty of Bucharest ended Second Balkan War.
1914 June 28th	Assassination at Sarajevo.

Cross-reference

For a map of the **Balkans**, look back to page 124.

The long-standing issue of the **Black Sea Straits** is outlined on page 119.

Cross-reference

To recap on Russia's defeat in the Far East, refer back to pages 136–7.

The **Bosnian Crisis** of 1908 is discussed in the next section.

The understanding between Russia and Britain and the **Triple Entente** are detailed on pages 137–8.

Key profile

Count Aehrenthal

Aloys Lexa von Aehrenthal (1854–1912), was an intelligent and ambitious Austrian statesman who had served in Paris, St Petersburg, Bucharest and Vienna before being appointed Foreign Minister in October 1906. He was an untiring worker and well thought of by the Emperor Franz Joseph. In office, he was determined to preserve the interests of Austria-Hungary in the Balkans, but he was prepared to negotiate with the Russians over the annexation of Bosnia and Herzegovina in 1908. Despite the dispute this provoked with Russia, Aehrenthal gained international acceptance of the annexation and was rewarded by being given the title of 'Count' in August 1909. In Vienna, he opposed the group, led by the Chief of General Staff, Conrad von Hotzendorf, which championed an unashamedly aggressive foreign policy, particularly against Serbia. He preferred a diplomatic or more subtle approach and while insisting on the independence of Austria-Hungary, sought to maintain and strengthen Austria's German Alliance. He secured a victory in 1911 when Hotzendorf was forced to resign. He died on 17 February 1912 and was succeeded by Berchtold.

Fig. 2 *Turkey was further weakened as Bosnia and Herzegovina were placed under Austrian administration*

The 1908 Bosnian Crisis

In 1908, there was a rebellion within the Turkish Empire led by a group of young Turkish army officers, who had become frustrated by the failures and weakness of the Sultan. They forced Abdul Hamid, the Turkish Emperor, to accept a Turkish parliament, abandon censorship, dismantle the spy network and promise of equality for the different races within the Empire, whether Christian or Muslim. This development sparked Austro-Hungarian fears of a resurgence of Turkish power, which could threaten their ambition to absorb Bosnia and Herzegovina. When these two provinces were invited to send representatives to the new Turkish Parliament, this seemed to undermine the justification Austria had hoped to offer for their annexation – namely the need to protect them.

Aehrenthal believed the Empire's only hope was to act quickly and take full control in the provinces before the Turks were ready to mount a challenge. His anxiety to incorporate them was flamed by the desire to forestall Serbia's ambition of forming a union with them and there were other influential voices within Austria who hoped that the action might provoke Serbia to war, so giving Austria an opportunity to crush Serbia once and for all.

Before risking war with Serbia, however, the Austrians needed to be sure that the Russians would not intervene against them, in defence of its ally and the South Slavs' interests. Although

Russia had, in theory, approved an Austrian annexation, Austria could not feel sure of the Russians, particularly since the resurgence of Russian Pan-Slavism after the 1905 revolution.

On 15–16 September, Aehrenthal held discussions with the Russian Foreign Minister, Izvolsky, at Buchlau Castle in Moravia. No records have been preserved of the discussions but it would seem that a deal was struck. Aehrenthal was granted Russian approval for the annexation, in return for a promise to bring about a revision of the Black Sea Straits agreements in favour of Russia. Both men took some steps towards fulfilling this deal but on 5 October 1908, Austro-Hungarian troops marched into the provinces and on 6 October Aehrenthal announced the annexation, without any further reference to Russia. There was panic throughout Europe. The Russian government, which had not, at that stage, been fully informed of Izvolsky's negotiations, condemned Austria's action outright and threatened to send troops in support of the outraged Serbia. Panic spread through Europe as Izolvsky tried to save face by demanding an international conference.

In January 1909, Austria-Hungary reached an agreement with Turkey, whereby the Turks accepted the annexation in return for £2m compensation, but Serbia's troops remained mobilised, awaiting Russian support to force the Austrians out. Von Bülow, the German chancellor, announced Germany's intention to support Austria and General Moltke, Chief of the German General Staff, wrote to General Hotzendorff, Chief of the Austrian Staff, on 19 March 1909 declaring:

> As long as Austria and Germany stand shoulder to shoulder we will be strong enough to break any ring around us.

The Kaiser put it rather more flamboyantly when he promised that if Austria were attacked *'a knight in shining armour'* would be found at her side. This was the first time Germany had made such a promise to its ally and it placed Russia in an extremely difficult position. Although Russia had begun a major rearmament programme in 1906, in the wake of defeat in the Russo-Japanese War, the country was not yet ready to face both Austria and Germany.

Germany went on to take the initiative on 21 March, sending Russia a note threatening that if it did not accept the annexation and end support for Serbia, events would *'run their course'*. Ten days later, under pressure from Russia, Serbia withdrew its objections and made promises of good behaviour to Austria-Hungary. It was a complete climb-down for Russia and Izvolsky was forced to resign.

Results of the Bosnian Crisis

The crisis fuelled the ambitions of the Balkan States. Serbia, in particular, was determined to fight back from this humiliation. The Serbs saw the annexation as a deliberate act of hostility towards their 'legitimate' ambitions and they set about borrowing money for railway building from France and laid track to the Austro-Hungarian border. Artillery guns were also purchased from the French, increasing the strength of the Serbian army. Serbia grew more open in her support of the South Slavs and did nothing to stop terrorist organisations forming within its borders and acting in the southern provinces of the Empire. Among these extreme nationalist groups was the 'Union of Death', better known as the 'Black Hand', founded in 1911. This group was committed to the liberation of all Serbs living under foreign rule by whatever means were necessary – including acts of terrorism. In Austria, some, such as General Conrad

■ Exploring the detail

Bosnia and Herzegovina

Bosnia and Herzegovina lay on the southern border of the Austro-Hungarian Empire, and adjoined Serbia. They contained a mixture of races of which 40 per cent were Slavs. The Empire had occupied and governed the states since 1878, and in 1881 Austria-Hungary had won the secret agreement of Germany and Russia to keep these provinces permanently. However, in 1897, Austria had promised Russia that there would be no change to their status unless the Ottoman Empire collapsed entirely. In 1903, that promise had been renewed, but only for a period of five years.

■ Exploring the detail

The Young Turks

The 'Young Turks' followed the ideas of 'The Ottoman Society for Union and Progress', set up in 1889, by a group of army medical students. Their aim was to re-establish Turkey's Great Power status and reclaim lost territories, by modernising the country and establishing constitutional government. Their activites led to the overthrow of Sultan Abdul Hamid in 1908 and the accession of his brother Mehmed V, but they tended to destabilise, rather than strengthen the Empire. There were many nationalist risings, some violently anti-Christian, and in April 1909, 30,000 Christians were slaughtered in two weeks by a 'Young Turk' mob.

■ Cross-reference

The **1905 Revolution** is the subject of Chapter 4.

The attempt to win support for a revision of the Straits Agreement, 1908

After his discussions with Aehrenthal, Izvolsky gained Bulgarian agreement in return for support for Bulgarian independence. He then visited the other European leaders to win support.

26 September The Germans agreed, in return for Russian support for the Berlin–Baghdad Railway.

28 September The Italians agreed, in return for Russian support for Italy's claim to Tripoli and part of the Balkans.

4 October He failed to gain French support. (5 October – Bulgaria declared its independence.)

9 October He visited London, but was told that Britian would only support if Turkey agreed, which it did not.

■ Cross-reference

The **Russo-Japanese War** is detailed on pages 136–7.

■ Did you know?

The Black Hand

The Black Hand was formed in Serbia in May 1911. It was a secret society committed to acts of terrorism in order to bring about the, 'unification of all Serbs'. It was led by Colonel Dragutin Dimitrijevic (codename Apis), Chief of the Intelligence Department of the Serbian General Staff. After a failed attempt to assassinate Emperor Franz Joseph in 1911, Muhamed Mehmedbasic was sent to kill General Oskar Potiorek, the Governor of Bosnia-Herzegovina, but this also failed. By 1914, the Black Hand had around 2,500 members including many junior army officers and some lawyers, journalists and university professors.

von Hotzendorff, the Austrian Chief of Staff, argued that Austria should launch a pre-emptive war against Serbia.

Bulgaria also sought to profit from this demonstration of Turkish weakness. Since Russia was keen to create a barrier against further Austrian expansion, it sought closer relations with Bulgaria, which accepted Russian money to help pay Turkey the compensation agreed as a result of its declaration of independence. Russia also encouraged an alliance between Serbia and Bulgaria, and this was signed in March 1912 when the powers agreed their future stakes to Macedonia.

The Bosnian Crisis had a major impact for the future division of Europe. The Germans had shown their total commitment to Austria-Hungary, while the Russians were determined never to give in again. It indirectly drove Italy, although a member of the Triple Alliance, further from Austria. Italy's ambitions were, in part, contrary to those of its supposed 'ally' as it wanted border areas in the Tyrol which fell within the Austrian Empire but were largely Italian speaking. Thus, it was prepared to respond to Russia's quest for support in 1911, and signed an agreement with Russia whereby each agreed to consult with the other on any future settlement in the Balkans. The agreement was limited but was a pointer to Italy's future loyalties.

The Balkan Wars, 1912–13

First Balkan War, 1912

Taking advantage of the 'Young Turk' revolution which had weakened the Turkish government, the Italians declared war and successfully attacked the Turkish province of Tripoli in North Africa in 1911. This encouraged the Balkan states to advance their own positions while the Turkish government was occupied elsewhere and Turkish resources were diverted.

In May 1912, the Greek statesman, Venizelos, formed the Balkan League of Greece, Serbia, Montenegro and Bulgaria, all committed to opposition to Turkey. This, however, was as far as their agreement went, for each power had a different view of the future of the Balkans. Bulgaria, for example, wanted an independent Macedonia that would look to Bulgaria for protection and the port of Salonika on the Aegean Sea, while Serbia favoured dividing up Macedonia and was primarily interested in gaining Albania and an outlet to the Adriatic sea. Greece also coveted Macedonia, which was predominantly peopled by Greeks.

In September 1912, when Albanian riots, which the Turks were unable to control, spread through Macedonia, the League's members mobilised their forces. However, it was Bulgaria which, without consulting its allies, first declared war on 7 September. Montenegro followed on 8 October, and Serbia and Greece on 18 October. The Turks were in no position to resist, but the rivalry between the Balkan powers was evident from the beginning. The Bulgarian forces rushed to Macedonia to seize the area before the Greeks could do so and went on to press southwards and, in a series of brilliant victories, forced the Turks out of Eastern Thrace and back to Constantinople. However, following warnings from the Russians of the possible consequences, they did not follow up their victory and move on to the Turkish capital.

While Bulgaria was fully occupied, their 'allies' were able to seize land for themselves. In the west, Serbia took Northern Albania while in the south the Greeks seized Salonika. Virtually all of European Turkey fell to the Balkan League. Four small countries with a population of 10 million had defeated a power of 25 million. On 3 December, an armistice was signed between Turkey, Serbia and Bulgaria. Fighting was renewed in early 1913, but eventually the Turks conceded defeat after the loss of Adrianople in April 1913.

Fig. 3 *Trouble in the Balkans, 1912*

Activity

Group activity

Divide your group into two. One half are Russian journalists, the other half, German journalists. You have been asked to produce an article reporting on the Bosnian Crisis of 1908. What would you write?

Cross-reference

For a map of the **Balkans**, see pages 124 and 156.

The **'Young Turk' revolution** is detailed earlier in this chapter, page 152.

Although Germany, Austria and Russia had initially avoided intervening in the war (the former believing wrongly that the Turks would defeat their rebellious peoples), by November 1912 both Austria and Russia, alarmed by Turkey's rapid disintegration, had begun to mobilise. Peace talks began in London in December 1912, and after the renewed fighting was brought to a conclusion a peace agreement was finally concluded in May 1913.

Treaty of London, 30 May 1913

The peace treaty was a result of the negotiations between the major powers of Europe rather than the Balkan states and they were not well received by those whom they affected. It was decided that:

- Greece would receive Crete, Salonika and Southern Macedonia (even though it was mainly peopled by Bulgars)
- Bulgaria would keep Thrace
- Serbia would receive Central and Northern Macedonia
- Albania would become an independent state on the Adriatic coast.

Serbia was very resentful of the Austrian insistence on the creation of an independent Albania. This closed a stretch of coastline to possible Serbian expansion and kept Serbia a land-locked state. Serbia also felt entitled to a greater share of Macedonia and resented Bulgaria's support for Austria. A Serbian diplomat complained, *'Bulgaria, her shores washed by two seas, denies us a single port.'* However, the Bulgarians felt that, as they had borne the largest share of the fighting, more of Macedonia should be theirs. Both Serbia and Bulgaria were determined to win back what they felt they rightly deserved and on 1 June 1913, Serbia formed an alliance with Greece, to this end.

Second Balkan War, 1913

Bulgarian anger and frustration led to an attack on Greece and Serbia on 29 June 1913. However, they were soon outnumbered as Romania and

Activity

Revision activity

Create your own map of events in the Balkans between 1908 and 1913. Start with a set of outline maps of the area and use these to fill in the developments and boundary changes that took place through this period.

Turkey joined in on Serbia's side. The Turks were hoping to be able to use this dispute between their former enemies as an opportunity to win back something of what they had lost and succeeded in regaining Adrianople. In August, Bulgaria asked for peace terms.

Under the Treaty of Bucharest (10 August 1913), signed by Bulgaria, Romania, Greece, Montenegro and Serbia, Bulgaria lost most of its recent gains. A further agreement – the Treaty of Constantinople (13 October 1913) – required Bulgaria to return Adrianople to Turkey.

Table 1 *The partition of Turkey, 1913*

Gains	Territory	Population	Area (sq miles)
Greece	Epirus, South Macedonia, Salonika, Crete	1.7m	17,000
Serbia	Central Macedonia	1.5m	17,000
Romania	South Dobruja	0.25m	10,000
Bulgaria	Eastern Macedonia	0.15m	2,700
Montenegro	Novibazar	0.2m	2,100

The humiliation of Bulgaria boosted the Serbs' confidence and in September they invaded Albania in the hope of fulfilling their ambition to take a coastal strip. Only when Austria-Hungary threatened intervention did they withdraw, and some Greek troops remained stationed in this area until 1914.

Impact and aftermath of the Balkan Wars

Fig. 4 *The growth of Serbia to 1913*

The wars had divided the Balkan states more than ever before. Serbian prestige had grown while the Bulgarians had emerged frustrated and embittered, especially after their early military successes in the

First Balkan War. Bulgaria had incurred heavy losses for little reward and resented Greece's acquisition of Salonika. By 1913, it was clear that Bulgaria would never assist Serbia in any future conflict.

The wars also worsened relations between the Austria-Hungarian Empire and Serbia. Serbia had been angered and frustrated by the Austrian insistence on the creation of Albania at the Treaty of London, and its continued opposition, even after Serbia's success in the Second Balkan War.

Since further conflict seemed likely, all the powers tried to manoeuvre to improve their positions. To the dismay of France and Russia, in November 1913, the Turks invited a German general, Liman von Sanders, to undertake the reorganisation of the Turkish army in Constantinople. With military and economic assistance from Germany, the 'Young Turk' government prepared for retaliation for the loss of more than 90 per cent of its European Empire.

The same year, the Austrians attempted, unsuccessfully, to gain Italian support for an attack on Serbia while in June 1914, the Russians tried, equally unsuccessfully, to win a promise of Romanian support for Serbia in the event of a contest with Austria-Hungary. The Romanians did, however, agree to helping Russia should the Straits be closed by a Greek-Turkish war.

Fig. 5 *A cartoon of the Balkans as an explosive bomb. What do you think is happening in this picture?*

In June 1914, Germany and Austria held their own joint discussions on future Balkan policy. While Austria-Hungary favoured friendship with Bulgaria and Turkey, Germany preferred to support Serbia, Greece and Romania. No decisions could be reached before events decided the outcome.

Activity

Thinking point

Could the Balkan Wars have been resolved in a way that would have preserved peace? If so, how?

Summary questions

1 Explain why wars broke out in the Balkans in 1912–13.

2 How important were events in the Balkans in increasing tension in Europe in the years 1908–13?

The outbreak of war in 1914

The final clash between Austria and Serbia came at Sarajevo, the chief city of Bosnia, on 28 June 1914. The assassination of Archduke Franz Ferdinand of Austria-Hungary and his (Czech) wife, Sophie, was believed to be the work of the Black Hand and the assassin was Gavrilo Princip, a 19-year-old Bosnian Serb student.

Key chronology

The lead-up to war in 1914

28 June	Assassination of Archduke Franz Ferdinand and his wife in Sarajevo.
5 July	Germany assured Austria-Hungary of German support – the 'Blank Cheque'.
20–22 July	Visit of French President Poincaré to St Petersburg.
24 July a.m.	The French urged Russia to support Serbia and promised French support if a war broke out.
24 July p.m.	Russia ordered partial mobilisation along the border with Austria-Hungary.
27 July	Austria-Hungary mobilised.
28 July	Austria declared war and Russia moved to 'State Preparatory to War'.
29 July	Austrian forces bombarded Belgrade; Russia mobilised.
31 July	German ultimatum to Russia; Austria-Hungary mobilised.
1 August	French troops mobilised; Germany declared war on Russia.
2 August	Britain promised help to France; German troops entered Luxembourg.
3 August	Germany declared war on France and troops entered Belgium.
4 August	Britain declared war on Germany.
6 August	Austria-Hungary declared war on Russia.

Cross-reference

To review the assassination of **Archduke Franz Ferdinand** and his wife, revisit the opening of this chapter.

Fig. 6 *Archduke Franz Ferdinand and his wife Sophie leaving the town hall in Sarajevo just before the fateful shooting*

Key profile

Gavrilo Princip

Gavrilo Princip (1894–1918) was the son of a postman from Bosnia. He was one of nine children, six of whom died in infancy. He had always suffered very poor health and it is believed he was recruited by the Black Hand to undertake Franz Ferdinand's assassination because, like the two companions he travelled with from Serbia, he was suffering from tuberculosis and was willing to sacrifice the little life he had left for the nationlist cause. He carried a revolver, two bombs and small vial of cyanide with which to commit suicide after the assassination. When the opportunity presented itself, he fired several times at the royal couple from no more than 2 metres. He shot the Archduke in the neck and Sophie in the abdomen. He tried to kill himself but a man behind him seized his right arm and he was easily arrested. Under interrogation, he gave the names of fellow conspirators and eight men were charged with treason. However, since he was under 21 years old, Princip was only given a sentence of 20 years and he died of tuberculosis on 28 April 1918.

A closer look

The Black Hand and the assassination at Sarajevo

It is believed that when the Black Hand organisation learnt of Archduke Franz Ferdinand's visit to Sarajevo they immediately put plans in motion to assassinate him and in June 1914, Gavrilo Princip, Nedjelko Cabrinovic and Trifko Grabez were sent from Serbia to carry out the deed. Nikola Pasic, the Prime Minister of Serbia gave orders for the three men to be arrested as they tried to leave Serbia but no action was taken. However, the records are scanty. Princip told investigators that the plot had been 'born in our hearts', suggesting he and his seven associates who stood on the streets of Sarajevo on the fateful day were actually acting alone. In the event, only two of the potential assassins actually took action on 28 June. One hurled his bomb at the Archduke's car in the morning, swallowed the cyanide he was carrying and jumped into the River Miljacka. However, he was rescued and survived to face trial. Princip happened to be standing on the corner where the royal car reversed in the afternoon. He was thus able to fire into the car several times fatally wounding both the Archduke and his wife. It was only in subsequent interrogation by the Austrian authorities that the Black Hand leaders, Dragutin Dimitrijevic, Milan Ciganovic, and Major Voja Tankosic, were implicated. Although Serbia initially ignored Austrian demands to disband the Black Hand (although it had agreed in principle), it was dissolved in December 1916. Dragutin Dimitrijevic and several of the leaders were arrested and executed the following year.

Whether or not the Black Hand had carried out this assassination, and whether or not the Serbian authorities were aware of the plans, it provided the Austrian authorities with an excuse to crush Serbia. The Serbs had allowed Princip and his associates to cross into Bosnia and they had failed to prevent the activities of the Black Hand. This seemed justification enough and Germany was immediately approached for a guarantee of support. A letter from the Emperor stated that:

> The Sarajevo affair was a well-organised conspiracy, the threads of which can be traced to Belgrade. Even though it will probably prove impossible to get evidence of the complicity of the Serbian government, there can be no doubt that its policy, directed towards the unification of all the Southern Slav countries under the Serbian flag, is responsible for such crimes and that the continuation of such a state of affairs constitutes an enduring peril for my house and my possessions. Serbia must be eliminated as a factor of political power in the Balkans.

The Kaiser responded through his chancellor, Bethmann Hollweg, on 5 July with a promise that:

> Austria can rest assured that his Majesty will faithfully stand by Austria-Hungary as is required by the obligations of his alliance and of his ancient friendship.

2

This promise has become known as a 'Blank Cheque', because it implied that Germany would back Austria-Hungary in whatever actions the Empire chose to take. No stipulations or provisos were made. Austria-Hungary could make the cheque – her demands – as big as it wanted! Whether Germany realised the full implications of this at the time is an area of debate. It could be that, since the 1912 war council had believed Germany's best chance of war would be in 1914, Germany too saw this episode as the moment they had been waiting for. On the

Cross-reference

The 1912 war council is detailed on page 46.

Cross-reference

The **events of 1908** are covered earlier in this chapter, on pages 152–4.

Activity

Class debate

Imagine that the powers of Europe had held a conference at this crucial time, in the second week of July 1914: Choose a country to represent and prepare a short speech about what you feel should happen and why. Hold a class conference and debate the ideas put forward.

Activity

Group discussion

Before reading further, discuss Serbia's likely reaction to this ultimatum in groups. Which points do you think Serbia would be prepared to accept and which might be rejected? Compare your ideas.

other hand, it is possible that the Kaiser and his advisers believed that when faced with a united Austria-Hungary and Germany, the Russians would back down, just as they had in 1908 and that this declaration of support was nothing more than a way of calling Russia's bluff.

The Austrian cabinet debated their action, while in Belgrade, the Austrian envoy, Baron von Wiesner tried, without success, to discover evidence of the Serbian government's complicity in the plot.

By 14 July, Austria had decided on war and by 20 July, an ultimatum had been prepared, but it was not despatched until the French President, Poincaré, who happened to be visiting St Petersburg at this time, had left Russia.

On 23 July, the Austrians sent the ultimatum to the Serbian capital, Belgrade. They demanded a satisfactory answer within 48 hours.

The Austrian Ultimatum

The history of recent years and in particular the events of 28 June last have shown the existence of a subversive movement with the object of detaching a part of the territories of Austria-Hungary from the Monarchy. The movement had its birth under the eye of the Serbian government. The Royal Serbian government shall therefore publish the following declaration:

'The Royal government of Serbia condemns the propaganda directed against Austria-Hungary and regrets that Serbian army officers participated in it'.

By 5 July:

- All newspapers and publications hostile to Austria to be suppressed.
- The national Defence Society to be dissolved.
- All schoolteachers hostile to Austria to be dismissed.
- All army officers hostile to Austria to be dismissed.
- Austrian police officials to be admitted to Serbia to investigate the assassination.
- Austrian lawyers to participate in judicial proceedings against suspects.
- Frontier guards to be punished for allowing conspirators to enter Bosnia.
- An apology to be given for anti-Austrian remarks by Serbian government officials since the assassination.

3

Serbia was placed in an exceedingly difficult position. Russia claimed that the ultimatum was tantamount to an Austrian takeover of Serbia and a partial mobilisation was ordered on 24 July, along the border with Austria-Hungary.

However, Serbia was prepared to make concessions and initially considered giving way on all counts. Nevertheless, spurred on by Russia, they played for time by rejecting the demands that Austrian police officials enter Serbia and Austrian lawyers participate in judicial proceedings. Such demands were felt to be an unreasonable challenge to Serbian sovereignty. They wrote:

As far as the cooperation in this investigation of specially delegated officials of the Imperial and Royal government is concerned, this cannot be accepted, as this is a violation of the constitution and of criminal procedure.

4

Most of Europe, including Germany, believed that Serbia's conciliatory response would be accepted by the Austrians, although Serbia had begun a partial mobilisation in case of an Austrian attack. On 25 July, the Russian Imperial Council decided that it would back Serbia, even though it had not consulted either France or Britain over the decision.

On 27 July, the Austrians began to mobilise against Serbia. Sir Edward Grey, the British Foreign Secretary, with the support of France called for a conference to discuss the crisis, but neither Germany nor Austria were prepared to come to the table. The Austrians declared war on Serbia on 28 July and on 29 July as the Austrians bombarded Belgrade, the Russian mobilisation began. Negotiations between Russia and Austria were abandoned, and although Bethmann Hollweg of Germany tried to revive them, it was in vain. The timetable to war was set to unravel:

Key chronology

The path to war

Date in 1914	Development
29 July	Austrian forces bombarded Belgrade (capital of Serbia); Germany requested British neutrality (refused). The Tsar ordered a general mobilisation against Germany and Austria. However, the order was changed to a partial mobilisation against Austria alone, when he learnt of Germany's attempts at mediation. Nevertheless, as troops were already moving, it proved impossible to reverse the order.
31 July	Germany requested French neutrality (refused). A British request that the Germans respect Belgian neutrality was refused by Germany. Germany sent an ultimatum to Russia demanding withdrawal of forces aimed at Germany within 12 hours. Austria-Hungary declared a general mobilisation.
1 August	French troops mobilised; Germany declared war on Russia.
2 August	Britain promised help to France; German troops entered Luxembourg and demanded free passage through Belgium (refused).
3 August	Germany declared war on France and troops entered Belgium.
4 August	Britain declared war on Germany because Belgian neutrality (agreed in 1839) had been violated on 3 August.
6 August	Austria-Hungary declared war on Russia.

Exploring the detail

The violation of Belgian neutrality

By a treaty of 1839, to which Britain had been party, the independence and neutrality of Belgium had been guaranteed. However, this was an outdated treaty and Britain was not legally obliged to take up arms in support of Belgium.

Revision activity

Look back over this chapter and the last and provide a list of bullet points for each of the following questions about July/August 1914:

1 Why did Germany support Austria?

2 Why did France support Russia?

3 Why did Britain support France?

Constructing a flow diagram

Make a flow diagram of the path to war between June and August 1914.

Sir Edward Grey

Sir Edward Grey (1862–1933) came from an aristocratic background, was educated at Winchester and Oxford and entered Parliament as a Liberal. He was Foreign Secretary in Asquith's government from 1906–16. He was a scholar who loved fishing and bird-watching and had no desire to involve Britain in foreign entanglements or war. He was uneasy about German ambitions but not openly hostile to Germans and had even been planning to travel to Germany to consult an occulist there about his failing eyesight in 1914. By 3 August, he had made it clear that Britain's neutrality was dependent on Germany withdrawing the threat to Belgium and the channel ports. His decision to involve Britain in war on 4 August remained controversial – several members of his cabinet disapproved, including Lloyd George, the Chancellor of the Exchequer, although he was praised by Winston Churchill at the Board of Trade.

Thinking point

Once Austria went to war against Serbia, was there any way a full European war could have been avoided?

Reasons for the First World War

Although the steps leading to the outbreak of war are relatively easy to understand, the underlying reasons for the outbreak of war are harder to fathom. Entwined within them are issues of responsibility and guilt. A fair appraisal has been made all the harder by the fact that Germany was declared responsible for starting the war at the subsequent peace negotiations at Versailles in 1919.

A consideration of developments within the various European countries can provide some indication of their relative responsibility. All faced huge economic and social pressures in the early 20th century and it is reasonable to argue that internal developments played a significant factor in the mix which saw Europe's leaders decide to risk everything on initiating armed conflict. However, it is important to remember that in 1914, the final decision on war or peace lay in the hands of a very small group of people within these countries.

Fig. 7 *By 1914, there was enormous pressure encouraging war in Europe*

Activity

Group activity

Divide the class into groups. Each group should choose a different country to blame for the outbreak of war. They should prepare a speech showing why their allocated country was the most responsible for the outbreak of war. After the various speeches have been delivered, have a follow up class debate and try to apportion blame fairly.

The following diagram provides some suggestions for this activity:

Cross-reference

The issue of **Alsace-Lorraine** is discussed under Revanchism on page 140.

Plan XVII is covered on page 144.

Germany, under Kaiser Wilhelm II, was an aggressive, military power with dreams of world domination, as exemplified by its policy of Weltpolitik.
Germany expanded its army and navy, with little regard for the consequences.
Germany expanded its colonial Empire and was greedy for trade.
Germany sought alliances and claimed others were encircling their nation.
Germany encouraged Austria-Hungary at every opportunity and was behind the decision to take a firm line over Serbia in July 1914.

Within France, there were influential voices, determined to avenge the loss of Alsace-Lorraine to Germany in 1871.
The French war plan – Plan XVII – was based on revenge for Alsace-Lorraine.
By allying with Russia, the French increased the Germans' feeling of encirclement.
France had suffered waves of strikes since 1910 and sought a diversion.
French activity in the colonies (e.g. Morocco) antagonised the Germans. The French brought the war to the west by mobilising in support of their ally Russia.

Russia wanted to avenge losses in the Russo-Japanese war and divert attentions away from troubles within the country.
Russian support for Serbia forced the alliance system into operation.
After the Bosnia Herzegovina showdown, Russia was intent on war.
Russian mobilisation plans dominated behaviour in July 1914.
Russia was the first country to mobilise.

Britain set the example of imperial power and expected to be able to dominate the seas.
Britain's reaction to German naval building sparked the naval race and encouraged German aggression.
Britain allowed itself to become entangled in the alliance perceived as encircling by Germany.
At home, Britain faced deadlock over Ulster and the Conservatives had promised to drop opposition in the event of war.
War offered an opportunity to avoid the break-up of the Empire.
In July 1914, Britain failed to take a firm line in response to the crisis in the Balkans, so encouraging German and Austrian action.
Britain's decision to enter the war turned the conflict from a central European war into a World War, because of the Empire.

Austria-Hungary was determined to preserve its Empire and expand to incorporate Bosnia-Herzegovina and to combat Serbia's ambitions.
Austria-Hungary was determined to control the ethnic minorities within its own Empire.
Austria-Hungary acted in an unnecessarily aggressive fashion and delivered the ultimatum that produced the war.

The Balkan States, particularly Serbia, were over-ambitious and unable to look beyond their own petty squabbles.
Serbia was particularly aggressive and was not prepared to concede.

Turkey could not keep control of its own territories.
Turkey allowed the annexation of Bosnia and Herzegovina and was unable to prevent the Balkan Wars.

Fig. 8 *Reasons for war*

Cross-reference

The **Pan-German League** is introduced in pages 54–5.

The **Black Hand** is detailed earlier in this chapter, on pages 158–9.

The **Bosnian Crisis** is covered in pages 152–4.

The **Agadir incident** was part of the First Moroccan Crisis.

Activity

Thinking and analysis

Look at the bullet points and:

1 try to decide the order of importance of the various trends which contributed to war and explain your reasoning

2 make a diagram to show the causes for the outbreak of war, indicating how the various factors are interlinked. You might like to put the short term factors of July 1914 in the centre, the general trends around the edge and between the two, specific developments in individual countries which link both to long term trends and to behaviour in 1914.

Another way of looking at the reasons for war is to examine trends which helped create war:

■ The development of the alliance system divided Europe into two armed camps. Although the original treaties were defensive and sometimes only concerned with colonies, they led to military discussions between nations and by 1914 they had grown into far firmer commitments. It was the alliances that turned war in the Balkans into a European/World conflict.

■ The arms race brought huge armies and new technology which were waiting to be tested. It created competition and a reckless confidence. Stockpiling weapons was dangerous and inviting war. Connected to this was the development of mobilisation plans by army generals. These were responsible for the outbreak of the war itself as they demanded speed and prevented political debate and reflection.

■ Nationalism, which had grown strongly at the end of the 19th century, was a dangerous concept. It bred a fierce patriotism which brought to the fore organisations like the Pan-German League and the Black Hand. The popular press extolled Nationalism in all countries. Russia's humiliation over the Bosnian affair or Germany's over Agadir, was seen as an affront to national values. The nationalism of the various races within the Austro-Hungarian Empire threatened to destabilise it and encouraged the Austro-Hungarian leaders to act firmly to crush ethnic minorities. They may have seen the war as a way of doing this.

■ Imperialism encouraged nations to seek colonies and power beyond the confines of their states. Colonies bred conflicts (e.g. Morocco) and provoked humiliations and instability. This activity encouraged the view that a 'show-down' was necessary.

Activity

Thinking and discussion

The following provides some suggestions as to why Germany and Russia may have gone to war. Debate them with a partner and try to decide which are the more important/likely.

Germany's key decision makers had different reasons for wanting war. 'Innenpolitik' or internal politics meant different groups wanted war for personal reasons.

■ Conservatives feared the growth of socialism within Germany. They believed mobilisation might heal division.

■ Wilhelm saw war as an opportunity to advance his personal status.

■ The Prussian Junker class believed it an opportunity to restore the prestige of the old Junker elite and escape the increasing demands for taxation.

■ The German General Staff (army leaders) believed in the strength of the German army and felt that the Schlieffen plan had its last chance of success in the summer of 1914.

Tsar Nicholas and the majority of his advisers also believed that war would preserve his regime from internal collapse.

■ War would unite the country and elevate the peasantry over the disruptive urban workers.

■ Ministers and the military wanted to avenge the humiliation of the 1908–9 Bosnian Crisis.

■ The Russians had their War Plan 19 – which needed to take swift effect if war seemed likely.

However, the Russians were not initially pressing for war in 1914. The Tsar and his advisers were aware of the economic and political demands of war and some still believed Russia's focus should be on Asia. Furthermore, Russia's military plans were not complete. Ideally, Russia needed another two to three years before it was ready for war.

A closer look

Historiography and the outbreak of the First World War

In the aftermath of the First World War historians began investigating the causes of the conflict. In Russia, the communists came to power in 1917, and argued that the war was the product of capitalism and its greed for colonies, markets, land and power. In Germany, writers wishing to disprove Germany's sole guilt for war offered other explanations. In 1926, G. L. Dickinson emphasised the role of alliances and secret clauses, as a cause of war. Others emphasised Germany's fear of becoming encircled by hostile powers, Russian ambitions in the Balkans and the French desire to retake Alsace-Lorraine. An American, Sidney Fay, writing in 1930, even suggested that the war was simply a series of unfortunate accidents.

However, in the 1960s, the German historian, Fritz Fischer published a number of books in which he placed the blame firmly on Germany and its 'Flottenpolitik' (building up a German navy), and 'Weltpolitik' policies. He claimed that Germany's actions since 1911 were all steps along a determined path to war. In the 1970s, Immanuel Geiss supported these views. Not all historians agree. The balance of military power and the influence of the military, the significance of war plans and problems associated with mobilisation have all received attention. A. J. P. Taylor played down the role of the alliances and wrote:

> The very things which are blamed for the war of 1914 – secret diplomacy, the balance of power, the great continental armies – also gave Europe a period of unparalleled peace. It's no good asking: 'What factors caused the outbreak of war?' The question is rather, 'Why did the factors that had long preserved the peace of Europe fail to do so in 1914?

| 5 | *From A. J. P. Taylor, **The Struggle for Mastery in Europe**, 1954* |

A few historians have sought to lay the blame elsewhere. Professor Herwig believed that it was the fault of Count Berchtold of Austria who witheld information from the German government in July 1914, in case they withdrew the 'Blank Cheque'. Gordon Martel has also put more of the blame on Austria-Hungary and Serbia with their military/nationalist ambitions.

Yet another line of enquiry has been to look closely at the tensions within European society, linking foreign to domestic policies rather than relying on purely diplomatic and military explanations.

Activity

Research activity

Try to find out more about different historians' ideas on the causes of the First World War. You might hold a class debate about the various explanations and try to answer the question posed by A. J. P. Taylor in Source 5 above.

Learning outcomes

In this section you have examined the ways in which Germany, Russia and the other countries of Europe became embroiled in war in 1914. You should now be able to assess the relative importance of the alliance network, the arms race and imperialism in bringing about that war and should have an understanding of how and why events in the Balkans provoked the outbreak of conflict.

You should also be able to relate the developments in international affairs, studied here, to the internal developments within Russia and Germany studied in Sections 1 and 2. Finally, in considering the reasons for the outbreak of war you should have become aware that events in history can be subject to many different interpretations and you will have had the opportunity to debate these interpretations and to formulate your own judgement.

 Examination-style questions

(a) Explain why Austria-Hungary declared war on Serbia in July 1914.

(12 marks)

In answering part (a) you will need to provide a short summary of both long and short term factors that explain Austria's declaration of war. The immediate factor was Serbia's failure to comply to the terms of the Austrian Ultimatum and a good answer might start with this, together with a comment of Germany's 'Blank Cheque' support for an Austrian declaration of war. These factors might then be linked to Serbian nationalist aggression and Austria's determination to preserve the Empire from racial break-up. The assassination was, of course, the trigger that led from general hostility to war and might well be emphasised as the crucial development.

(b) How far was Germany responsible for the outbreak of the First World War?

(24 marks)

In part (b) you will need to supply evidence of Germany's responsibility, but you should also point to evidence which shows that other countries were at least partly to blame. Austria gave Serbia the ultimatum, Russia knew how high the stakes were when a full mobilisation was ordered and France encouraged Russia. Britain failed to declare its interests and by maintaining an official position of neutrality (even though Lord Grey and the Foreign Office believed Britain must support France against Germany) allowed the war to escalate. Try to decide what your argument will be so that you can follow it through your answer to a clear conclusion.

4 Conclusion

By 1914, both Russia and Germany were very different countries from those of 30 to 40 years earlier. During that time, both had undergone an economic transformation, faced and survived political battles and had emerged, if not unscathed, confident enough to embark on a war, one with the other.

The Germany of 1914 had come a long way since its founding in 1871. Once united, Germany had been able to exploit its abundant natural resources and manpower to the full. Many parts of Germany had already experienced rapid economic growth before 1871 and this had continued as internal barriers had disappeared, a vast banking, education and communication substructure had been established and, as more railway lines criss-crossed the countryside, both the old and newer industries had grown as never before. This industrial expansion had been aided by state protection from 1878 and had been given considerable state encouragement, for example in allowing the establishment of cartels and in the signing of trade treaties. The population had increased and towns and cities had swelled. Prosperous and strong, Germany's economic growth had assured it a place of power and influence in Europe.

Entering late onto the European scene, and already some way behind other nations, such as Britain and France, in the colonial race, Germany had tried to make up for lost time. Weltpolitik had been a calculated policy to demonstrate Germany's status as the foremost power of continental Europe and so, fully deserving of a 'place in the sun'. Such ambitions had also promoted the growth of military strength and this too had acted as a stimulus to industrial development. The tragedy of all this was that the Kaiser, Wilhelm II, to whose lot it had fallen to run the show, possessed the pride and ambition but lacked the vision and common sense to see, as Bismarck had done, that peace, not war, was the key to Germany's political and economic domination of Europe.

These years also saw another, internal miscalculation by the German rulers, and in this, Bismarck was almost as much to blame as Wilhelm II. In 1871, Bismarck had set Germany on the path of constitutionalism. He had given Germany a Reichstag, manhood suffrage and a constitutional arrangement that placed at least some restrictions on the power of the ruler and his ministers. In so doing, Bismarck had opened the way for the growth of political parties and had provided the basis from which Germany might develop as a liberal western democracy. However, Germany had always had one foot in the east. Prussia's heritage was of 'enlightened despotism', and a powerful ruler backed by conservative Junkers and a strong army. Kaiser Wilhelm I and, even more forcefully, Kaiser Wilhelm II brought this heritage to the new Germany. Even Bismarck himself grew alarmed at the processes he had set in motion and, from 1878, tried to pull back. None had proved prepared to see the Reichstag grow in power and dominate governmental processes and when faced with a political party of which they disapproved – the SPD – all had resorted to repression.

The situation in Russia had both similarities and differences. 1881, for Russia, was less a moment of triumph than of despair. The Tsar, Alexander II, who had set out with high hopes of bringing Russia out of the timeless gloom into which it seemed to have settled, had been assassinated. His efforts to emancipate the serfs and reform local government, education and the army had brought internal unrest, while, internationally, Russia had still not recovered from its humiliating defeat in the Crimean War and the enforced revision of the Black Sea Straits Treaty, to its disadvantage, in 1878. Alexander III's reign was, from its inception, marked by a determination to set the wheels in reverse and to halt what he saw as the frightening influence of western reformist ideas within his Empire. Tsarist autocracy had been reaffirmed, the Okhrana had been sent into action and, in the absence of a constitution, the overwhelmingly peasant population could expect to till their subsistence plots, without rights or representation.

Yet, ironically, it was during Alexander III's reign, far more than under the reformist Alexander II, that Russia took its most modernising steps. Like Germany, Russia had plentiful natural resources and a large population but before the 1890s, they had remained unexploited through a poor communication network, a largely peasant population and a lack of capital investment. Under the able direction of Witte, all this had changed. Thanks largely to external investment, and a squeezing of the peasantry, Russia had gone through a huge and rapid industrial revolution which had propelled the country foward at an unprecedented pace. While Alexander III and, from 1894, the earnest but weak-willed Nicholas II were desperately trying to cling to the political autocracy of their forebears, the huge industrial advances had transformed sections of Russian society and so placed even greater pressure on these inadequate rulers for political modernisation.

While the state had encouraged industrialisation, it had done little to provide for its growing class of urban workers, who were largely unskilled and underpaid. Nor had it shown much humanitarian sympathy for the plight of the rural peasants, who were taught to love the Tsar as their 'little father'. While Stolypin instituted some important agricultural reforms between 1906 and 1911, giving peasants mobility and the means to buy land, 'Stolypin's neck tie' (the gallows) was the means by which he had ensured compliance and quelled unrest. Abroad, the attempt to recover lost prestige in a war against the Japanese (1904–5) had all gone disastrously wrong and only in the depths of defeat had the Tsarist regime made any attempt to respond to the demands of the growing proletariat and institute a Duma, following the 1905 revolution.

In the years leading to 1914, the pressure to restore Russia's damaged international prestige must have been enormous. The rebuff experienced by Austria-Hungary's seizure of Bosnia-Herzegovina in 1908, coming so soon after the problems of 1905, proved the last straw. From 1909, Russia looked to exert itself in the Balkans and bolstered by its new-found industrial strength, overestimated its power to make gains out of war there. What Russia most needed, after the upheavals of 1905, was stability. Its enormous potential had still not been fully exploited by 1914 and a period of peace might just have enabled the country to move forward politically, even if the signs from the last two Dumas had not been promising. What it got, of course, was war, and as its rulers should have known from their studies of Russian history, the effects of a damaging war rarely brought anything other than internal crisis.

Thus, Germany's and Russia's paths followed some similar patterns. A semi-autocratic or autocratic regime, with an inept ruler at the helm, faced the forces of industrialisation and the rise of a militant working class and rather than conceding change, looked to gain prestige in exploits abroad. However, there, the similarity must end.

Internally, Germany had proved better able to cope with the consequences of change than Russia. In Germany there had been state-led schemes of social welfare, beginning with Bismarck's 'state socialism' and while the conditions in industrial cities may not have been pleasant, by 1914, the worst was well over and living standards were rising in town and country. There were certainly those who were discontented with their lot, but they were not forbidden to speak out or hounded by a secret police and they did have the opportunity to form trade unions and vote – even if the outcome was not quite as they would have wished.

For the majority of Russians, despite all the advances, there remained a very rigid social structure, the stultifying presence of the Orthodox Church and, for most of the period, no legal outlet for their frustrations, through unions or a franchise. Their brief experience with a more democratic form of government from 1906 had been emasculated before it had really begun and as demonstrated in the tercentenary celebrations of 1913, Tsar Nicholas II believed in the autocracy every bit as firmly as his ancestors had done.

Externally, it was Germany that was the more aggressive and the more determined. Germany's behaviour was that of the youngster determined to take its place with the 'grown-ups'. Nevertheless, Russia could not afford to let its 'grown-up' status slide. Both nations had confidence and pride. Germany's arrogance knew no bounds under Wilhelm II and while the Russians would have preferred to avoid conflict in 1914, there was little doubt in the minds of the Tsar and his ministers that the loyalty of the people to provide a 'Russian steamroller' would bring victory.

It is easy, from a latter day perspective, to assume that the war and the ultimate collapse of the political structures of these two states were bound to occur. This would, however, make for a very limited appreciation of the twists and turns of the 1871–1914 era. In many respects, the last years of Empire in both Russia and Germany were impressive. Russia was home to great writers, such as Tolstoy, Dostoevsky and Chekov, musicians like Tchaikovsky and Rimsky-Korsakov, its industrial changes emulated the west, the lot of its peasants was improving and it had made liberal progress since 1905. Germany was a mighty, rich, economically modern and scientific state. The Kaiser's court might not quite match the Tsar's – but he put up a pretty good show for the foreign ambassadors and dignitaries whom he entertained. To the outside world in 1914, it might have been assumed that these Empires would last forever.

Through your reading of this book, you should now be able to answer the two questions which have underpinned this history of the development of Russia and Germany between 1871 and 1914. Why did neither Russia nor Germany prove able to match their political growth to their economic development and respond to the need for change? Why did international relations follow such a collision course in the years up to 1914 and so provoke the outbreak of war? Neither question has an easy answer, but it is hoped that your study of these two fascinating countries will have enabled you to develop a greater appreciation of the circumstances which moulded both states and the forces which restricted the decision makers' freedom to manoeuvre. You should, in short, be in a position to form judgements of your own about the issues, events and developments which this book explores and in so doing, appreciate the lessons that are there to be learnt from this study of major change tempered by underlying continuity.

The End of the Empires

Fig. 1 *The storming of the Winter Palace in Russia, October 1917*

Fig. 2 *The proclamation of the Weimar Republic to cheering crowds outside the Reichstag in Germany, November 1918*

Glossary

A

Anti-Semitic: actions or words displaying hatred of Jews.

Absolutism: refers to complete and undisputed authority in the hands of a monarch. This was the normal style of government in 18th century Europe, although some rulers, such as Friedrich II of Prussia (1740–86), turned their monarchies towards 'enlightened absolutism', by granting some freedoms.

Agrarian League: a pressure group founded in 1893 to represent the interests of the large landowners of Germany. It was politically conservative and sought protectionist tariffs.

Autocracy: all power in the hands of one person.

B

Balance of power: the idea that peace is best maintained by ensuring that no power feels superior and so strong enough to challenge another. A traditional aspect of British policy, but also one used by Bismarck, from Germany's point of view.

Bund: another word for a league. In Germany, the federation of 38 states set up in 1815 is usually referred to as the 'Bund'.

Bundesrat: the name given to the Federal Council of the North German Confederation established by Bismarck in 1867 and, from 1871, of the Empire. It had 43 members during the time of the Confederation and 58 under the Empire. In both cases, Prussia had 17 of the seats and the rest were divided between the other Länder. It is sometimes referred to as the Reichsrat.

C

Centre Party: founded in 1870 to represent the German Catholics and the minorities opposed to Bismarck. It is known in German as the Zentrum or Z. The party was strong in the southern German states, particularly Bavaria and also in the Rhineland. It was determined to preserve the position of the Catholic Church, especially in education. It was conservative regarding the constitution and favoured greater decentralisation, but it was quite liberal in its attitude to social reform.

Chancellor: head of the government. In the German Empire he was deemed the 'highest official of the Reich'. He was appointed by the Kaiser and led a government directed by 'state secretaries'. He presided over the Bundesrat. Most chancellors were also Minister-President of Prussia, although Bismarck gave up that post briefly in 1872–3 and Caprivi in 1892–4.

Chauvinistic: a display of extreme or aggressive patriotism; a chauvinistic act demonstrates an exaggerated (and sometimes war-like) determination to act for the country to the exclusion of everything else.

Communism: derived from Marxism and refers to an economic and social system in which everyone works together for the common good. In a perfect communist society, all would be equal and there would be no need for any money. Government and states would wither away and society would be classless. Communists saw this 'perfect' state as the ultimate stage in human history.

Conciliation: a policy of making concessions to win favour.

D

Diet: an assembly or parliament.

Diocese: a district under the control of a bishop.

Duma: the Russian term for an elected council. Originally, a Duma was a municipal council but between 1905 and 1917 the Duma became the elected legislative council of state.

F

Free Conservatives or (from 1871) Reichspartei (FKP): the Freikonservative Partei was founded in 1866. It represented landowners, industrialists and businessmen. Its members were strong supporters of Bismarck and it attracted a number of former liberals. It changed its name in 1871 but had no real party organisation or programme until 1906. It had an influence greater than its numbers and favoured an assertive foreign policy. It opposed radical reform at home although it was prepared to accept cautious modernisation.

Free trade: when goods can pass freely across borders and boundaries without tariffs (customs duties) being levied.

G

German Conservative Party (Deutsch Konservative Partei or DKP): this party adopted the name in 1876. It mainly represented the Protestant and aristocratic Prussian Junker landowners. It was the most right wing of the political groups of the imperial period and detested the Reichstag because it was elected by universal suffrage. It was dominant in the Prussian Landtag (state government).

German Workers' Association (ADAV): this group was led by Ferdinand Lasalle, and was committed to a socialist programme which included the redistribution of wealth and the abolition of private property. It had 15,000 members by the middle of the 1870s.

H

Hereditary: refers to something that is passed down from one generation to the next. It may refer to personal matters passed down in the genes (as in the case of haemophilia) or to land and property.

J

Junker: a term used to describe Prussian aristocrats. The Junker class was specifically the class of large Prussian landowners who lived east of the River Elbe and dominated the institutions of Prussia, and more indirectly, of the Reich. They were involved in runnning the army and manning the bureaucracy and were conservative in outlook.

K

Kaiser: the German word for Emperor (deriving from the Latin 'Caesar', which also gives rise to the word Czar/Tsar).

Kulturkampf: this means literally a struggle for culture and was, in practice, Bismarck's attack on the Catholic Church and its political influence in Germany.

L

Liberalism/Liberal: a political concept spread by the French revolution that encouraged personal and economic freedom. Personal freedoms included the right to property and the freedom of speech, of religion and of participation in politics. Economic freedoms included free trade and non-interference in working relationships. The term 'liberal' came to imply those in favour of representative, elected government. In Germany, the liberals came to form the National Liberal Party (see below). In Russia, the Zemstva was the natural home of the Liberals.

M

Marxism/Marxist: refers to the political ideology deriving from the theories of Karl Marx who taught that all history is driven by economic forces which creates class struggles. In the 19th and early 20th centuries, most Marxists wanted to further the stage of history whereby the proletariat (workers) would rise against the bourgeoisie (capitalists).

Mir: the Russian word for the village commune where the peasants worked. After 1861, the peasants were not allowed to leave the mir until their redemption dues were paid.

N

National Liberal Party (Nationalliberale Partei or NL): this party was founded in November 1866 by members of the Progressive Party in the Prussian Diet who left to support Bismarck. This was the Party of the Protestant middle classes. It was supported by wealthy, well-educated men such as bankers, merchants and civil servants. It favoured free trade, a strong Germany and a constitutional liberal state. After 1875, it grew more conservative as its members felt threatened by the growing strength of the Social Democratic Party.

Nationalism: this implies loyalty to a nation, rather than to a ruler or ideology and it became a major force in 19th century Europe, following the defeat of Napoleon and the economic changes of that century. Nationalism manifested itself in the unification of both Germany and Italy, in the drive to Empire through colonisation and in the determination to acquire and maintain 'Great Power' status.

Navy League: the Deutscher Flottenverein was founded in 1898 following the campaign for the first Navy Law and was one of a number of right wing pressure groups at that time. It was mainly controlled by businessmen and conservative politicians with a lower middle class nationalist following. By 1914, it had over a million members.

O

Okhrana: the name given to the Tsarist secret police force, which replaced the Third Section in 1880.

P

Pacifist: refers to a dislike of war and a preference for settling disputes by peaceful means.

Pan-Slavism/Pan-Slav: the Pan-Slavist movement favoured uniting all Slavs into a single country. Pan-Slavs felt sympathy for their fellow Slavs elsewhere and wanted to help them.

Particularism: permitting a minority in a federation to pursue its own interests at the expense of the unity of the whole.

Polycracy: a system of government in which there are many competing power-bases.

Pope: head of the Roman Catholic Church, residing in Vatican City in Rome.

Progressive, or Progress Party (Deutsche Fortschrittspartie or DFP): founded in June 1861 by a radical group that broke away from the Liberals in the Prussian Landtag. It was led by landowners and educated middle classes and precipitated the crisis over the Army Bill, which brought Bismarck to power, by refusing to approve Wilhelm I's budget. The party believed in a liberal, constitutional state but disliked centralism and militarism and so was not very supportive of Bismarck. Its members wanted to extend the powers of the Reichstag and in 1884 the left wing broke away in more open opposition. This was the only middle class grouping to oppose Bismarck.

Protection: the reverse of free trade. Protection involves placing duties on goods to protect home industry and prevent unwanted foreign imports.

R

Realpolitik: a concept promoted by Bismarck that the exercise of power should not be influenced by some abstract desire for glory, honour or shaped by past allegiances but that a country should pursue its own interests in accordance with the situation in which it found itself.

Reich: the German word for an empire or state. It was used to describe the Holy Roman Empire (the First Reich), the German Empire of 1871–1918 (the Second Reich) and the Nazi regime of 1933–45 (the Third Reich).

Reichsfeinde: a term used in the Bismarckian era to describe 'enemies of the Reich'. In practice, these were the more progressive forces in the state, such as the Progressive Liberals, the Socialists and the Centre Party. By labelling such as

Reichsfeinde, Bismarck inhibited the growth of responsible political parties representing all areas of life.

Reichstag: this term was used of the Parliament of the North German Confederation from 1867 and then the parliament of Germany from 1871–1945. From 1871, the Reichstag was the principle parliamentary body. It was directly elected on the basis of a franchise for all males over 25 years. However, it was not fully representative as there was no redistribution of seats to take account of demographic change. It also had only limited power over the chancellor's government (until the last weeks of the First World War).

Revanchism/Revanchist: refers to a movement in France that wanted to reclaim Alsace-Lorraine which the Germans had taken after the Franco–Prussian War (1870), and restore France's former glory.

Right wing/Left wing: in politics it is quite normal to talk about 'the left' and the 'right' or left and right wing. This division derives from the time of the French Revolution when deputies who supported the monarchy sat on the right, while more radical opponents, who wanted change, sat on the left in the Assembly. Thus 'right' has come to mean conservative – and, at its most extreme, authoritarian and in favour of strong rule – while left means pro-reform, in favour of the workers and, at its most extreme, communism.

S

Serfs: there were various categories of serfs in Russia before 1861, including state serfs, household serfs and privately-owned serfs. All were the personal property of their masters could be bought and sold. They were required to serve their masters in various ways and had to apply for permission, for example, to marry or to travel. After 1861, there were technically no serfs in Russia.

Social Democratic Party (Sozialdemokratische Partei Deutschlands or SPD (also SAPD): this was formed in 1875 in Gotha by the merger of the General Workers' Association (ADAV) and the SDAP (the Social Democratic Workers' Party), the new party was at first known as the SAPD. This party represented the working classes and worked with the trade unions. It supported a reduction in the power of the elite and the extension of welfare reforms. Its most extreme members wanted a total overthrow of the constitution, but the majority were prepared to work within it in order to bring about better conditions for the masses. In Russia; the Social Democratic Workers' Party was formed in 1898 and was a Marxist party. It split in 1903 and from it emerged the Bolshevik and Menshivik political groupings. Both believed in the class struggle and the overthrow of the Tsarist regime but differed in the means whereby this would be brought about.

Social Revolutionary Party: a Russian political grouping founded in 1901 which primarily championed the cause of the peasants and land redistribution (following the Populist tradition). It also believed that the urban proletariat could lead revolution. Its members advocated terrorist methods including assassination.

Socialism: seeks to achieve greater equality by reducing private profit, extending opportunities and spreading welfare reforms. In its most extreme form socialism is generally referred to as Marxism or communism. However, more moderate socialists are prepared to work through representative bodies to advance the cause of the down-trodden.

Soviet: a council, usually of workers, soldiers, sailors and perhaps peasants, who tried to take control of the local area. One was set up in St Petersburg at the time of the 1905 revolution.

Stratification: literally means organising into layers. Society can be stratified when there are pronounced divisions between the classes.

T

Tariffs: another word for customs duties. (See Free trade and Protection.)

Trade unionism: trade unions are organisation of employees set up to lobby employers and the governing powers for better conditions of both work and living for their members.

Tsar: derives from the Latin word 'Caesar' (as does 'Kaiser') and refers to an Emperor. It was the title given to the Emperor of Russia.

W

Weltpolitik: a German term which literally means 'World Policy' and refers to the drive to acquire colonies and power throughout the world in the time of Kaiser Wilhelm II.

Z

Zemstva: the name given to the elected local government assemblies set up in Russia by a decree of 1864. They were the first type of 'democratic' institution to be established in Russia but while often effective in their local areas, their tendency to criticise central government led Alexander III to rein in their powers and restrict the popular vote to these in 1890–2.

Zollverein: the name given to the customs union established between 18 German states and Prussia in 1834 to create a free trade area. it was gradually extended to other states and was a force promoting the economic advance and eventual unity of Germany.

Bibliography

General coverage

Cooper, D., Laver, J., and Williamson, D., (2001) *Years of Ambition: European History 1815–1914*, Hodder Arnold.

Joll, J. (1990) *Europe Since 1870*, Penguin.

Lee, S. J. (1982) *Aspects of European History 1789–1980*, Routledge.

Morris, T. and Murphy, D. (2004) *Europe 1870–1991*, Harper Collins.

Pugh, M. (1997) *A Companion to Modern European History 1871–1945*, Blackwell.

Simpson, W. O., and Jones, M. (2000) *Europe 1783–1914*, Routledge.

Stone, N.(1999) *Europe Transformed 1878–1919*, Blackwell.

Biographies and first hand accounts

Clark, C. (2000) *Kaiser Wilhelm II*, Longman.

Feuchtwanger, L. (2002) *Bismarck*, Routledge.

Lerman, K. (2004) *Bismarck*, Longman.

Lieven, D. (1994) *Nicholas II Emperor of all the Russias*, Pimlico.

Palmer, A. (1997) *The Kaiser: Warlord of the Second Reich*, Weidenfeld.

Röhl, J. G. (1996) *The Kaiser and his Court*, Cambridge.

Taylor, A. J. P. (2003) *Bismarck: The Man and the Statesman*, Sutton Publishing Ltd.

Germany, 1871–1914

Abrams, L. (1995) *Bismarck and the German Empire*, Routledge.

Berghahn, V. R. (2004) *Imperial Germany 1871–1914*, Berghahn Books.

Carr, W. (1991) *A History of Germany 1815–1990*, Hodder Arnold.

Craig, G. A. (1999) *Germany, 1866–1945*, Oxford University Press.

Farmer, A. (2007) *The Unification of Germany 1815–1919*, Hodder Murray.

Kitson, A. (2001) *Germany 1858–1990*, Oxford University Press.

Layton, G. (1995) *From Bismarck to Hitler: Germany 1890–1933*, Hodder Murray.

Lee, S. J. (1999) *Imperial Germany 1871–1918*, Routledge.

Lerman, K. (2004) *Bismarck: Profiles in Power*, Pearson.

Porter, I. and Armour, I. (1991) *Imperial Germany 1890–1918*, Longman.

Rohl, J. C. G. (1999) *The Kaiser and His Court Wilhelm II and the Government of Germany*, Cambridge University Press.

Simpson, W. O. (1995) *The Second Reich*, Cambridge.

Stiles, A. (2001) *The Unification of Germany 1815–1890*, Hodder Murray.

Sturmer, M. (2002) *The German Empire*, Weidenfeld.

Wehler, H. U. (1997) *The German Empire 1871–1918*, Berg.

Williamson, D. (1997) *Bismarck and Germany*, Longman.

Russia, 1881–1914

Darby, G. (1998) *The Russian Revolution 1861–1924*, Longman.

Figes, O. (1997) *A People's Tragedy: The Russian Revolution,1891–1924*, Pimlico.

Freeze, G. (2002) *Russia, A History*, Oxford University Press.

Hite, J. (2004) *Tsarist Russia 1801–1917*, Causeway Press.

Hutchinson, J. (1999) *Late Imperial Russia*, Longman.

Laver, J. (2002) *The Modernisation of Russia 1856–1985*, Heinemann.

Lynch, M. (2nd New Ed. 2005) *Reaction and Revolutions: Russia 1881–1924*, Hodder Murray.

Mosse, W. (2nd ed. 1995) *Alexander II and the Modernisation of Russia*, I B Tauris.

Offord, D. (1999) *19th century Russia: Opposition to Aristocracy*, Longman.

Oxley, P. (2001) *Russia 1855–1991*, Oxford University Press

Rogger, H. *Russia in the Age of Modernisation and Revolution 1881–1917*

Service, R. (1991) *The Russian Revolution 1900–1927*, Macmillan.

Waldron, P. (1997) *The End of the Imperial Russia*, Macmillan.

Wood, A. (2007) *The Romanov Empire 1613–1917*, Hodder Arrnold.

International relations

Berghahn, V. R. (1993) *Germany and the Approach of War in 1914*, Bedford.

Clay, C. (2007) *King, Kaiser, Tsar: Three Royal Cousins Who Led the World to War*, Hodder Murray.

Henig, R. (2001) *The Origins of the First World War*, Routledge.

Lieven, D. (1984) *Russia and the Origins of the First World War*, Macmillan.

Lowe, J. (2001) *Rivalry and Accord: International Relations 1870–1914*, Hodder.

Martel, G. (2003) *The Origins of the First World War*, Longman.

Photographs

Kurth, P. (1998) *Tsar: The Lost World of Nicholas and Alexandra*, Back Bay.

Moynahan, B. (2000) *Russian Century: A Photographic History*, Weidenfeld.

Sturmer, M. (2000) *The German Century: A Photographic History*, Bison.

Acknowledgements

The authors and publisher would also like to thank the following for permission to reproduce material:

p3 Quoted in Ryan, J. (ed), *The Russian Chronicles*, 1998; p14 Quoted in Lee, S., *Imperial Germany*, 1999; p16 Quoted in Mitchell, I. R., *Bismarck and the Development of Germany*, 1980; p21 Stiles, A., *The Unification of Germany*, 1989; p23 Simpson, W., *The Second Reich*, 1995; p23 McKichan, F., *Germany 1815–1939: The Rise of Nationalism*, 1992; p25 Quoted in Stiles, A., *The Unification of Germany*, 1989; p26 Prince von Bülow, *Memoires: Early Years and Diplomatic Service 1849–1897*, 1932; p28 McKichan, F., *Germany 1815–1939: The Rise of Nationalism*, 1992; p34 Layon, G., *From Bismarck to Hitler: Germany 1890–1933*, 1995; p34 Stürmer, M., *The German Empire*, 2001; p35 Simpson, W., *The Second Reich*, 1995; p36 Lee, S. J., *Aspects of European History 1789–1980*, 1988; p37 Craig, G., *Germany 1866–1945*, 1981; p37 Porter, I., and Armour, I., *Imperial Germany 1890–1918*, 1991; p37 Lee, S., *Imperial Germany*, 1999; p40 Traynor, J., *Europe, 1890–1990*, 1993; p42 Simpson, W., *The Second Reich*, 1995; p43 Lee, S., *Imperial Germany*, 1999; p45 Pinson, K. S., *Modern Germany: Its History and Civilisation*, 1966; p45 Fischer, H. W., *Private Lives of Kaiser William II and his Consort*, 1909; p45 Wolfson, R., *Years of Change: European History 1890–1945*, 1978; p46 Wolfson, R., *Years of Change: European History 1890–1945*, 1978; p46 McKichan, F., *Germany 1815–1939: The Rise of Nationalism*, 1992; p47 Table 2 Lee, S., *Imperial Germany*, 1999; p47 Table 3 Stapleton, F., *The Kaiserreich – A Study Guide*, 2002; p 47 Table 4 Lee, S., *Imperial Germany*, 1999; p52 McKichan, F., *Germany 1815–1939: The Rise of Nationalism*, 1992; p50 Table 6 Adapted from Simpson, W., *The Second Reich – Germany 1871–1918*, 1995; p57 Quoted in Ryan, J. (ed), *The Russian Chronicles*, 1998; p58 Quoted in Ryan, J. (ed), *The Russian Chronicles*, 1998; p59 Wolfson, R., *Years of Change: European History 1890–1945*, 1978; p63 Oxley, P., *Russia 1855–1991*, 2001; p66 Quoted in Ryan, J. (ed), *The Russian Chronicles*, 1998; p66 Wood, A., *The Romanov Empire 1613–1917*, 2007; p69 Mack, D. W., *Lenin and the Russian Revolution*, 1970; p70 Flannery, E., *The Anguish of the Jews: Twenty-Three Centuries of Anti-Semitism*, 1965; p72 www.worldfuturefund.org 2008; p73 Figes, O., *A People's Tragedy*, 1996; p74 Figes, O., *A People's Tragedy*, 1996; p81 Quoted in Ryan, J. (ed), *The Russian Chronicles*, 1998; p82 Figes, O., *A People's Tragedy*, 1996; p82 Figes, O., *A People's Tragedy*, 1996; p82 Figes, O., *A People's Tragedy*, 1996; p89 Figes, O., *A People's Tragedy*, 1996; p89 Quoted in Ryan, J. (ed), *The Russian Chronicles*, 1998; p90 Figes, O., *A People's Tragedy*, 1996; p93 Quoted in Ryan, J. (ed), *The Russian Chronicles*, 1998; p94 Figes, O., *A People's Tragedy*, 1996; p97 Wood, A., *The Romanov Empire 1613–1917*, 2007; p98 Table 4 Adapted from Murphy, D., and Morris, T., *Russia 1855–1964*, 2008; p98 Quoted in Ryan, J. (ed), *The Russian Chronicles*, 1998; p101 Quoted in Taylor, A. J. P., 20th century History Magazine no 3 p83, 1969; p101 Wood, A., *The Romanov Empire 1613–1917*, 2007; p101 Figes, O., *A People's Tragedy*, 1996; p103 Figes, O., *A People's Tragedy*, 1996; p104 Oxley, P., *Russia 1855–1991*, 2001; p104 Table 5 Adapted from Murphy, D., and Morris, T., *Russia 1855–1964*, 2008; p105 Table 6 Wood, A., *The Romanov Empire 1613–1917*, 2007; p107 Table 8 compiled from Evans and Jenkins, *Years of Weimar and the Third Reich*, 1999 and Cook and Stevenson, *Modern European History 1763–1991*, 1987; p110 Quoted in Ryan, J. (ed), *The Russian Chronicles*, 1998; p117 Davies, N., *Europe – a History*, 1996; p127 www.firstworldwar.com/source/dualalliance.htm; p131 Simpson, W., *The Second Reich*, 1995; p139 Morris, T. A., *European History 1848–1945*, 1995; p140 Morris, T. A., *European History 1848–1945*, 1995; p145 Porter, I., and Armour, I., *Imperial Germany 1890–1918*, 1991; p147 Bates, B., *The First World War*, 1984; p149 Turner, L. C. F., *Origins of the First World War*, 1970; p149 Turner, L. C. F., *Origins of the First World War*, 1970; p153 SALLY; p153 Wolfson, R., *Years of Change 1890–1945*, 1978; p155 Edwards, A. D., and Bearman, G. W. L., *Britain, Europe and the World 1848–1918*, 1971; p156 Table 1 Edwards, A. D., and Bearman, G. W. L., *Britain, Europe and the World 1848–1918*, 1971; p159 Wolfson, R., *Years of Change 1890–1945*, 1978; p159 Wolfson, R., *Years of Change 1890–1945*, 1978; p160 Edwards, A. D., and Bearman, G. W. L., *Britain, Europe and the World 1848–1918*, 1971; p161 Wolfson, R., *Years of Change 1890–1945*, 1978; p165 Taylor, A. J. P., *The Struggle for Mastery in Europe*, 1954.

Many of these quotations and tables have been adapted by the author to be suitable for AS students

Photographs courtesy of:

Ann Ronan Archive pp15, 18, 28, 34, 47, 69, 82, 88, 106, 121, 123, 127, 162; Bundesarchiv p31; Edimedia Archive pp10, 29, 53, 70, 75, 76, 81, 134, 137, 138, 141; Mary Evans Picture Library pp65, 67, 86, 98; Photo12 pp17, 44, 57, 85, 93, 95, 155, 157, 158, 117; Topfoto pp3, 77, 105, 108; World History Archive pp6, 14, 20, 22, 24, 27, 37, 40, 42, 52, 83, 90, 102, 111, 113, 119, 131, 145, 146, 150, 152, 169, 169.

Cover photograph © RIA Novosti/ The Bridgeman Art Library / Getty Images

Photo research by Unique Dimension Researchers: Samuel Manning, Dora Swick, Alexander Goldberg. Special thanks to Ann Asquith and Jason Newman of ICC and Martyn Blankenburg (Intercontinental Group, Berlin). Copy editing by Susannah Fountain.

Index